ISBN 978-1-330-45847-1
PIBN 10065143

English
Français
Deutsche
Italiano
Español
Português

www.forgottenbooks.com

Mythology Photography **Fiction**
Fishing Christianity **Art** Cooking
Essays Buddhism Freemasonry
Medicine **Biology** Music **Ancient**
Egypt Evolution Carpentry Physics
Dance Geology **Mathematics** Fitness
Shakespeare **Folklore** Yoga Marketing
Confidence Immortality Biographies
Poetry **Psychology** Witchcraft
Electronics Chemistry History **Law**
Accounting **Philosophy** Anthropology
Alchemy Drama Quantum Mechanics
Atheism Sexual Health **Ancient History**
Entrepreneurship Languages Sport
Paleontology Needlework Islam
Metaphysics Investment Archaeology
Parenting Statistics Criminology
Motivational

CHAIN STORES

THEIR MANAGEMENT AND OPERATION

BY

WALTER S. HAYWARD, A. M.

RESEARCH ENGINEER

AND

PERCIVAL WHITE, A. M.

RESEARCH ENGINEER, AUTHOR OF "MARKET ANALYSIS, ITS PRINCIPLES AND METHODS"

With chapters by

JOHN S. FLEEK, M. B. A.

AND

H. MAC INTYRE

FIRST EDITION
SECOND IMPRESSION

McGRAW-HILL BOOK COMPANY, INC.
NEW YORK: 370 SEVENTH AVENUE
LONDON: 6 & 8 BOUVERIE ST., E. C. 4
1922

THE MAPLE PRESS - YORK PA

PREFACE

The purpose of this book is to set forth the principles of chain store operation, organization, management, and control. It is intended not only for the use of the executive at chain store headquarters, but it is also particularly addressed to the branch store manager and his assistants. Furthermore, it is hoped that the book will prove stimulating to independent retailers and to others who are interested in the possibilities offered by the chain store movement.

In the opinion of the authors, this movement is characteristic of all that is best in tendencies towards combination and scientific control. It is thoroughly American. It stands for scientific management as applied to the great function of retail merchandising.

Although this movement is still in its infancy, the chain store is probably the most highly developed exemplar of modern distribution methods.

The first chapter is offered as a brief summary of findings, the intention being to give the reader a perspective of the subject before he comes to the more specific and detailed examination of the various phases of the problem.

As a further means of clarifying the reader's ideas, an outline is placed at the head of each chapter, setting forth its main points in topical form. It is hoped that these outlines will prove valuable for anyone desirous of obtaining in the most direct fashion a comprehensive knowledge of the subject.

Without the assistance of many friends it would have been impossible to complete this work. In addition to those mentioned in the text, grateful acknowledgment is made to the following for their assistance:

Messrs. F. B. Barton, of Akron, Ohio, Robert M. Updegraff, of the Displays Company, New York City, Malcolm P. McNair, Instructor in Marketing, Prof. Donald K. David, Assistant dean and assistant professor of marketing, Graduate School of Business, Harvard University, Philip Remington, Lyman Armes, of Wood, Putnam & Wood, Allen Wood, of Wood, Putnam & Wood, Alden C. Kenyon, of Wood, Putnam & Wood, Frederick J. Mullen, of the *Boston News Bureau*, Philip Burbank, of the H. B. Humphrey Advertising Agency, Mort Hamburger, of the Federal System of Bakeries, Charles Coolidge Parlin, of Curtis Publishing Company, H. C. Parson, president ·the Woolworth Co., Charles E. Merrill, of Merrill, Lynch & Co., W. T. Grant, president of the W. T. Grant Company Department Stores, Benjamin F. Meyers, editor of *The Haberdasher*, Harold Snyder, of Spear and Company, New York City, S. H. Ditchett, editor of the *Dry Goods Economist*, Alexander New, president of the Mercantile Stores Corporation, Inc., Alfred H. Beckmann, secretary-treasurer of the National Chain Store Grocers' Association, Paul J. Mandabach, editorial director, *Drug Store Merchandising* and *Confectionery Merchandising*, B. B. Wilson, associate editor, *The Music Trade Review*, E. Hubbard, associate editor, *The American Hatter*, Richard D. Wyckoff, J. B. Levey, general sales manager, United Shirt Shops, Wm. Henry Smith, of the United Shoe Machinery Corporation, H. J. Schuell, general manager, *The Druggists Circular*, H. B. Hanser, assistant general manager, *The Variety Goods Magazine*, Bertrand L. Chapman, manager of Merchandising Department, the *New York World*, Kingman Brewster, attorney, D. Walter Morton, Educational Department, J. C. Penney Co.

Thanks are also due to Mrs. Walter S. Hayward for the preparation of illustrations and for editorial assistance, and to Charles G. Wheeler for his invaluable help in reading manuscript.

F. J. Arkins of the Alexander Hamilton Institute has been of great assistance, not only in supplying bibliographical data but in actual constructive suggestions and reading proof.

As it is the intention of the authors to keep this book up-to-date, they would appreciate suggestions from readers calculated to be of assistance in making revisions.

WALTER S. HAYWARD.
PERCIVAL WHITE.

NEW YORK, N. Y.,
May 15, 1922.

CONTENTS

vii

CHAPTER I

THE PRINCIPLES OF CHAIN STORE OPERATION

OUTLINE

Chain store principles of four kinds.
   1. Physical aspects of store location and construction.
   2. Methods of operation.
   3. Men.
   4. System of control and coördination.
Physical aspects.
   1. Locate
      (a) According to analysis of product.
      (b) According to analysis of traffic.
   2. Standardize.
      (a) Appearance of store.
         1. Store front.
         2. Size.
         3. Stock.
         4. Window trims.
Methods.
   1. Purchase
      (a) At headquarters
      (b) Direct from manufacturer.
      (c) For cash.
      (d) Enough and no more.
   2. The warehouse
      (a) Keep adequate and fresh supply of stock.
      (b) Fill orders with speed and accuracy from well-arranged stock.
      (c) Keep warehouse overhead down by standardization of method.
   3. Sales methods.
      (a) Suit product to wants of community.
         1. Carry only standard sizes.
         2. Avoid style articles.
      (b) Mark prices in accordance with
         1. Cost to chain.
         2. Overhead expense.
         3. Sales expense.
         4. Necessary profit.
      (c) Keep every line turning at a profit.
   4. Eliminate unnecessary expenses.
      (a) Conduct business on cash basis.

    (*b*) Charge extra for deliveries.
5. Take advantage of benefits of publicity.
    (*a*) Display.
    (*b*) Advertising.

Men.

1. Choose men carefully
    (*a*) Who have interest in work.
    (*b*) Who show signs of promise.
2. Train men carefully.
    (*a*) Start at bottom and work up.
3. Pay personnel adequately.
    (*a*) By some form of bonus on sales, profits, etc.
4. Promote men on merit alone.
5. Maintain morale
    (*a*) By discipline.
    (*b*) By infusing spirit of goodwill.

Control and coördination

1. Keep careful and complete records
    (*a*) Of warehousing and purchasing.
    (*b*) Of overhead expenses.
    (*c*) Of independent store statistics.

CHAPTER I

THE PRINCIPLES OF CHAIN STORE OPERATION

What is a chain store? This term is generally applied to a group of two or more retail stores, dealing in the same line of goods, and under the same central management. Each store, although a separate unit, has certain features in common with the rest, whether in purchasing, merchandising, or accounting. The degree of independence possessed by the individual stores varies from almost complete independence, as in some dry goods chains, to the closest inter-dependence, in those cases where the manager is hardly more than a head clerk.

How does a branch house differ from the chain store? In many cases this is hard to define since the ordinary branch store is in reality a chain store. The term "branch" is frequently applied to the several links of a manufacturer's chain. An independent retailer with two or three stores commonly calls them "branches," although they are in reality members of a chain.

An agency is not a chain store, although frequently this term is applied to such organizations as the United Drug Co.'s agencies. A "Rexall" store, it is true, handles the manufactured products of the United Drug Co., but there is no executive control. The individual agency is an entity in itself and is self-governing. No chain store can ever run counter to the policy of the organization to which it belongs.

In discussing the general principles on which chain stores are conducted, it is difficult to include only methods and policies of unique application. Many of these principles can be applied equally well to an independent retailer. In the last analysis, a chain is nothing more than a collection of retail stores dealing in the same products and guided by the same policies, profiting by the same economies and correcting the same mistakes.

The principles of chain store operation may be divided into four sections, the first dealing with conditions already existing, the second with merchandising policies, the third with chain

3

personnel, and the fourth with the control of chain activities through records and statistics and the interpretation and application of these data.

The Physical Aspects.—Under this first heading come all those factors which are outside the power of the chain to create but by which it can profit if it will take advantage of them. Of all the principles involved these are perhaps the most fundamental because they deal with unalterable facts. The correct location of a store, for example, is always an essential factor. Again, there is a size for a store which is just right to accommodate its traffic and trade. Anything larger would be waste; anything smaller would be inefficient.

These physical aspects are known conditions, possible to estimate and forecast. The man who first put them to practical use, George J. Whelan, became a millionnaire. The example of success is irresistible. Today, all scientifically managed chains realize that the physical aspects of retailing must be reckoned with. If no use is made of location, then some other method, notably advertising, must be used to attract trade .

There are three steps involved in the problem of locating a store.

1. Analyze the product.
2. Analyze the locality.
3. Analyze the traffic.

There is a proper site for the store and it can be found by using this method. If the products to be sold are mainly convenience goods, that is, goods which are the same wherever purchased, such as cigarettes, groceries, notions, etc., the site should be on the stream of traffic. If the products are "shopping lines," or if there is something in the article or the service which will induce people to leave their accustomed path to purchase, the store may be away from usual traffic. But, in this event, it must resort to publicity and advertising to acquaint people with what it has to offer.

Next, analyze the locality. Who are to be your neighbors? What do they sell? A five and ten cent store can be found close to the department store like the pilot fish by the shark. Which side of the street is the shady side? Women prefer it.

Last of all, analyze the traffic. Note the number of passers-by and the direction in which they are going. Note the hours at which this traffic is heaviest and the relative number of women and men of which it is composed. Last of all, note the character of the traffic. Is it mainly composed of men and women going to and from work? Of shoppers? Of commuters? What is their rank and station? It is the buying power of the traffic which we must determine.

Thus, the first principle of chain store operation is to locate the member stores in relation to the nature of the products to be sold, the character of the locality, and a careful analysis of the traffic. There is a right place: find it.

The second principle is to suit the store itself to the product, the locality, and the traffic.

Take advantage of the principles of display. Design a store front in harmony with the character of the organization and the localities in which it sells. Make the exterior of the store combine with the location to act as a drawing attraction for the public. Make the interior of the store large enough to utilize every inch of working space, and no larger. Arrange the stock so that it appears at its best. Furthermore, arrange it so as to make the most of the points of sales vantage. Traffic, in a store as well as outside, follows certain channels. And when the "one best way" for arranging a store has been determined, the same plan can usually be used as a model throughout the chain.

The window display is one of the most important points in the physical appearance of the member store. More people buy as a result of what they see than for any other reason. Good window displays, and good table displays sell goods. And last of all, keep stores neat and attractive. This will create favorable notice.

The essence of this part of chain operation is to take advantage, as far as possible, of things as they are, and of people as they are. This is a study in human nature and psychology. Choose the proper location and your customers will come to you.

Merchandising Policies.—The purpose of all chain store policies is to sell goods at a profit. As all other retailers are in business with this same purpose in mind, it follows that the most efficient will be the most successful. How is this efficiency to be obtained? The independent retailer makes a success by personal supervision and by personal service. He can vary his policy to suit his customer. But the chain is more impersonal. Its policies, like its store fronts, must be standardized. And this principle pervades the whole chain structure. Appearance, arrangement of stock, price, wages, everything is standardized. Instead of personal service, we have standard practice. Human nature cannot be standardized, but almost everything else can.

The merchandising policies of a retail chain are chiefly confined to obtaining products of the highest quality at the lowest price, and selling as large an amount of them as possible at the lowest expense and the largest profit consistent with rapid turnover.

Purchasing.—As far as possible, all buying for the chain should be done at headquarters. There are several reasons for this. In the first place, the larger the purchase, the greater the quantity discount. In the second place, the purchasing agent of the chain can buy direct, and in this way save the jobbers' discount as well as obtain the quantity discount. Although at one time there was much reluctance on the part of manufacturers to accede to this policy, there is less objection offered at the present time.

The purchasing agent of the chain, if he is not located or directly represented at the market, should go where the article he wishes to buy is, and offer cash for it. If the manufacturer fears it will be impossible to make the goods to retail at the price the chain wishes to sell them for, the purchasing agent may be able to show the manufacturer how it can be done. The question of how much to buy is a problem facing all purchasing agents, and in the case of the chain is scientifically determined by records, as explained later.

The principles of chain store purchasing may be summed up under four headings:

1. All purchasing should be done through headquarters,
2. Buy as directly as possible, preferably from the source,
3. Pay cash.
4. Do not overload.

Overloading, and other evils, will be minimized by proper executive control, and the coördination between departments.

Warehousing.—In an effort to simplify distribution, the majority of chain stores have taken upon themselves the warehousing function. That is, they store all goods purchased and delivered until such time as they are requisitioned by the member stores. This reduces freight charges, and gives assurance that goods will be available when needed.

The warehouse must be located with respect, first to the routes by which articles are received, and second to the position of the member stores. If the jobber's profit is to be saved this is exceedingly important.

The main principles of warehouse management are three:

1. Maintain an adequate and fresh supply of stock. On this point depends the efficiency of distribution to member stores. Articles listed as being in stock must actually be in stock. Of course, there will be unavoidable cases where goods will get out of stock, but these must be kept at a minimum.

2. Orders from member stores must be filled with speed and accuracy. If there is any lapse in the rapidity of distribution lost sales will be the result.

3. Expenses must be kept down. The expense of warehousing is taken care of in the central organization, and it forms a part of the general overhead expenditures. That is, each store must bear a certain percentage of this cost of storing and distributing goods.

All stock in warehouses should be arranged logically with consideration to the frequency with which it must be moved and the actual labor of moving. Heavy goods, for example, should be nearest the loading point. A regular position for each article of merchandise helps in speed of handling, and eliminates mistakes. By placing old goods in front, the stock can constantly be kept fresh. In the warehouse, as in the store, the layout may advantageously be standardized.

Sales.—Study the sales records and take advantage of the information they have to offer. No other documents are so valuable or so easy to read. Analyze the daily sales. See how sales for Fridays and Saturdays compare with those of other days. Many chains find that their sales are almost double on these days and they make preparation accordingly. Study also the influence of weather on the volume of trade. Learn how to distribute the seasonal rush over a period of time in order that no sales may be lost through overcrowding.

Minimize sales resistance by giving the public what the public wants. Sales resistance eats up profits. Therefore, study the product from the sales angle. Is it in demand? Is there another product which the public prefers?

A chain organization, because of its impersonal character, and the nature of its organization, should stock only standard goods. Odd sizes, unknown brands, style goods, are all too much of a risk, regardless of the amount of the profit. The wise chain store executive always remembers that it is not the length of the profit but the rapidity of the turnover which counts in the long run. And he, therefore, limits the number of lines offered to the public. He limits these, furthermore, according to the desires of the public. Where possible, a chain deals in packaged goods. There are few successful chains dealing in bulk products. The selling expense is too high.

The chain store should cater to the majority of its customers and let the few who wish special services or special products go elsewhere. The loss of a few customers will be more than made up by the increased efficiency in the management of the store and the ability to satisfy the wants of the great bulk of the customers.

Should a chain store manufacture and sell its own private brands? So many of them follow this policy that the idea has almost become inseparable from that of chain store operation. No set rule on this point can be laid down.

The arguments in favor of private brands can be reduced to three. First, it allows the chain to make extra profit, since it permits a manufacturing profit as well as the jobbing and selling profits. Second, the private brand is often of immense advertising value. Third, private brands give the chain a source of supply independent of any manufacturers. Against this, it can be argued that the public as a whole will ask for nationally advertised goods. The reply of the chains is to stock the nationally advertised goods and allow their own goods to compete on a quantity and price basis, the method used being display.

Pricing and Turnover.—The retail price should be uniform in all stores, except, perhaps, for a difference justified by additional freight rates. This principle is almost self-evident. It would be disastrous to the chain if a customer were to find that at Store No. 10 prices were different from those at No. 15. The price of goods should be fixed when possible by marking up the value a certain percentage over cost. This mark-up will vary with the nature of the product and the competition. Price cutting is always dangerous. It instils doubt in the mind of the customer as to the genuine values offered by the store and it makes it more difficult to sell the product later at the normal price.

The larger the turnover, the less profit it is necessary to make on each sale in order to show satisfactory results. That is, volume of sales reduces overhead and increases profits. Turnover of merchandise is increased by increasing sales, while the stock remains stationary or increases less rapidly.

But volume of turnover is not sufficient. There is one other element. Keep every line turning. Do not stock lines that will not sell. If some line is in stock which will not move, try to shift it to some store where it will. Such a store can usually be found in a chain of any size. If the stock of the article is too large for such methods, or if there is no such store to be found, reduce the price and turn the goods, even at a loss.

The chief merchandising appeal of the average chain is price. A low price is secured by efficient purchasing, low overhead, and large turnover. The first two yield in importance to the last. Also, as chains grow, and their goodwill increases, a reputation for quality and service make as strong an appeal as price.

Expense and Profits.—Each store in a chain will show the same amount approximately for expense as its independent competitor, less the economies effected by increased turnover, and the elimination of credit accounts and deliveries. When sales are large the overhead goes down, because the turnover has increased. By increasing the average sale, profits are increased also, due to decreased selling expenses.

Profits come with standardization of method. Generally, overhead is larger in small chains and smaller in large chains because of this very factor of standardization. Chain standards and practices are evolved slowly by experience. A new chain cannot hope to accomplish in a few months what normally takes many years.

Generally speaking, chain stores find it the best policy to do business for cash. This eliminates bad debts and simplifies accounting practice.   In almost every case where credit has been eliminated, the result has been increased net profits for the organization.

The question of deliveries is harder to settle.   Some chains deliver on payment of a certain amount extra, sufficient to cover delivery charges.

Watch the individual stores.   Ascertain the reasons why certain of them pay well month after month.   The lessons learned in this way can be applied with benefit to those which do not pay well.

Every store should earn a profit, unless there is some strong reason, such as competition, which makes it impossible.   A new store will take a certain length of time to become established. If an old store shows consistent losses, and no other reason can be found except lack of adequate volume of sales, this store should be closed and a new one started in some better favored location. The wise chain executive knows how to take a loss as well as make profits.   Mistakes are made in spite of the highest degree of standardization.   It is his business to see that these mistakes occur as seldom as possible.

Keep expenses down.   Establish percentages, based on records, which can be applied to all member stores.   Investigate any store the itemized expenses of which exceed the allowed percentage. By means of daily reports, see that expenses are reduced to a minimum, keep every line of goods turning at a profit, and profits for the entire organization should be forthcoming.

Advertising.—Every retailer must let the public know where he is located and what he has to offer.   This can be done in one of two ways.   The first is to establish the business where the traffic will pass, and to display the goods in the windows so that all who pass may see.   The second is what is technically known as advertising, that is, giving the people the same information through the medium of magazines, newspapers, theatre programs, etc.   All chains use the first method to a greater or less extent. Few chains have used the latter method in the past, more are using it now, and the probability is that in the future the majority of chains will use paid space in certain media of publicity.

The type of advertising done by the chain depends on

1. The size of the chain,
2. The type of product or products sold,
3. The location of the store.

The larger the chain, the better use it can make of advertising. The more elastic the demand for the products sold, the more stimulus can be given to sales by advertising. The type of advertising necessary depends a great deal upon the location of the store. Stores out of the line of traffic must do more advertising to attract trade.

Advertising should be initiated at headquarters as far as possible, although local conditions may make special advertising necessary. In local or semi-local chains, advertising can be standardized. In larger chains, allowance will be made for local, sectional, climatic differences, etc.

Few chains can advertise nationally with profit. But few chains can afford not to undertake some form of local advertising.

Personnel.—Are methods or men more important in chain store operation? This question has long been argued and seems no nearer settlement than before. The methods are necessary, but the men to carry them out are even more important. No matter how well standardized the procedure and the policy of a chain may be, it will not operate profitably unless there is a coördinating personal influence which binds the whole together, making it work in harmony.

Like the great railway magnates of the past century who virtually created opportunity out of what they saw, the pioneer chain executives have built up vast retailing enterprises against the strongest competition. They built the machine, but, as with the railways, they had to have men to run the engines. The chain store locomotives are the local store managers. From this local store there is a direct line to the central office which must be kept clear. Merchandise must go forward, daily reports must come back. The district manager sits at his desk like a train despatcher signalling a clear road for the trains in his district.

The function of each man in a chain store organization should be clearly defined, from the chief executive down to the humblest clerk. And each member of the organization must feel an interest in his work. How shall this interest be created? By giving each member a monetary profit in the operations of the concern, and making this profit commensurate with the work he himself does. Even the clerk will sell more goods if he or she receives extra profit for so doing.

It pays the chain to employ brains, even at a high price. The executive, the buyer, the window trimmer, the accountant, all are experts in their line, and worthy of their hire.

Training and Promotion.—Choosing the right man in the beginning saves much trouble. The chain store's employment department should pick and choose carefully only those men and women whom it considers as possessing the requisite characteristics for success in the organization.

It will pay the company to train the clerk before actually putting him behind the counter. He should be taught the standardized sales policies and methods of the chain, the nature of the product he is selling, the arrangement of the stock in the store, the habit of being courteous to customers under all conditions, etc. This preliminary training will result in more sales for the company and a larger bonus for the clerk.

Start all men at the bottom and let them work up. Do not look outside the organization to fill executive positions. There should be plenty of good executive material under training at the moment, possessing the great advantage of a thorough knowledge of the chain and its ways. Avoid labor turnover. If men are anxious to leave the employ of the chain, there must be something wrong. A concern that makes adequate allowance for the store cat but starves the store manager will find in the long run that its economy has been ill-directed.

Promotions should take place mainly on merit. Length of service is seldom a substitute for ability.

Morale.—The chain organization is held together by morale. Morale is a combination of discipline and teamwork which carries out methods and even betters them. A proper system of morale makes every individual in the organization morally and financially responsible for the duties of his position.

The higher the morale, the less necessity for policing. Chains should keep careful watch on all activities of their personnel, but the best safeguard for it is the morale of the organization. Morale creates teamwork and coöperation. It makes it easier to coördinate the various functions of the business. It fuses the sales activity and creates goodwill towards the management among the employees.

Morale should be inspirational and instructive, without cheapening the effect by using the style of language so frequently encountered in sales bulletins. Every man likes encouragement and it costs little to give it to him. Every man works better when he is interested in his work. Make him interested. Let him know he will receive a bonus for his sales efforts. Let him know that what he does is appreciated.

It is not laid down as a principle that a chain should publish a house organ, but it is laid down that there should be some established method of publicity by which the central office can let the member stores know what is going on both at headquarters and among the other stores. The larger organizations frequently publish house organs as a way to solve the difficulty. Smaller concerns send out sales bulletins and letters. In local chains, the owner can pay a daily visit, or keep in touch by telephone.

In handling the personnel, the problem resolves itself into one of training and choosing men of the type which can take charge of a retail store and operate it by routine methods, with partial supervision. It offers a large field for the great number of men who must always work under someone else's guidance. Choose your men carefully, train them properly, and keep up the level of the morale.

Control.—All the manifold activities of the chain can be controlled only by means of records. Records are a fundamental necessity in every chain. By means of them the purchasing agent buys goods to sell through retail stores and estimates the quantities necessary to keep on hand in the warehouse. By means of records, the sales manager keeps track of the sales in various stores and can tell at a glance which stores are doing well and which are falling behind. By means of records, the auditor tells whether overhead expenses are too high. Lastly, by means of records the executive control is exercised.

The average small retail store keeps few accounts, because the facts are supposedly contained in the head of the owner. But all the necessary information in the chain is tabulated. It undergoes a regular digestive process until it is finally served up to the chief executive in the form of percentages and profits.

The records of the chain are one of its most valuable possessions. Extending back over a series of years, they contain in essence the results of past experience. By looking back, the chain can tell approximately what to expect in every line and phase of its activity. Should it plan to start another store, the records should tell what a store in such a location should earn. When sales are reported each month, the sales manager can see whether the amount is less than it was a year ago at the same time, or more.

All chain stores should keep a continual, automatic inventory of stock on hand in warehouses, and in some cases in each store. Adequate turnover of all lines can be controlled in no other way.

Records fall into three main divisions:

1. Warehousing and purchasing records,
2. Accounting records, overhead, salaries, etc.,
3. Records of individual retail stores.

Taken collectively, they form the basis of the chain's operation, and the person in authority knows daily exactly where his company stands in every detail. Thus, the principle follows that the chain should have records so complete in every detail as to allow the executive at any time to ascertain the exact status of any store in the chain, any warehouse, any manager's record, and all overhead expenses.

The Principles of Growth.—Everything previously discussed leads us to this point: A successful chain grows larger. It adds more links; it takes in more territory.

Ordinarily, a chain should expand naturally by utilizing the profits made in old stores to start new ones. The great majority of chains have been financed in this way, and this is without doubt the soundest method.

But a chain can also expand by absorbing other chains and by adding them to its organization.

Lastly, a chain can borrow money and start a number of retail links at one time. This is the most hazardous method, and should be carefully investigated before being attempted.

Chains grow not only as their financial resources expand,

but also as their trained personnel grows larger. New stores must be opened for new potential store managers, as they become trained in the methods and policies of the organization.

Chains are found chiefly in congested centers of population, and they occupy this territory principally because the physical advantages are greater. The traffic being heavier, the volume of trade per store is greater. When urban locations are taken up, those chains the member stores of which require a minimum of population for successful operation extend their activities to the suburbs. A grocery store, for example, can operate on a population of ten thousand successfully. (There are some chains, of course, which purposely confine themselves to the smaller towns.)

Watch the normal growth of population if you wish to extend your program. Natural causes, or unusual stimulus to growth, make new sites continually available. If you do not take advantage of this some one else will.

Conclusions.—Out of the mass of specific principles for chain store operation, two fundamentals emerge, one having to do with methods primarily, the other having to do primarily with men. In other words, the fundamentals are those of standardization and of coördination. Chain store practice should be standardized as far as possible. The chain store personnel should coördinate effort and practice.

All other principles must be connected one with another so as to make the process of operation smooth. The major part of this book is devoted to showing how methods and practice may be standardized and how all activities may be united into a smoothly functioning organization through the mechanism of records. Records are always a means; never an end. The chain does not exist to make records, but to use them. The routine of chain store operation merely supplies the necessary cogs which will make the whole function smoothly and in unison.

CHAPTER II

THE CHAIN STORE FIELD

OUTLINE

Classification of chain stores.
  1. Geographical.
  2. According to policy.
  3. Type of organization.
  4. According to product sold.
Geographical.
  1. National chains.
      (a) Comparatively few.
      (b) Follow lines of population.
  2. Sectional.
      (a) Larger number.
  3. Local chains.
      (a) By far the greatest in number.
Operating policy.
  1. Saving in price by cutting out
      (a) Credit.
      (b) Deliveries.
      (c) Telephones.
      (d) Miscellaneous.
  2. Self service stores.
      (a) Thus far limited to grocery lines and restaurants.
Organization.
  1. Closely centralized.
      (a) Authority of store manager closely limited.
  2. Loosely connected.
      (a) Authority of store manager broad.
  3. Partnership type.
  4. Manufacturers' chains.
  5. Agency plan.
Type of product sold.
  1. Material products.
      (a) Necessities.
      (b) Semi-necessities.
  2. Services.
Trends.
  1. Combination.

16

    (*a*) Secures additional capital.
    (*a*) Allows new operating economies.
        1. Reduced overhead.
        2. Increased purchasing power.
    (*c*) Increases rate of expansion.
    (*d*) Increases territorial extent.
    (*e*) Relieves pressure of competition.
2. Manufacturing by chains.
    (*a*) Private brand.
        1. Gives chain unfailing source of supply of uniform quality.
        2. Tends to reduce cost of advertised articles.

CHAPTER II

THE CHAIN STORE FIELD

The chain store movement is as yet in its infancy. Judged by the comparatively recent origin of the movement, its rapid and unchecked growth, there is an economic place for chain stores in the life of the community. They help in no small way to keep the cost of living down and to stabilize retail prices. For example, when prices fell after the war, the canners reduced their prices. The jobbers passed on the saving to the small retailers, and there the saving stopped. The small retailer could not see far enough ahead to realize that he must pocket his loss and reduce his prices. But the chain grocery stores, buying direct of the canner, immediately revised prices in line with the new quotations.

The economic trend of the times is towards more direct distribution and a more rapid reflection of the course of wholesale prices in the retail field. The chain stores are working in accordance with this tendency and not against it. So far, the experiment has been limited to comparatively few types of products, but each year sees new chains in new fields, apparently prospering in the venture. Most independent retailers have ceased declaiming against the chain store and predicting its failure. They are accepting it as an accomplished fact, and their aim is to imitate, as far as possible, the methods used by the chains in obtaining their success, even to the extent of starting chains themselves.

The field of retailing has been immensely broadened. It now offers opportunity to men of ambition and vision. Brains came first, and then capital. The great founders of the present day chain stores created them out of profits. Capital was slow in following the lead or realizing that a new field had been created for exploitation. Capital had been too much occupied with the profits of production and had paid little attention to those of selling. The past century was the great age of productive effort in the world. The present century seems to be turning towards scientific sales effort. The chain store organizations have gone farthest with their experiments towards creating an efficient method of bringing the product to the consumer.

The Inception of the Movement.—The credit for founding the first large chain of stores belongs to George H. Hartford, the originator and, until his death, the president of the Great Atlantic & Pacific Tea Co. In 1857 he was in the hide and leather business in New York, and in 1859 he added tea as a sideline. This venture was so successful that in 1864 he organized the Great American Tea Co. Then it occurred to him that it would be possible to have a chain of retail stores throughout New York and Brooklyn and in a few years he had a chain of 25 stores, called the Great Atlantic & Pacific Tea Co.

The dates of founding some of the more important chains are as follows:

Great Atlantic & Pacific Tea Co	1859
Jones Tea Co	1872
F. W. Woolworth Co	1879
James Butler	1882
Hanan Shoe Co	1885
Acme Tea Co. (Now part of American Stores Corporation)	1887
S. S. Kresge Co	1897
United Cigar Stores Co	1900
J. C. Penney Co	1902

The greater part of the development of these chains has taken place within the last 20 years, but it is interesting to note that all the earlier chains have attained considerable size and prominence. The Great Atlantic & Pacific Tea Co. is still far ahead of all others in the number of stores operated. The date of the Hanan Shoe Co.'s starting its chain of retail stores shows that the idea of a manufacturer's chain was conceived comparatively early in the development, and the far greater expansion of the purely retail chains makes it seem that these chains will be the ultimate type.

Types of Chain Stores.—Chains may be classified in several ways, each one of which offers valuable points for analysis. They are:

1. *Geographical Extent.*—Under this heading chains may be divided into
    (a) National.
    (b) Sectional.
    (c) Local.
2. *Policy*—Under this heading come those particular sales and merchandis-
    ing principles according to which the chain is operated.
    (a) Cash and carry.
    (b) Self service.
3. *Organization.*—Chains have shown considerable variation on this point,
    due to difficulty in standardizing both men and methods.
    (a) Closely centralized type.
    (b) Loosely connected.
    (c) "Penney" type.
    (d) Combination of types.
4. *The Product Sold.*—This question of the product was at first compara-
    tively limited, but in recent years it has been extended to such
    intangible products as places of amusement, barber shops, hotels,
    and other institutions offering service rather than a tangible product.

Chains Considered Geographically.—There are few national
chains, if by national we mean operating stores in every or nearly
every state in the union. Among the large chains, the Great
Atlantic & Pacific Tea Co., the F. W. Woolworth Co., and the
United Cigar Stores Co. are the outstanding examples. Each
of these chains has followed a policy of locating in the larger
centers of population first.

The F. W. Woolworth Co. claims to have a store in every
town containing 8,000 inhabitants or over. Figure 1 shows how
their stores are distributed. The great majority of these stores
are located in New England and the Middle Western States,
with New York and Pennsylvania in the lead. The growth of
this chain will obviously follow the lines of population, and if
the inhabitants of the South or the West gather more in the future
in cities and towns, the Woolworth stores will follow them.

A great many chains are sectional, that is, they have outgrown
their purely local character and have extended into the neighborhood. Some of these sectional chains, such as the Louis K.
Liggett Co., show signs already of becoming national. The
Liggett Co. with fifty-five stores in New York City and nineteen
in Boston, eight in Philadelphia, and eight in Washington, has
already extended its operations as far South as Georgia and
Florida, and as far West as Oklahoma and Minnesota. Many

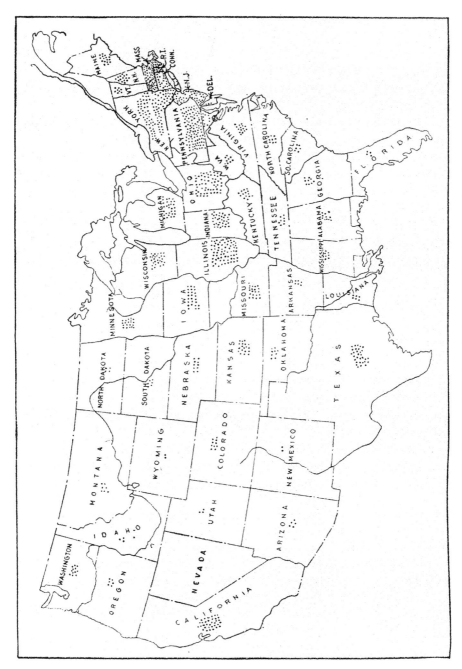

Fig. 1.—Distribution of Woolworth stores. Each dot represents a store.

grocery chains are sectional, such as the Kroger Grocery & Baking Co. in the Middle West, the John T. Connor Có. in Massachusetts, and the Mayflower Stores in Rhode Island.

Last of all, come the local chains, which form the bulk of the field, chains with two, three, five or ten links, all closely connected in the city or its immediate surroundings.

Few chains are started with the definite idea of making them national or even sectional. The growth is usually gradual and the steps in the growth perfectly logical. The local chain, which is superior in its methods, becomes sectional. The sectional chain keeps on expanding until it becomes too large to be called sectional, and becomes national.

Chains Considered According to Operating Policy.—The chain store's great appeal to the public has been saving in price. To attain this end, chain managements have been constantly scheming how to sell their goods at a greater saving. In 1912, the Great Atlantic & Pacific Tea Co. did away with telephones, deliveries and credits, and the company claims that from this change a 65 per cent. increase in business has come about. This policy met, in fact, with instant approval from the purchasing public, a large part of which was willing to do without the extra services if it could obtain the saving in price. This policy has been generally adopted by chain store organizations and the name chain store at this time is almost synonymous with "cash-and-carry."

Richard M. Decker, treasurer of Chas. M. Decker & Brothers of Orange, N. J., explains as follows the reasons which led them to change radically the type of their organizations:

"The company of Chas. M. Decker & Bros. has operated so-called service grocery stores since 1871. However, due to changing conditions, the demand for this class of store was decreasing, rather than increasing, in this territory. Therefore, in the early part of 1918 we decided to enter the chain store business for ourselves. Since that time, we have closed all but three of our service stores and have opened, either ourselves or through the purchase of another company, approximately one hundred and sixty odd thrift stores.

"In 1920 we organized a new company to take over the operating thrift stores of Chas. M. Decker & Bros. and to open additional ones as times and conditions should warrant. Two companies are now being operated but with one centralized purchasing and administrative organization. We have different schedules of prices in the two chains of stores; and it is needless to say that there is a difference in our accounting systems.

"At present we consider the thrift stores the most satisfactory, but we also feel that there is enough demand in certain localities for a service grocery store; and whether the service grocery store should be continued depends of course upon whether there is sufficient demand. We would also add that in our service stores we carry a much greater assortment of merchandise than in our thrift stores."

Here, in a nut shell, is an answer to arguments against the chain cash-and-carry stores. The public prefers them to the service stores. The people who can afford to pay for extra services are comparatively few, compared to those who prefer to carry their purchases home and save the money.

There has been one further development in cutting down expenses and this is the self-service store, as evidenced by the phenomenal growth of the Piggly Wiggly stores. Since 1916, the Piggly Wiggly Co. has opened 600 stores. There is saving on clerk hire as well as the customary savings on delivery and credits. The plan is very simple. There are turnstile gates through which the customer enters. Goods are all placed on open shelves with prices plainly marked. The customer opens the refrigerator and takes out whatever he or she wishes. It is impossible to leave the store without passing through all the aisles. When the customer reaches the out-turning wicket a clerk records the amount of the purchase and the customer pays this to the cashier.

Although the Piggly Wiggly stores appear to fill a certain need in retail merchandising the rapid growth of the idea has brought about certain financial difficulties. The Manhattan Piggly Wiggly Corporation, one of the groups operated under separate franchise, is in the hands of a receiver. The future of the self-service idea as embodied in the Piggly Wiggly stores is not yet certain.

The Dry Goods Economist quotes the following remarks about the profits and economies made by the Piggly Wiggly Co. from the use of the self-service idea:

"The first Piggly Wiggly store in Memphis, Tenn., was opened in a building formerly occupied by one of a chain of twenty stores. For the six months immediately preceding the taking over of the building by the Piggly Wiggly concern, the sales of the former chain store had approximated $34,000 with an approximate expense of $5,200. The Piggly Wiggly organization retained the clerks formerly used in the other store and had the same management, but put into effect its self-service system and its own equipment. In the first six months of the Piggly Wiggly occupancy, $114,000 business was done at an expense of $3,400. The self-service system cut $300 per month from expenses, and showed a gain of $80,000 in sales. Under the old system the overhead had been 15 per cent; the Piggly Wiggly overhead was three per cent. For two months, June and July 1920, this store did an average of $6,000 per week, while it carries $8,000 worth of merchandise at all times, giving it a thirty-nine-time turnover yearly."

The above account is obviously written from the Piggly Wiggly angle. Now listen to what a chain store which tried out the self service method has to say:

"We tried out the Piggly Wiggly idea of a self-service store, and it worked. In fact, it is one of our best stores. However, we find this is true: there is no tremendous saving in the payroll, as might be expected. We like this one store in its location, down town, and feel that it takes care of the afternoon rush more efficiently than the old style of store ever could. But for a residence neighborhood, we feel the self-service store would never work. Women like to have things explained to them. The personal factor is too valuable to warrant having a lot of mechanical stores without real human beings behind the counter."

This sounds strangely like the arguments that were put forth against the chain stores themselves in the early days, when it was freely predicted they could never be a success because of the lack of this very personal element which is brought up here against the self-service store. Actually, it is too early to speak with certainty as to the future of this development. It would seem that there should be a place for such a store in nearly every community, and the success of the Piggly Wiggly Company itself would seem to bear out this assumption.

Whether the self-service idea can be adapted to forms of merchandise other than groceries has not yet been attempted.

If the self-service plan is to be restricted to the grocery field, its importance will be restricted, but if it can be extended to other fields, there is no limit to its possibilities.

Type of Chain Organization.—There is no standard type of chain organization. It varies all the way from the most closely connected organization possible under the circumstances to a very broad authority vested in the local manager. The grocery chains, the drug chains and other chains dealing in staple commodities are ordinarily very closely knit together. In other cases, each store is dependent on the head organization only for certain things, in others being a unit in itself, such as the hotel chains. Between these two extremes there is a wide gradation.

A different type of organization is usually required for chains that have several stores in each community than for that in which the links are widely scattered. It takes a larger percentage of population to support a chain candy store than it does to support a chain drug or grocery store. The proximity of the various links in a grocery chain makes it easier to superintend their operation and makes it unnecessary to invest the branch manager with any great amount of authority.

The Penney system is explained at length later in the book. This partnership type of organization seems to fit the dry goods field particularly well, although there seems to be no inherent reason why it should not be applied to other fields with equal success.

The manufacturer's chain brings in so many new problems not existing in the average retailer's chain that the subject has been treated separately in Chap. XXI.

The agency plan as instituted by the United Drug Company seems outside the ordinary chain store field since the agencies are not under one central executive control as are all other types of chains, including the manufacturer's chain.

The Type of Product.—In the last analysis, the greatest point of differentiation between chains is the type of product they sell. As previously mentioned, the chain idea has spread from the grocery and the five and ten cent stores, until now it enters into many retailing lines. Following is a classification of some businesses successfully operating under chain store principles and practices.

Bakeries	Hardware
Barbers	Hats
Butchers	Hosiery
Cloaks and suits	Hotels
Clothes	Men's clothing
Candy and confectionery	Optical
Dairy products	Pianos
Drugs	Restaurants
Dry goods	Shirts
Dyers and cleansers	Shoes
Five and ten cent stores	Tailors
Florists	Theaters
Fruit	Tobacco
Garages	Typewriters
Groceries	Waists
Haberdashery	

It is not too much to say that all operating policies and methods depend on the nature of the product or service to be marketed, not only the method of accounting, the type of clerk, and the degree of supervision necessary but also the location and the methods of publicity. The nature of the product will also determine the type of customer to whom the chain must appeal.

Chain Store Trends.—It is difficult to tell what the ultimate outcome of the chain store movement will be. It seems definitely established that it is to be one of the most important elements in retailing and, as pointed out before, it is growing because its principles are in harmony with the spirit of the times.

There are two major tendencies which deserve particular mention. The first of these is the tendency to combination which is observable, and the second is the increasing policy of the chain organizations to manufacture as much as they can of what they sell.

1. *Combination.*—It seems to be a principle of chain store growth that a chain will attain a certain size by carefully plodding ahead on the most conservative lines and then suddenly merge with another chain of the same size, or one slightly smaller.

There have been three great chain mergers. In 1912, the F. W. Woolworth Co. was formed to take over and operate six five and ten cent store chains, viz:

	STORES
F. W. Woolworth & Co	318
S. H. Knox & Co	112
F. M. Kirby & Co	96
E. P. Charlton & Co	53
C. S. Woolworth	15
W. H. Moore	2
Total	596

At one stroke the F. W. Woolworth Co. became a national chain, for the various components had each developed a separate section of the country. The motives for the merger were plain. It gave at once a stronger financial organization, much greater buying power, and a consequent wider range of articles which could be sold at five and ten cents, and lastly it increased operating efficiency. Since the merger, the number of stores in the Woolworth organization is nearly double the 596 stores operated at that time. The sales, however, have almost trebled, going from $52,616,123 in 1911 to $147,644,999 in 1921, a space of just ten years.

The second great merger was in the grocery field in Philadelphia when the following five chains combined to form the American Stores Co. The merger took place in 1917.

	FOUNDED	STORES
The Acme Tea Co	1887	433
Robinson-Crawford	1891	186
The Bell Co	1890	214
Child's	1883	268
Dunlap & Co	1888	122
		1,223

This total of 1,223 stores made the American Stores Co., the second largest grocery chain in the country, and the only chain operating more than 1,000 stores which was not national in scope. The results are substantially the same as in the case of the Woolworth combination.

The mergers of small chains which take place constantly are rarely discussed. They are not large enough to cause much stir in the commercial world. But this process, which goes on unceasingly, and has been more rapid of late years has enormously increased the number of chain stores. No sooner do two or more chains combine than a new chain arises to compete with them. No chain has yet succeeded in having a monopoly because the same fields in which it operates are open to its competitors.

The third and most significant combination of the three took place in 1919, when the United Retail Stores Corporation was formed by the Duke-Whelan interests. It was not a combination of several companies dealing in the same product, but a combination of companies retailing different products. The statement to the stockholders concerning the attitude of the management said:

"For several years the outstanding feature of business development in the United States has been the growth of chain store merchandising. It has been steady and permanent and promises to have greater expansion during the next ten years. The United Cigar Stores Co. was among the pioneers in the development of the chain store idea and during the growth of the company a splendid organization, efficient in methods of systematic checking and progressive store management was built up.

"As all chain store development rests primarily on securing suitable locations, it was realized by the management that the large real estate department pretty well covering the country could, without much additional expense, secure stores for other lines of business besides cigars. Also, as fundamentals of chain store operation apply to most lines of merchandise, the experience of the successful heads of various departments of the company could be applied to any field of chain store management considered desirable.

"In short, the management felt that by securing additional capital, and being placed in a position to finance new enterprises, expansion most profitable to the stockholders would be assured."

The new company started out with three chains. The United Cigar Stores Co. was taken in first. Gilmer's, Inc., a dry goods chain operating chiefly in the South was acquired. And lastly the United Retail Candy Stores Co. was formed which already has over twenty-five stores in operation. In addition to these three chains, Montgomery Ward & Co., the second largest mail order house in the country, was acquired. In this way the corporation felt that the retail outlet problem was solved. It is planned to have each of the subsidiary companies manufacture a great deal of what it sells. The United Cigar Stores Co. already was ensured a supply of its own branded goods and the Furst & Kramer Co. was bought to supply its own brand of candy to the United Retail Candy Stores. A retail drug chain, the United Retail Chemists Corporation, operates eighteen stores mostly in New Jersey.

Each line of business will be run as a separate entity. The parent corporation will furnish capital and funds. About half the stock in each company will be sold to the members of that company and the public. In addition to the cigar stores, the candy stores, the drug stores and the department stores, the corporation may start grocery stores or any other type of retail store for which it sees a need. The United Retail Stores Corporation plans to furnish the accounting system, locate sites for retail stores, and furnish men.

The corporation has no intention of confining its operations to the United States for its charter reads: "To extend and carry on generally in the United States and throughout the world a manufacturing business and a system of retail stores for merchandising of all kinds." In the full course of expansion the corporation was hit by the post-war deflationary movement and plans were, if not suspended, at least modified, to meet the new conditions.

2. *Manufacturing by Chains.*—When the chain stores first came into conflict with manufacturers on the questions of buying direct and maintaining manufacturers' prices, the result was that in many cases the chains started factories of their own to manufacture a certain portion of their products which they found it difficult to obtain outside. These manufactured products they labeled with a brand of their own invention and placed them in competition with the advertised articles.

On the part of the grocers, the business of manufacturing their own brands was taken directly from the practice of the jobbers and wholesale grocers, 75 per cent. of whom had for a long time been manufacturing. The war, shutting off as it did a great deal of importation from Europe, was a great stimulus to chain manufacturing. The Woolworth Co., particularly, took this opportunity to start manufacturing many articles.

The United Drug Co., an association of manufacturers, has provided for the sale of its products not only through its own chain of stores, the Louis K. Liggett Co., but through an extensive chain of agencies. The United Cigar Stores Co., which manufactures many of its own brands, pursues this same policy of extending sales through agencies into districts which are hardly large enough to support one of the company's own stores. The Winchester Stores Co. has attempted this same scheme of obtaining distribution for manufactured products and this method is used by the majority of the manufacturers' chains. The goods manufactured by the chain are sold at lower prices:

1. It gives the chain an unfailing source of supply of goods to sell, in uniform quantities, and of uniform quality,

2. It tends to keep the price of advertised articles down.

But independent manufacturers need have no fear that the manufacturing policy of the chain will do away with all demand for their products, provided they are merchandised properly. The customer of the chain store can be sure of getting what he asks for.

Conclusions.—The chain store movement is still in the growing stage. Differentiation is bound to occur. That is, the science of retailing has only in the past few years passed the experimental stage. Standardization is brought about by increased competition and the resulting elimination of the unfit. Thus, in the future, chain store practice will become even more standardized than it is today, granting, of course, individual and minor differences in policy or the guiding influence of a great executive.

It is difficult to forecast the future further than to say that it is full of opportunity and promise. The experiment of the United Retail Stores Corporation brings in a new and highly interesting development. This company maintains that it is possible to standardize chain store practice sufficiently to run several retail ventures of different kinds under the same executive control, and furthermore, that the business of manufacturing is necessary for the greatest success of the chain.

CHAPTER III

LOCATING THE STORE

2. By sex.
 (*a*) Male.
 (*b*) Female.
3. Traffic entering neighboring stores.
4. Amount of traffic carrying bundles.
5. Type of traffic.
 (*a*) Shoppers.
 (*b*) Commuters.
 (*c*) Miscellaneous.

The building.
1. Construction.
 (*a*) Number of stores.
 (*b*) Material.
 (*c*) Condition.
 (*d*) *H*eating.
 (*e*) Water supply.
 (*f*) Miscellaneous.
2. Present occupants.
 (*a*) Character.
 (*b*) Length of leases.
 (*c*) Degree of success obtained in location.
3. The store.
 (*a*) Floor space.
  1. Necessity of new partitioning.
 (*b*) Fixtures.
 (*c*) Display windows.
  1. Arrangement.
 (*d*) Entrance.
  1. Up steps or level.
 (*e*) Lighting.

Renting or owning.
1. Dependent on
 (*a*) Size of chain.
 (*b*) Capital.
 (*c*) Rate of expansion.
 (*d*) Policy.
2. Possibilities of profit from owning and renting remainder of building to tenants.
3. Advisability of special realty department to
 (*a*) Collect rents.
 (*b*) See to improvements.
 (*c*) Make rentals and new leases.
 (*d*) Miscellaneous.

CHAPTER III

LOCATING THE STORE

No matter whether a merchant is locating his second or his two hundredth store, the location of it is of first importance. Probably more has been written about locating the chain store than any other phase of the subject. The reason is simple. There is no other aspect of the business which is calculated so much to catch the public interest, always alive to novel merchandising methods. There is something out of the ordinary in the idea of a man or several men standing on a street corner and clocking the passers-by. Yet this was the method initiated by the United Cigar Stores and widely imitated over the whole country.

Many chain store systems maintain real estate departments which are organized to a high degree. A department of this sort not only picks the sites, but it takes care of the buildings, makes improvements, renews leases, in a word, takes entire charge of the company's property. A separate real estate department, of course, is possible only for chains possessing a large number of stores and facilities for increasing this number at a comparatively steady rate.

But location is not always a matter of finding out where the largest number of people pass during the day. Some large chains rely little on this factor to secure patronage. An example of such a chain is the J. C. Penney. Penney wants low rents. It seldom rents a store in what is supposed to be the best locality, although much depends on the town and the character of possible customers. It tries to locate in a fairly central position in the town but rarely on the main street. It will go to the very edge of the business district if the downtown side streets are too expensive. This policy is justified for this company which finds that people will come without much regard to location. This rule must be modified occasionally. As one of their officials says, a farmer will walk a block to save a few cents, but a miner will not. Therefore, in mining districts the Penney policy has to be made to suit conditions.

General Principles of Location.—In the old days a merchant bought or rented a store where he could get it. He hung out his sign and waited for customers. If such a policy were tried today, he would still be waiting. If the modern merchant is not prepared to make his presence known by advertising or by cut prices or special sales, he must put his store where the largest number of potential customers will see it.

The first thing to do when locating a store is to analyze the business and see exactly to whom the goods are to be retailed and how trade is to be attracted. One of the experts in locating sites divides merchants into two classes:

1. *Those Who Advertise.*—Such merchants can afford to take a chance on location. He gives such notable examples as Lane Bryant in New York, maternity garment merchandizers, who cater to a Fifth Avenue public, although located half a block away from Fifth Avenue on 38th Street. Another example is Spear & Co., furniture retailers, New York, who have made a big success although located on what is technically the wrong side of the street. A furniture store, to be sure, has a somewhat different problem from the ordinary retailer, and can sometimes afford to locate out of the main traffic.

2. *Non-advertisers.*—This second type of merchants must select locations which naturally obtrude on the public vision. The circulation of traffic may be compared to a river which has overflowed its banks. The main current flows steadily on while in the backwaters there is little motion or perhaps an eddy. The merchant who succeeds in locating on the main artery of commerce and whose merchandizing plan is otherwise suitable must be successful, while the merchant around the corner finds little traffic coming to his door.

Cigar and drug stores endeavor to locate near some point where traffic is heavy. In fact, a cigar store finds it difficult to make a success unless it is on a corner. The United Cigar Stores have gone so far as to make it a rule that their stores shall all be on corners. A drug store can take an inside location provided that the traffic does not have to go out of its way more than a short distance.

The first principle of locating a chain store is this: If the traffic cannot be made to come to the store by special inducement, such as advertising, or price, then the store must be located in the path of traffic.

The Locality.—Almost every chain has a definite objective when going into a community. It knows exactly where its store ought to be. Rarely is it possible to obtain this location at once. Often it is a case of waiting years. One chain has a lease on property in San Antonio which will not go into effect for seven years. Another lease made in Norfolk starts in five years. The real estate department is looking well into the future.

The future of the community must be considered a fundamental factor in determining location. Some cities are constantly moving, others are safely anchored. Wherever the high-class residence district is, the high-class business district will follow. Business has gone out Euclid Avenue, in Cleveland, Woodward Avenue in Detroit, and East Avenue in Rochester, N. Y.

But where there are physical obstacles to this, such as in the case of a steep hill in Providence, Rhode Island, or rivers, as in Pittsburgh, the business section cannot move except in certain directions. As a general rule populations grow up hill. If office buildings predominate in a locality, stores selling goods with a shopping appeal will be found elsewhere.

Charles Nicholls, Jr., president of the Chain Stores Leasing Co., gives an interesting resumé of the method by which he establishes the value of a piece of property:

1. Ascertain the population.
2. Determine the type and habits of the people.
3. Investigate main industries to see whether location is good for men or women. Youngstown, Altoona, and Akron are good for men. Fall River, Lowell, and New Bedford are good for women, because of the large number of women employed in the factories there.
4. Investigate bank deposits and clearings. These give an excellent history of business conditions. However, it is necessary to ascertain how these are divided among the population. It might be in a medium-sized town that the majority of the clearings were due to a small number of individuals.
5. Find out the number of different industries. Find out also the proportion of workmen to clerks. Washington, D. C., for example, has a

large clerical population, while Schenectady has a large number of skilled and unskilled workmen.

6. After having considered the above points, the proper method is to study the prevailing local rental conditions. The available business blocks are investigated with relation to the traffic. Men's locations are differentiated from women's. When the block has been chosen, secure definite and reliable information on each piece of property and the possibility of securing it. The value depends mainly on the volume of actual business. One location might be worth $3,000 to one man, $4,000 to another. In addition, it is necessary to take into consideration the drawing power of the surrounding territory.

The above outline of method sets forth the general course of procedure. It brings out clearly the salient points to be investigated.

Analyzing the Traffic.—The value of analyzing the traffic passing by a potential chain store site lies in the fact that statistics have been worked out carefully by the different chains on which they can form judgments. They can compare conditions existing in the old stores. They know the percentage of people passing a given point who will enter a store such as theirs. For example, the United Cigar Stores Company has a fairly definite idea, after it has analyzed the traffic, not only how many men will enter its store, but also how many will buy, and the average sale to each one. Knowing this, it is comparatively easy to figure out what an individual store will earn, or better the volume of sales each individual store will make. In each case allowance is made for the type of the locality, the traffic, etc.

The most spectacular feature of choosing the chain store is undoubtedly the clocking, that is, determining how many people pass a given point, to what type they belong, whether they carry bundles, their sex, age, or any other information which may be desired. Anywhere from one to four men is required to gather this information. It is not only gathered for one day but for several days and even weeks. Some chains will not establish stores unless it is found that at least 15,000 people a day pass the point where it is proposed to establish the store.

Figure 2 shows the questionnaire which the investigator for a bakery chain had to fill in. It is to be supposed that some definite site was already in view when the investigator was sent out to cover some location. Here the hourly traffic was gauged,

How near is shopping centre.....................................

State nearest bakery...

Distance of store from United Cigar Store.........................

Distance of store from Liggett's Drug Store.......................

Distance of store from Schulte Cigar Store........................

Will owner agree to run necessary **two-inch gas pipe** from oven......

DETAILS OF TRAFFIC HOURS	MALES	FEMALES	HOW MANY PEOPLE CARRIED PACKAGES	TOTAL NUMBER
7 A.M. to 8 A.M.............				
8 A.M. to 9 A.M.............				
9 A.M. to 10 A.M.............				
10 A.M. to 11 A.M.............				
11 A.M. to 12 Noon.............				
12 Noon to 1 P.M.............				
1 P.M. to 2 P.M.............				
2 P.M. to 3 P.M.............				
3 P.M. to 4 P.M.............				
4 P.M. to 5 P.M.............				
5 P.M. to 6 P.M.............				
6 P.M. to 7 P.M.............				
7 P.M. to 8 P.M.............				
8 P.M. to 9 P.M.............				
9 P.M. to 10 P.M.............				
10 P.M. to 11 P.M.............				
11 P.M. to 12 Midnight.............				
Grand totals.............				

REMARKS...

....

....

....

....

....

....

Investigator's Signature

....

Approved

....

Approved

FIG.. 2.—Questionnaire used by bakery chain to determine attractive store sites.

divided by sexes.   It was also important to ascertain how many people carried bundles.

Some such plan as this should be followed in nearly all cases where new stores are to be opened.   It is especially important to know in advance the size of this volume of traffic where the store does not rely on other means of attracting trade.   Department stores, women's ready-to-wear stores, specialty shops, and some shoe stores, can afford to take a chance of making up traffic deficiencies by their own efforts, but this means money expended and it is always a debatable question whether increased rents and more traffic are not better than lower rents and increased advertising with decreased profits.   A mistake in location may prove costly because often stores are taken on long term leases. The United Retail Stores Corporation finds it profitable in some cases to take a location, formerly devoted exclusively to retailing tobacco products, and make it a candy store, devoted exclusively to the retailing of confectionery.

The investigators for many chains have to go much further in analyzing the traffic than is indicated in this bakery questionnaire.   They take into consideration the direction of the traffic both in general and at special times of the day.   There are very definite currents of traffic which it is possible to set down statistically.   In some cases the number of people entering other stores in the same line of business is noted as well as the number of persons leaving that store with bundles.   In suburban districts it is frequently found valuable to analyze the number of persons returning home from the city with packages, indicating that purchasing is done elsewhere.   In many cases this may prove an inducement to the chain store to enter that locality, accepting this foreign purchasing as an index that prices in the district are too high.

Grocery stores ordinarily go in for cheaper locations.   In the majority of cases they are a strictly neighborhood proposition, the prevalent cash-and-carry feature making this almost universal. In some cases, however, stores in the heart of the business district have been found exceedingly profitable, particularly when run in connection with some lunch room or restaurant feature.

Location and Buying Habits.—It is quite possible that 15,000 people might pass a given location daily, yet that location prove useless, simply because the people and the product were not suited. People going from the railroad station to the business district to work will often stop and purchase tobacco and candy, but they rarely would have time to shop in a department store.

Mr. Nicholls says: "I analyze the travelling population carefully. I notice where people get on and off the cars. I classify the general types. I can tell the 'drop in' type, which is quite different from the type which comes prepared to purchase. There is also the station traffic, the commuters. These are always in a hurry."

Every location will have a certain type of purchaser, and this type of purchaser varies at different times of the day. Now from this it is possible to draw rather definite conclusions. It is evident that some locations are particularly fitted to some types of stores. For example, the five and ten cent store does 90 per cent. of its business with women. Its usual policy is to locate as near as possible to a department store, thus getting the benefit of the department store's great drawing power. If a department store is not available, some other magnet which draws people such as a theatre or a drug store will do although the latter are not considered nearly so effective. Since a five and ten cent store in itself is not important enough to draw people to it, it must rely on putting itself in the way of its potential patrons. It will not be a success in the office district where the great majority of pedestrians are men.

It has long been known that sides of the street differ from each other in the amount and nature of business done. Ordinarily the shady side of the street is given over to women's trade and rentals are 25 per cent. higher. Department stores are an example of this. There are exceptions in Boston on Tremont St. where the Common makes it impossible to seek the shady side, and in Rochester, N. Y., where the sunny side was originally chosen and no change has since been made.

In similar fashion, one side of the street may be good for candy stores and fatal to shoe stores. Going even further, one side of the street may be good for expensive shoes and bad for cheap shoes, and vice versa. A cigar store which was a failure on one side of the street might be successful on the other side;

and this can be predetermined to a great extent by analyzing the traffic.

Going back for a moment to the population of the city, we find it is possible in many cases to determine the per capita consumption in a given city or district of a given product. By gathering statistics such as these, George J. Whelan, founder of the United Cigar Stores, was able to establish his locations in more scientific fashion than would otherwise have been possible. For example, he made up the following list of the per capita consumption of tobacco in the largest cities:

San Francisco	$4.06	Rochester, N. Y.	$0.99
Atlantic City	2.55	Chicago	0.63
New York	1.74	Spokane	0.60
St. Louis	1.21	Milwaukee	0.22

Such figures are readily ascertainable by the ordinary methods of commercial research. By a glance at the above table it is evident that a great many more people would have to pass a United Cigar Stores location in Milwaukee than in San Francisco before the same volume of sales could be obtained.

Such a list as the above is of only temporary value and must not be relied on too far. Buying and consuming habits are constantly changing. New styles, new people, new industries, all have a bearing. Therefore, such figures must be constantly kept up to date. An increase in per capita consumption would mean more stores, a decrease a policy of curtailment or of artificial stimulation of consumption.

City and Suburban Locations.—In the earlier stages of the chain store development, many stores were located hit-or-miss. Some of them succeeded and some of them failed. But those that failed went out of business for good and sufficient reasons. There was nothing intangible about their failure. Many of them succeeded because they could not help doing so. The business was forced upon them. But, in general, the larger chains have always followed a standard policy in choosing locations, and the smaller chains can only hope to compete by doing the same. Locations are always becoming available through growth in population but, generally speaking, locations are becoming scarcer and competition keener.

Chains normally start in large cities, spread in that city and then jump to another large city. This was the manner in which the Great Atlantic & Pacific Tea Co. started as well as the United Cigar Stores. Later they return and comb up the smaller communities. Woolworth started* in a small town and then spread to larger communities. Penney follows a policy of clinging preferably to the smaller communities, and in this way effects many economies, at the same time having a monopoly of the chain department store field in these localities.

In cities, the most likely locations are taken first. Expansion then extends to the suburbs, and finally to the smaller towns nearby which fall within the warehouse radius. In obtaining data on suburban locations, a favorite method is to watch the delivery route of some independent competitor and, if it is judged that the volume of trade is heavy enough, a store is opened. Some grocery chains have had surprising successes in quality suburban locations, seemingly well filled with flourishing businesses.

Individual Policies.—It is an interesting psychological fact that customers dislike walking upstairs to make a purchase. Women will always go down to the basement rather than up to the second floor of a department store. The United Cigar Stores Co. has capitalized this trait. It avoids raising the level of the store either a step above or below the street, making it exactly even. In fact this is now becoming standard practice among many retailers.

Furthermore, the store entrance is set at an angle so that traffic on either street can readily see into the store. In this way, the corner location is made to yield full value. In addition, it prevents congestion as well as giving a pleasing impression. The United people never hesitate to open one store across from one of their own shops already operating if traffic conditions seem to warrant. Wherever this policy has been followed, it has been found that there was no falling off of business in the old store.

As a matter of fact, chain stores show a tendency to cling together in localities. Chain grocery stores often occupy the same block, and frequently are located next to each other.

Location Experts.—There has been much controversy as to how efficient the chain store leasing experts actually are. It has been claimed that only a local real estate man is able to appraise the value of a piece of property at its true worth. There is no doubt that the chain store realty man is over-charged because it is well known the chains are able to pay. It is even possible that a chain store is willing to pay more for a certain location than the previous independent occupant. But it is usually for good and sufficient reasons. When a chain store expert has analyzed a location, he *knows* whether that location is going to prove satisfactory and the company is willing to risk its money on the accuracy of his judgment.

One chain store company had seventeen stores in operation. Before opening the eighteenth, it called in an expert. He picked out a location and submitted an estimate of the first years' sales which, in actual practice, turned out to be only $8,000 less. The United Cigar Stores scouts have done even better than this. So highly developed are their methods that they have often given estimates of the first six months' business which came within $200 of actual sales.

When it is possible to obtain such accuracy as this, there seems little possibility of failure. But chain store location experts must be highly paid. Their ability to forecast is not obtained immediately, but is the fruit of long and tedious observation. They are assisted by a large number of records, some companies having statistics in their files on almost every city of size in the United States.

One of the largest five and ten cent stores believes that intuition and "horse sense" have much to do with opening new stores, coupled with the usual standard investigations. It rarely happens, according to them, that an overestimate is made. Occasionally, in opening up a new location, the "percentage lease" is resorted to, the lessee paying as rent a certain percentage of his gross sales.

The Real Estate Department.—Many of the larger chain store systems, as has been said, maintain a highly organized real estate department to take care of property and buildings, make improvements, close leases, improve property, etc. But it is only the larger chains that can afford to install a special organization for this purpose. In the smaller chain, one or two individuals may have charge of the real estate, while

Date..................

City................................Population............

Number of Railroads....................Names................

....

Number of Street Car Lines..............Names................

....

Description of Property..

....

Location..

....

Condition of Store..

....

Dimensions..

Term of Lease...

Rental..

Allowance by Owner..

Owner's Name..

Agent...

Date when possession can be had...............................

Time necessary to make repairs and alterations...................

Give list of adjacent stores in block both sides...................

....

....

How long has present store been vacant?........................

Inquire of three adjacent store owners..........................

....

....

How many vacancies in block both sides?   No...................

How many tenants in present store in last five years?.............

Give reason for change of tenants..............................

Do you approve of store for   Bakery?....................

Give your reasons...

....

How many bakeries in town?....................................

What brands of bread sold?....................................

How near are markets?...

....

FIG. 3.—Report on possible property for use by chain bakery.

in the very small chains it forms only a portion of one person's duties.

The location expert locates the store. He may have done all that was in his power to ensure the prosperity of this link in the chain by the exercise of his experience and judgment; but the real estate department must carry on his work. Many events occur which may have more or less important bearing on the future of the chain. If the business falls off it is not alone the function of the sales department to ascertain why, but it also comes within the province of the realty department. Populations are not stationary. They move. Residential areas gradually become business sections. A large factory will change the character of a neighborhood in a few years. A foreign speaking population may come in whose habits of living are utterly unlike those of the previous population.

If the realty department finds some such event as this taking place, and the store manager is usually well acquainted with neighborhood events, it may be highly inadvisable to renew a lease for a long period at the same rent.

But neighborhoods do not always deteriorate. In many cases, locations in the outskirts, which apparently now are worth little, and which handle but a fraction of the trade turned over by the down town establishments, may, in the course of ten years, be the centers of large and thriving populations.

Figure 3 shows how carefully the same bakery chain mentioned before reports on real estate locations, in addition to clocking and analyzing the traffic. The population of the city, the number of railroads and street car lines, the condition of the property, the rental, time of possession, adjacent vacancies, everything that can throw light on the real value of the location, is put down. The number of times tenants have changed in the last five years, and the reasons for their changes, are found out.

No detail which will augment the success for the chain is too small to consider. In real estate dealings, as elsewhere, it is the spirit of efficiency, of standardized operations, which must make itself felt. Some idea of the detail involved in the problem of locating a store is indicated by the questionnaire form in the following five pages:

REAL ESTATE REPORT

City...........................State.....................

Retail Zone Boundaries, by street...............................

....

Traffic Points...

Principal Retail Streets

1........from........to........side........front ft. rate......

Class of establishments............................

General Character Foot Traffic.....................

2........from........to........side........front ft. rate......

Class of establishments................................

General Character Foot Traffic..........................

3........from........to........side........front ft. rate ....

Class of establishments................................

General Character Foot Traffic..........................

IN OUR JUDGMENT BEST LOCATION FOR A RETAIL STORE FOR WOMEN'S

ARTICLES WOULD BE:

1........from........to........side........front ft. rate......

2........from........to........side........front ft. rate......

IN OUR JUDGMENT BEST LOCATION FOR A RETAIL STORE FOR MEN'S

ARTICLES WOULD BE:

1........from........to........side........front ft. rate......

2........from........to........side........front ft. rate......

IN OUR JUDGMENT BEST LOCATION FOR A RETAIL STORE FOR A GEN-

ERAL LINE WOULD BE:

1........from........to........side........front ft. rate ...

2........from........to........side........front ft. rate....

Best local broker or correspondent...........................

REMARKS...

....

....

Suitable for: { Men's line / Women's line / General line

BUILDING No...........................

Available..

between....................and.............................side

.........story...........................Erected.............

Constructed of..

Condition..

Other tenants...

....

Neighbors: Right...

        Left...

        Opposite...

        Others...

Sidewalks, kind...........................Width..............

Street, kind................Width........Lighting............

Water Supply..............Toilets.............................

Heating..

Fire Protection...

Store self-contained or sub-divided?.........................

Partition walls...

Insurance rate on building...................Fixtures..........

Insurance rate on merchandise...............................

Restrictions, if any..

Building owned by..

Remarks..

....

....

Suitable for: { Men's line | Women's line | General line

STORE

..........Feet front..........feet deep.   Ceilings............feet

..........Feet wide in rear ....

Display Windows: Style......................................

How many?..

Size...............................Lighting.................

Remarks...

Fixtures, if any..

....

Shelving..

How is store entrance?......................................

Level or steps from sidewalk................................

Rear or shipping entrance...................................

Windows...

Lighting..

Heating...

Condition of floor.......................Load.............. ..

Condition of side walls.....................................

Condition of ceilings.......................................

Remarks...

....

Basement

..........Feet front..........feet deep.   Ceilings...........feet

....

Stairway..

Elevator..

Outside entrance..

Fixtures..

Shelving..

Floor: Material...

        Condition...

Drainage..

Windows...

Lighting..

Condition of side walls.......................................

Condition of ceilings...

Remarks...

Sub-basement..

....

Any storage yard to building?.................................

....

Any storage shed outside?.....................................

....

Suitable for: { Men's line
Women's line
General line

SECOND STORY

..........Feet front..........feet deep.   Ceilings...........feet

....

Stairway to main floor: Width..........Height of steps..........

Number of steps..................Finish.........................

Balustrade.........................Landings...................

Front Display Windows..

Other Windows...

Any large central opening to main floor?.......................

....

If not, the possibilities for such an opening..................

....

Partitions..

Fixtures...

Shelving..

Condition of floor.....................Load...................

Condition of side walls.......................................

Condition of ceilings...

Lighting...

Heating...

Remarks...

What are floors above?..

Renting Stores.—How much rent can a chain store afford to pay? This is a difficult question to answer. But it has been established by experts that there are certain percentages of gross receipts which should govern the rent paid by different types ·of businesses. For example, high class retail stores which are large advertisers can afford to pay six per cent. of gross receipts. These figures should be taken as applying over a considerable period, possibly for the entire period of the lease. During this period, receipts should increase in proportion to rent.

Taking the ratios up in more detail, Mr. Nicholls has compiled the following list:

Shoe stores	8
Department stores	3
Five and tens—non-advertising	5
Non-advertising specialty stores	8
Theatres and hotels	9
Drug stores, candy, fruit, etc	10
Grocery stores	10
Cigar stores	6–8
Barber shops, shoe shining establishments, etc	12
Cloak and suit	6

With such a wide variation, it is apparent that few varying types of chains will desire the same location. Such a table as the above is valuable in making estimates for new locations and in judging the performances of old stores. A great many stores may do better, but if one does less, it is a sign of trouble.

Many policies are followed in regard to renting stores. Some chains prefer to secure sites that will do for purchase. Then they rent superfluous space to other retailers. In some cases, this policy has resulted in the chain store's obtaining its portion of the building free of charge, the overhead of the building being carried from rent derived from the other stores.

The United Cigar Stores are famous as an exponent of this policy. The real estate department purchases a corner, remodels the stores, takes its own portion on the corner and rents the rest. Since the formation of the Retail Stores Corporation, it has been possible for them to secure locations and use them for either candy or cigar stores, and, in course of time, it is quite possible that their retail activities will embrace further lines of retailing. In this case, the same block might hold several retail stores operated by different chains, all subordinate to the holding company.

Locations which the real estate department pick up cheaply may be sold at a profit and still provide for the future of the company's chain store in that location.

The real estate department has frequent occasion to scrutinize buying habits. If it buys a building, it wants to know whether the location is suitable for a grocery, a drug store, a department store, a bakery, etc. It is almost as important that the other stores surrounding the chain store be prosperous as that the chain store be prosperous itself. Prosperity attracts trade. If the chain store selects its own neighbors, as it can often do by calling the attention of non-competing businesses to excellent qualities of the location, it can ensure the class of trade to which it wishes to appeal. That is, to its own pulling power is added the combined pulling power of all the other stores and, since the buying appeal of the chain store is largely to the eye and the pocket book of the customer, any increase in purchasing traffic by the store is advantageous. It is well known that people who come to buy in one store often buy articles which they need in adjacent stores rather than go elsewhere.

Wherever the chain store realty department decides to hold on to the property, it collects all rents and reports to the central organization. It also collects rent from the chain store itself. This is often necessary since, although the chain realty department should operate at a profit, it is often necessary to operate at a loss due to large expenditures in improving new locations, purchasing property in advance of the city's growth, etc.

The Childs Company has data on practically every place suited to its needs in the United States. This detailed information renders it fairly easy for it to keep ahead of its expansion programme. It is devoted to the policy of making long term leases, from 21 to 99 years.

When a chain store organization attains any size, there is no lack of locations offered for its inspection. One of the chain store leasing companies has an average of five new locations brought to its attention daily, and each one of these is carefully investigated. One grocery chain of 50 stores in the Middle West says "our stores have attained such a standing in the community that the developers of every new allotment in the city come to us and offer us a center lot for one of our stores. Other people continually offer us vacant storerooms for rent, or try to sell us lots. Right now we own about 18 lots on which we shall build within the next three to five years. In the meantime, we will rent several stores if we find the kind we want, in the right location, and if the rent is not too high. If the rent is too high, we wait for it to come down, or look around for a place to build."

Building vs. Renting.—It is probably safe to say that the great majority of chain stores are rented, although this depends to some extent on the type of business. This avoids a great deal of trouble on the part of the company in looking after a large real estate department and the worries that a real estate department always brings with it. Then, after all, the primary function of the chain store company is retailing. Real estate is only a by-product of the industry, so to speak.

But many chain stores have peculiar requirements. They wish a standardized front to which the neighbors may object. Most chain store fronts are made in such a way as to be readily recognizable. Therefore, to get in certain locations it may be necessary to purchase and remodel.

Purchasing and building requires more capital and consequently a larger investment. There is more to lose if the property deteriorates, although there is also more to gain if it improves. The chain grocery store ordinarily prefers a one story building with a standardized front and standardized fixtures. A grocery chain, naturally choosing a low priced location, rarely finds it profitable to build additional stories to rent to tenants. The rental from the upstairs portion does not justify the added investment.

The problem of a local chain is, in a way, quite different from that of a national chain. The local chain officials, at the start, are well acquainted with the character of the townsmen, and the buying habits of the people. They know by daily experience what the national chain investigator has to learn from statistics. That they often fail to achieve true success does not disprove the fact that their initial opportunity is better for profits than the national chain. They are on the spot, they are known, they are compact, and their problems are comparatively simple.

Quality Locations.—For many years, in fact, until quite recently, chain stores were regarded as merchandising ventures exclusively devoted to the interests of the poorer classes. To be seen going in or out of a chain store was avoided. Merchants on the better streets frowned upon the advent of the chain store. When Childs bought their way on Fifth Avenue in New York City, there was great nodding of heads and portents of failure. But the Childs organization went ahead and erected a building, letting all but the ground floor. There was only room for 29 tables, 116 seats in all. But the profit on each of these 116 chairs was carefully reckoned within a cent or two on daily turnover. These statistics had been secured by applying the results of long experience to the traffic passing the door.

When the five and ten cent store decided on Fifth Avenue for its thousandth store, Mr. Woolworth went so far as to become a member of the Fifth Avenue Association. The bright red signs were kept but the window dressing was carried only half way up. It is reported the location makes no difference in the number of mousetraps sold and the luncheon counter is just as busy at noon as it is anywhere else.

It is said the United Cigar Stores pay $27,000 a year rent for one of its Fifth Avenue locations. The company's architect was told to design what would be the most beautiful cigar store in the country. The exterior is in black and gold marble with the name of the company in specially designed letters of bronze and gilt. The familiar red signs are made narrower and less conspicuous. The bases of the counters and the showcases are black and gold marble. The showcase frames and all decorations are of bronze. The windows are dressed with the care of a jewelry store.

Quality locations illustrate one very important trend in chain store development, and that is the tendency of chain store systems to break into the exclusive retailing sections and, what is more, make a success in their new surroundings.

Conclusions.—One of the reasons for chain store success may undoubtedly be ascribed to scientific locating of member stores. No retailer can afford to pass over the opportunity presented him to capitalize on the location. The fact. that the chains have been able to go in under the local retailers' noses and capture the best sites merely goes to show how badly new principles of retailing were needed in the community.

The congested districts, as a rule, offer the best opportunities because of their compactness. The product, however, and the chain policy, may determine otherwise. It may be desirable to obtain the place which the most people pass every day, such as is the United Cigar Stores policy, or the company may be willing to seek less public locations at a lower rent because of other facilities for attracting trade. Either extreme is unsafe. A great volume of sales will carry a large overhead, but without this large volume of sales the large overhead would be a constant drag. Again, low rent in a back street might be uneconomical because of the great opportunities for that store in a better location.

Every member of the chain organization should constantly be on the lookout for new locations. The man who sees opportunity first is the man who succeeds, and in many cases a desirable location means dollars to the chain which is first to come on the scene.

The whole question of location may be summed up in a few words. The site of the store should vary in distance from the traffic centers directly as the selling appeal of the chain. For example, men will not go out of their way to buy cigars, or candy, or razor blades, but they will go out of their way to get a pair of shoes or a suit of clothes. The first element in appeal is the nature of the product, whether it is a convenience article, that is, a necessity, or a shopping article, one which people will spend time to hunt for, the second is the price of the product, and the third is the publicity of the chain. The location of the store is almost inseparable from a discussion of these topics, as will be shown later.

CHAPTER IV

THE MEMBER STORE

OUTLINE

Size.
1. Large enough.
    - (a) To hold stock.
    - (b) To hold clerks.
    - (c) To hold customers.
2. Results of conservation of **space.**
    - (a) Saving in
        1. Rent.
        2. Expense of cleaning.
    - (b) Increased selling efficiency.
3. Special problems of smaller chains.
    - (a) Necessity of keeping stock in stores where warehouse is lacking or too small.

Appearance of stores.
1. The store front.
    - (a) Uniform
        1. **In color.**
        2. In lettering.
    - (b) **Distinctive**
        1. In appeal.
        2. **Easy to recognize.**
2. The interior.
    - (a) **Equipment standardized.**
        1. **Easy to equip new stores.**
        2. **Restore old equipment damaged by fire, flood, etc.**
    - (b) **A mathematical problem.**
3. Arrangement of stock.
    - (a) **Most in demand**
        1. **Near front of store**
        2. **Nearest clerk.**
    - (b) Aisles wide.
    - (c) **Arrangement with regard to**
        1. **Movement of traffic.**
        2. Lighting.

Display.
1. Of stock

    (*a*) In windows.

    (*b*) On counters.

 2. Importance of price tags.

    (*a*) Counter display.

    (*b*) Manufacturers' helps.

Window display.

 1. Difference in policies

    (*a*) Centralized at headquarters.

    (*b*) Managers allowed to trim.

 2. Importance of, in selling.

 3. Analyzing product for display purposes.

    (*a*) Influence of character of traffic.

    (*b*) Technique of window display.

    (*c*) Expense.

 4. The window trimmer.

 5. Teasers and window pasters.

Counter display.

 1. Tie up merchandising with display.

CHAPTER IV

THE MEMBER STORE

The chain idea may be likened to an octopus. The central organization is the head and the branch stores are the tentacles. If one tentacle is cut off, another grows to take its place. It is this way with the member stores. No one of them is vitally important for the organization, and if any store shows marked weakness, it can immediately be amputated, and another one started. This opening of new stores has become a real science in some chains. The process has been standardized so that nothing further is required than to start the machinery moving and in consequence on the appointed date the store is ready for occupancy by the selling force, complete down to the last detail.

We have discussed in a previous chapter the various problems connected with locating the store. This chapter is a logical continuation of the same topic. We investigate the amount of floor space required for various types of stores, the fixtures, the display, the window trims, and the general appearance of the store. We also discuss the stock and the arrangement by order of goods or by various departments. The keynote which is again sounded is standardization. The nearer alike one store is to another, the easier it is to make repairs, replenish stock, shift selling force, etc.

The success of a chain organization is almost directly proportionate to the care it takes of detail, and the size, equipment, and arrangement of stock in the retail stores is of very great importance. In a variety of ways, it eliminates waste, and eliminated waste means increased profits. Furthermore, it is just as important for the small chain to start with standard equipment as it is for the large chains, even although alterations may cost more.

The Size of the Store.—The store should be just large enough to hold the stock, the clerks, and the customers. Every inch of space over these requirements is waste. For an example of the utility of this practice, it is necessary to go back to the larger chains. In this case, the president of the United Cigar Stores, then George J. Whelan, decided that his stores must be compact. As a result, he saved rent, saved space, saved cleaning expenses, and brought practically every article for sale within reach of the clerk. The majority of the company's stores are one size, which makes it possible to use standard equipment in each store.

The owner of a small chain, or the owner of one retail store who is planning to branch out and establish one or more other stores may ask: How shall I know how large to make my stores? And what shall I do with the rest of the space? You've shown me how valuable it is to have a location in the right place, but the only location I can get there is much too large for the business I expect to do. The chains which make a practice of owning their own realty make their own stores the regular size and rent the rest of the space to others. If the store is too large, get the owner to turn it into two stores and thereby make more rent.

There is one note of caution to be sounded here. A small chain cannot, as a rule, concentrate its stock in such tiny spaces as the larger chains possessing much quicker turnover and adequate means of supplying deficiencies in stock almost immediately. This is one of the problems of the small chain—to have ample stock yet achieve rapid turnover. Thus a chain with two or three links may find it advisable to have slightly larger stores since it must keep its warehouse in the stores themselves.

For example, there is a big variation in the size of chain grocery stores. Many of them are mere holes in the wall, using bins for shelves and representing a very low investment. Other chains run larger stores and carry a much heavier stock. One problem the grocery chain has had to confront is the desire on the part of the customer for perishable goods. Not to carry vegetables, baked goods, etc. means a positive loss of trade and sales in the other staple dry groceries. A meat counter, for example, attracts a great deal of trade. The Sam. Seelig Stores, of Los Angeles, California, rents space in its stores to butter, fruit, and vegetable concerns. The main idea has been to cut out all perishable goods and cling to staple groceries but the value of the presence of these other merchandising activities in the same store is recognized, and the result has been a succession of chain concessions. Thus a meat man will operate meat counters in several of these stores in one town.

A middle western grocery chain has sublet a corner in some of its larger stores to meat markets. In three cases it built two stores side by side so that a meat market could be secured next door. A grocery, a market, and a drug store are all that are needed to form a small community. In one section this chain operated a grocery store next to a drug store. As a shrewd investment, the chain built a meat market next door and thereby secured enough additional rent to carry the overhead on its own store. It also increased trade, since people no longer had to go down town.

There are other exceptions to the standard size for a store. Frequently stores in the heart of a large city must be larger than stores in the suburbs or than stores in smaller cities or towns. These are but the exceptions which prove the rule. Make your stores as nearly alike in size as possible.

The Store Front.—Whenever a big chain secures a new site, arrangements are quickly made for erecting or altering the old store. When completed, the store has the same appearance, outside, as that of other stores of the chain.

A person can stand on the main street of almost any sizable city in the United States and, looking around, he can tell immediately what some of the stores within his radius of vision are. For example, on the opposite corner, he sees a store finished in red, with a shield beside the lettering. Clearly, this is a United Cigar Stores branch. Farther down the street is a much larger and broader red sign, with prominent gilt letters. Nearby, is a white store with script letters on the windows, gold letters on a white back ground over the store, and a pancake griddle in the window. Everybody would recognize these stores. But, in addition, there are any quantity of local chains which have their own color scheme, well recognized by the communities in which they operate.

A uniform store front is an asset which has been proved very valuable. Coming into a new community, the store finds patrons among those to whom its name is familiar or who have actually bought at its stores in other localities. Like the railroad station, the member chain store becomes a landmark.

This uniformity of appearance is nothing more than the idea of the signboard standardized. The store is picked out by the familiar color which can be seen much farther than the name. Red is a favorite color in grocery stores, The Piggly Wiggly stores are painted blue, brown, and yellow, with Piggly Wiggly in white letters on a blue background, and "All Over the World" printed beneath.

Not only is the color scheme of the exterior the same but the fronts and entrances wherever possible conform to the standard. In other words, every store in a chain is as nearly like the rest as possible.

Equipment.—The analogy can be carried out as far as the interiors of the stores are concerned except that here uniformity is not so much a matter of advertising importance as of expense, replacement, etc. Make your own equipment if possible. The larger chains do, and find that it pays. They also keep extra equipment on hand in case of opening a new store, a fire in an old one, etc. When the Federal Bakery at San Antonio, Texas, was ruined by the flood of 1920, in five days new equipment had arrived from Davenport, Iowa, to take its place. In a chain such as this, or the United Cigar Stores, or some grocery chains, it is possible to standardize equipment almost absolutely. Once given the amount of space in the store and the amount of goods to be carried, and the equipment is a mathematical problem of shelves, counters, etc.

But when it is a question of stores, the size of which may vary a great deal, such as a five and ten cent store, it is more a question of standardizing units. For example, the counters may be uniform, although their number may vary in the stores, according to size.

Figure 4 shows the interior of a Federal Bakery in Knoxville, Tenn. Here the local manager has used the standard equipment as a basis, and for $12.00 bought some laths and artificial flowers and added the extras himself. Note the display of goods and the compact arrangement, with just room in front of the counter for customers and just room in back of the counter for the sales girls to move around without interfering with each other.

Arrangement of Store.—Where shall the merchandise be placed? Experience has worked out rather definite positions for most merchandise. As a general rule, the merchandise most in demand is nearest the clerk. In the grocery store these articles are directly in back of the counter. In a store with a number of departments goods most in demand are at the front of the store.

Fig. 4.—Interior of Federal bakery.

This rule, however, is capable of exceptions. Mr. Kells, manager of the Metropolitan Stores, Inc., says, ."You have to know just what goods will sell in certain locations. Jewelry, for instance, will not sell in the basement, but must be well up towards the front door with plenty of light. Men will not hunt for things; therefore, their department must be easily accessible. Hardware is in the basement, music to the rear, quick sellers to the front."

If it is necessary to have aisles, these should be wide enough to avoid overcrowding. Narrow aisles tend to decrease sales of goods on display at the point of congestion. Arrangement of goods in one unit of a chain should be absolutely the same as in other units. In the Piggly Wiggly stores there is a place for every bar of laundry soap and every bottle of ketchup. Everything is arranged for convenience with the heaviest goods nearest the exit. One hundred and eighty-five customers an hour can be handled easily.

A. L. Townsend says, "at least 50 per cent. of the success of an institution, large or small, can be attributed to the stage management of the store and of the merchandise." In the chain, it is the reproduction of this efficient stage management in many stores that does so much towards standardizing sales and profits.

A sales manager of a chain store system is quoted as saying:

"Give me a certain line of drugs and toilet preparations. I will stock up ten average drug stores of the old regime and then build ten competitive stores of the new type. The latter will inevitably get the business, get it in a big way, despite the fact that the other shops keep-the same identical line. It is in the method of display, in spectacular stage dress of the store and the hundred and one details of service supplied to these stores."

The Fifth Avenue Store of the F. W. Woolworth Co. is one in which "stage" arrangement has been carried to the *nth* degree. Everything in this store has been arranged with an eye to the effect. Ribbons, jewelry, and candy are at the front. The store contains 34 departments, two more than usual, the two extra ones being the light lunch and the soda fountain. Several departments are duplicated on the main floor and in the basement on the theory that if customers pass an article on one floor they will buy it on the second.

J. B. Levey, General Sales Manager of the United Shirt Shops, says in an article in The Haberdasher:

"It is an established fact that the movement of customers in a shop affects the sale of merchandise. The fixtures are placed accordingly. In entering a store, we usually adhere to the law of traffic regulations, and keep moving to the right. Points of sales vantage are usually about 10 to 12 feet on the right at the entrance of the store and on the right center, where you can probably sell more merchandise than in any other part. Another good point of sales vantage is the extreme rear of the store, where people, having reached the turning point, naturally stop and look around. Personally, I believe the best selling spot in the store is where the incoming and outgoing traffics criss-cross. That point is a few feet from the entrance, on the right-hand side. Usually there is some confusion when people are walking in and out all the time, and it causes them to move more slowly than ordinarily, thus affording another opportunity to glance around."

All goods should be priced carefully and plainly. If the goods are on shelves, price should be directly underneath, or, if in trays, as in a variety store, the trays should be marked. All articles of a kind should be by themselves, not hit-or-miss anywhere, as was once a common occurrence in retail stores. If a woman wants breakfast food in a grocery store, she will see all the different brands and kinds grouped in one location, and that location she knows from habit.

Display.—If you want to sell your goods, put them where people will see them, and make them look attractive. This, like many other chain store principles, is nothing more than ordinary retail salesmanship. All goods cannot be displayed in the window, but all, or nearly all of them can be displayed on the counters. This, of course, is not an easy matter. A poor display repels rather than attracts. But it has long been known that there is no easier way of selling goods than by efficient methods of display.

Take, for example, the five and ten cent store. Once in a while, you may find trays that are out of order and messy, but you may be sure they will not remain that way long. You will note that counters are filled, but never junky, and that shop worn goods are surprisingly rare. Nor are there any rusty goods on the hardware counter. Probably display sells more articles in the five and ten cent stores than the name of the brand or the need for the object. People buy what attracts them on the counters. The price is negligible, and, as explained elsewhere, the five and ten cent stores pursue a rigorous policy of letting the goods sell themselves—by display.

The Piggly Wiggly Co. follows the same policy, and here the customers themselves pick out the goods they desire. Therefore, of necessity only those goods are sold which are in demand and consequently on display.

Note the Federal Bakery illustration on page 61, and you will see that baked goods are plainly and attractively displayed in racks.

Most chain executives believe that if the prospective customer can be got to enter the store, the display will do the rest. But he must first be induced to come in, and therefore the great importance of the window display.

Window Displays.—All chain authorities agree on the importance of the window display. Some chains centralize window dressing at central headquarters and pay large sums to experts for their services. Other chains delegate the duty of trimming windows to the store managers, who are thus allowed some scope for originality. The former method insures an even standard of excellence throughout the country while the latter allows more individuality and initiative. The United Cigar Stores have their corps of window dressers at headquarters.

Location and the window display take the place of advertising for the majority of chain stores. The location brings them the traffic, and the window trims attract the trade to the inside. Some corporations employ several chain experts, and keep them traveling over the country, visiting the several branches and teaching the managers the fundamentals of good window trims. Others do the same thing by mail. The principal features of a good window trim may be observed by referring to Fig. 5. Following are the instructions to managers:

"In presenting the above window display featuring 'Bringing Home the Bakin,' your attention is called to the holiday atmosphere which surrounds the entire display (for December). The holly background sets off the window attractively and conveys the holiday spirit. The large centerpiece featuring the trademark is finished in seven attractive colors. The display card has been handled in poster effect so that the striking colors will stop the passing crowds. Note how the two smaller cards tie up with the centerpiece, and carry out the 'Bringing Home the Bakin' message. The old window-trick of tying up the products with the display always commands attention because the eye naturally follows lines. In this particular display, note how easily you can work out this idea by drawing baby ribbon from the packages right to your products."

FIG. 5.—Tying up window display with the product

FIG. 6.—Japanese window display.

Now, what do we find in this window display?

1. A seasonal atmosphere, in this case Christmas, and shown by the holly.

2. An attention-attracting feature—in this case the poster effect of the display card.

3. Balance, secured by flanking the big card with smaller cards.

4 Products tied up with the display by ribbons.

5. The trade mark featured, which is good advertising.

Another window display of the Federal Bakeries is shown in Fig. 6:

1. The seasonal atmosphere here is changed to a national atmosphere, that is, Japanese.

2. The center display on the white background forms the feature which attracts the attention of passing traffic.

3. The fans on either side furnish the balance.

4. The product, in this case Tokio bread, is set off by the fans, which form a neat background for it.

5. The trade mark, "Tokio," coincides with the atmosphere, and is featured on the poster, on the fans, and on the lanterns.

Another point is that nothing but Tokio bread is shown in this display, while in the previous illustration a variety of products was shown.

There are two kinds of window display, the general display of products and the special feature display. In the general display, some particular article may have greater prominence, but if the selling effort is to be directed to one article, it is a better plan to devote all the window space to this product. Of course, this does not always hold true, depending as it does on the nature of the product.

Take a shoe store, for an example. It would do little good to feature some particular shoe, since individual tastes differ so widely. Therefore, show a large variety at a scale of prices. But in the case of a drug store, where even the smallest carry more than 3,500 different items and the large stores a great many more, a feature window display should be used. It may feature a brand of products, or a single product. In city stores, toilet products are more frequently featured than medicines. In small towns and country stores, medicines with well-known names are featured. One large advertising agency says the "question of whether a window can or cannot be obtained from a given druggist is largely a combination of the volume of sale the medicine commands plus the profit offered the druggist. If the sale is reasonably large and the profits fair, the druggists will use windows for these products at the height of the selling season."

In other words, if you sell one product, such as shoes or hats, etc., show a variety of styles and makes in your window trim. But if you sell a large variety of products, such as groceries or

Fig. 7.—Window pasters.

drugs, arrange a succession of window trims featuring a particular brand or product.

Pasters, Packages and Counter Displays.—Pasters put on the windows are a cheap and inexpensive method of attracting attention, particularly when stores are putting on special sales nearly every day. Grocery stores and drug stores frequently use these, the pasters, themselves, of course, being furnished by headquarters. Window pasters attract immediate attention, whether price or product is featured.

Figure 7 shows how the window paster was used in the same Tokio campaign previously illustrated. Friday and Saturday previous to the campaign, the paster was used as a "teaser" and was replaced by the regular paster the following week. A paster is primarily used to attract attention. People look at the paster before the window trim, as a general rule. In a city where the chain maintains several stores, the repetition of these pasters in each store is sure to arouse interest.

Packages are used as displays, inside and out. More and more manufacturers are coming to realize the value of display as connected with their own products. Consequently, the designing of packages has become almost an art. In the drug store, for example, many articles are sold solely by the package. It is especially true also in the grocery business that packages sell a great many goods, and hence the value of displaying well-known packages in window trims, etc.

In the Piggly Wiggly stores, as explained previously, the packages are merely arranged on the shelves and the customer allowed to take her pick. Where the chain manufactures its own private brands in competition with advertised brands, and where it does no advertising itself, it must rely almost wholly upon its package display for selling the goods. If the goods are out of sight, no one would ask for them, and, if in sight, more people ask in proportion to the display value of the package.

Some chains make a habit of using counter cards, either furnished by them or by the manufacturer, who often finds it very much to his advantage to tie up closely with the merchandising efforts of the various chains dealing in his products.

Show cards can frequently be used to good effect either in the windows or on the counters. In the ordinary store such a card would read something like this "Felt hats reduced to $3.00" or simply "Lux 10 cents." The sales department of the chain store organization ordinarily makes the message on the show card interesting enough to attract passers-by and customers. If the reduction in the price of the article is important enough to feature, there are surely some sales arguments which can be featured also.

The object of all display is to attract. Therefore, make your displays attractive. The more people you get in the store, the more sales you can make. Good display is merely another aspect of good merchandising. When you advertise in a newspaper the advertisement may or may not be read by the prospective customer. A far larger proportion look at the display material in the store by which they pass.

Appearance.—The chain store should and can excel in general appearance. Not only the exterior, the interior, the equipment, and the stock can be standardized, but the lighting and the general effect of neatness. The Piggly Wiggly stores have done away with window trims. The windows look right into the store, thus making the goods in the store serve as window trim, and relying on their general appearance of attractiveness as well as the novelty of their idea to attract people into the store. The United Cigar Stores, according to President Wise, notice an almost immediate influx of customers when it is possible to keep open the doors, and this is noticeable in congested districts especially. He also stresses the value of night lighting.

As a matter of fact, there is nothing which attracts the average customer more than cleanliness and neatness. If a chain had a monopoly on the trade in a district through its price appeal, cleanliness might matter less, but where there is such keen competition between chains, every factor which lends attractiveness to the store is exceedingly important. In a grocery store, for example, where the majority of the customers are women, this factor looms up. Broken boxes, sawdust, scraps of paper on the floor, flies, all of these detract from the store appearance.

Clean windows are another point to stress. "Were your windows clean?" is one of the first questions asked by the Regal Shoe Co. when one of its stores begins to fall off in sales. Clean paint is still another point. Fresh merchandise, no dust, orderly arrangement, each one of these factors has an incalculable but important part in helping to make the retail links of the chain successful.

There is a case quoted in New York where in one block there were seven places selling candy. A new chain candy store moved in. One of its competitors was selling goods of its own make, trade-marked, of course, but employing no special methods of selling, no novel containers, etc. There was another slightly higher-grade store of the same general nature with a shop neat and clean, but with nothing particularly remarkable. Candy was sold in two drug stores and three tobacco stores. When the new store moved in it stressed appearance at once. The windows were made bigger and brighter, each box on display was opened, prices were plainly marked, all showcases were uniform and so placed as to obtain the best display of the contents. All containers were designed to suit the brand of candy with vivid colors and attractive designs. Names and prices shown in the window were repeated inside.

To close this section, we quote from the statement of the policy of the Kroger Grocery and Baking Co. in regard to store appearance:

1. Fresh paint—plain name
2. Clean windows.
3. Clean interior.
4. Serviceable counters and equipment.
5. Small, well assorted, packaged stock.
6. Signs on windows—fresh daily.
7. Lots of plain price tickets.
8. No cluttered-up corners.
9. No goods on floor—everything in boxes or on shelves.
10. Neat, business-like, and polite clerk.
11. Special leader daily.

Conclusions.—This chapter has been devoted to the physical aspects of the member store. The location of the store and its physical appearance are inseparably connected. After finding the right location, it is necessary to let passers-by know what the store has to offer. Hence the enormous publicity value of the standardized front lies in the fact that its mere appearance on a city or suburban street signifies to the public the exact information and reputation which that chain has made for itself. The appearance of the individual, independent store is of value to that store alone, but the appearance of the individual chain store is of value to every other store in that chain, at present established or prospected for the future.

Throughout this chapter the attempt has been made to lay emphasis on the standardization of all the physical aspects of the store, of its exterior and interior, of the size and the arrangement of the stock for the best convenience of the clerk and the public. By whatever methods it is carried out, the following principle is universally applicable: "Make the member stores as attractive as possible, inside and out, and results will be commensurate with the effort."

CHAPTER V

PURCHASING

2. Duties.
    (*a*) To purchase goods for entire chain.
    (*b*) To purchase saleable goods.
    (*c*) To purchase goods on the lowest terms for the highest quality.
3. Requisites of chain store buyer.
    (*a*) An expert on certain line.
        1. Knows sources.
        2. Qualities.
        3. Price trends.
    (*b*) Wide circle of acquaintances.
    (*c*) Goes and looks for products where they are for sale.
4. Desirability of maintaining purchasing agents in various parts of country and abroad.

Buying policies.
1. Chains where all buying is done at headquarters.
    (*a*) Choice of goods and products wholly in hands of purchasing department.
    (*b*) Local managers with advisory voice in choice of articles.
2. Chains where some products bought locally by manager.
3. Chains where purchasing is done by member stores.

Buyer and manufacturer.
1. Possibility of coöperation.

CHAPTER V

PURCHASING

The controversy which has gone on for so long over the ability and the practice of chain stores in selling goods at a lower price than their independent competitors has revolved about the question of purchasing. The larger the organization, and the larger the orders which it can place, the better the price which can be obtained from the manufacturer. Jobbers were at one time very prominent in organizing and helping retail chains, but no class now is more outspoken as a whole in denunciation of the chains than jobbers. Just as soon as a chain organization feels itself strong enough, it stops buying from jobbers, wherever possible, and goes straight to the manufacturer or grower. Some chains are able to purchase the whole output of factories.

The ability to buy the right goods at the right prices is one of the first and most important requisites of chain store success. This ability, in the great majority of cases, is gained by a centralized purchasing organization and a trained staff of buyers. In fact, as mentioned previously, a central purchasing organization is one of the fundamental requisites of chain store success. The larger the organization, the more important and the more complicated do the duties of this purchasing department become. In this chapter, it is intended to discuss the general purchasing policies of chain organizations with specific reference to some of the most common policies. The accounting required in the purchasing department has been developed completely in a following chapter.

Buying Channels.—Generally speaking, the chain store buyer can purchase either directly—from the manufacturer, grower, etc.—or he can buy indirectly—from the jobber, wholesaler, broker, etc. In general, the chain store prefers to buy direct, because in this way the jobbers' margin, which in many cases is as low as two per cent., could be saved. Even two per cent. is a large consideration when several carloads of one item are used in the course of a year.   Naturally, the chain stores work to get on the direct selling list of all the manufacturers.   This is not an easy proposition.   Manufacturers, under the veiled or open threat of jobbers to discontinue their lines, hesitate.   They are uncertain as to the continued prosperity of the chain store and fear to find themselves shut out from the channels of distribution in case of failure.   This is especially the case where branded goods are concerned.   The manufacturers of Kellogg's Corn Flakes had a famous controversy over selling direct to chain stores.

As chain stores have become more powerful and the old-line jobbers have become weaker, conditions have changed so that now practically all chain stores are able to buy everything direct.   The inability to buy direct and the consequent entry of some chain stores into manufacturing will be discussed later.

So much for direct purchasing.   The attitude of the manufacturer has changed.   He prefers to create consumer demand for his product by judicious advertising rather than to shut himself out of a sure and steady retail outlet.

This, of course, does not mean that the jobber has been eliminated.   There are frequently articles needed which are used in such small quantities that it is found better policy to let the jobber carry the risk and pay him for it.   This is also true of articles the price of which is likely to fluctuate violently.   In some cases, the chain store prefers to let the jobber carry the risk.

The ordinary policy, let us repeat, is to buy direct.   But the following is the experience of one medium-sized grocery chain. These people usually buy canned goods direct from the officials of the canning companies.   But often they deal with a canned goods broker, who acts as the canners' salesman.   One broker, for example, sells them whatever they want from two Michigan canneries, and also represents the account of a sal-soda firm, a large pea-bean grower, a peanut growers' organization, etc. Naturally, this broker, with his varied lines of goods to sell, can afford to get around to his trade oftener than a representative of only one house.   In addition, this man sells them beet sugar when they want it.   They could buy beet sugar direct by telegraph, but as long as it does not cost any more to buy through a broker, it is a big advantage to have a broker handle the business.

He takes an interest in them, wants to see them make money, and frequently gives advice as to market changes that are well worth while.

The channels of purchase are more or less determined by the policy of the chain management. The Kroger Grocery & Baking Co., for example, one of the largest grocery chains, made it a cardinal point of their policy to buy direct, not only from manufacturers but from growers. Other chains will buy from wholesalers and jobbers where they consider the price is low enough, but these are ordinarily the small and medium-sized chains.

The "Five and Tens."—Nowhere is purchasing more important than in the case of the so-called five and ten-cent stores, where the ability of the store to stock articles is more or less dependent on the price at which these articles are purchased. During the war, all the large chain store organizations found it necessary to abandon the 10-cent limit with the exception of the Woolworth chain. This was due entirely to inability to purchase a large enough variety of goods to retail within the 10-cent limit. And the success of a five and ten-cent store chain is determined by the volume of sales it can attain.

Woolworth was able to maintain its price level throughout the war by the enormous volume of sales. For example, in one year they sold nearly 90,000,000 pounds of candy, enough to fill a train of freight cars 24 miles long. This was not inferior candy. But the enormous volume of sales enabled the manufacturer to make a profit on pure candy even at the low prices. Illustrating this point further, in one year Woolworth sold more than 9,000,000 yards of curtain material, 350,000 barrels of glass ware, 20,000,000 pieces of enamelware—enough to load a freight train 7½ miles long. In 1918, the year of the influenza epidemic, they sold 54,000,000 handkerchiefs at the regular price limit. Despite the fact that the cost of raw material kept shooting up like a rocket, this enormous turnover allowed sales to be made at a profit.

As the Woolworth Co. says, "The Woolworth stores buy their goods where goods are to be had, and are ruled by the same economic laws of manufacture and selling that govern every other retailer. The more of a thing that can be produced, the lower the price can be." They go on to illustrate their point and the example is well worth quoting, although it has been used before.

One of the Woolworth buyers saw a ring which retailed at fifty cents. ·He thought this ring would go well in the Woolworth stores· and accordingly approached the manufacturer.

"Absurd!" was the manufacturer's comment, "I can't make that ring so you can sell it at ten cents. Anyway—I am selling plenty as it is—more than 450 dozen this year."

The buyer merely said that he could sell a "great quantity" and by dint of persuasion got the manufacturer to try the experiment. During the first year 5,000 gross were handled, or 60,000 dozen. This is exactly the point. If the manufacturer only made 450 dozen, he had to get fifty cents at retail, but if he made 60,000 dozen the economies he could effect in manufacturing, standardization of processes, etc., offset the lowered retail price.

Most retailers base their selling price on the basis of the purchase and overhead cost, and this same policy is followed out by the five and ten-cent store chains.

Purchasing Terms.—J. C. Penney says the first principle of merchandise is to go where the article is for sale at first hand and then to offer cash. Here we strike another reason for chain store purchasing efficiency. The chain store pays cash. In this way it obtains a further reduction in price by discounting bills promptly.

In 1921, the Kroger Grocery & Baking Co. advertised in the produce papers stating that it was in the market for carload lots of apples, potatoes, onions, cabbage, sweet potatoes, peaches, melons, and oranges, bought direct or consigned by grower or shipper.

The American Stores Co. has also been steadily advertising along this line. The Kroger advertisement reads in part as follows: "The more than 950 Kroger stores form a direct outlet, Mr. Grower and Mr. Shipper, over our counters to the consumer. Our tremendous outlet will make a steady market for you."

The grower has the option of accepting cash or consigning at the highest market price.

In some cases a chain is given the privilege of future dating. That is, the bill is dated several weeks later than the date on which the delivery of the goods is made. Frequently the goods are already sold before the bill comes.

Chain stores have found that buying for cash is as advantageous as selling for cash. It ensures prompt service and delivery from manufacturers as well as saving in discounts and bookkeeping for the chain.

Buying Ahead.—Whether it is advisable to purchase far in advance is still a moot point in chain store operation. There are arguments on both sides. Generally speaking, however, there is much less risk in contracting ahead for staple articles than for products in which demand fluctuates or totally disappears.

For example, it has never been the policy of the J. C. Penney Co. to buy far ahead. Its policy is to buy frequently and for cash. It holds that it is no part of the merchandising function to speculate in goods values. It might be possible to make large profits and it might not, but, in any event, it would mean altering the present cost-plus price policy. As the system is arranged now, the stores turn their stock on an average of five times, and when any major change in price reaches them, the stock is already sold. Neither branches nor stores carry stock above current needs. This naturally means that there are no special sales.

A certain grocery chain which never makes merchandise contracts for a year ahead, and seldom buys even staple goods in carload lots, has evolved the following system. Suppose it buys laundry soap in 100-case purchases. At the same time, it stipulates that delivery shall be made in 10-case lots and by the time the whole has been received, it has been nearly sold. It always tries, however, to keep from 30 to 60 days' supply on hand.

If a chain overloads, it is usually in a far better position, because of its numerous retail outlets, to unload than is its independent competitor. Yet the evils of overloading are just as apparent. "Men's Wear" publishes an article showing how the chain men's furnishings shops over-expanded and over-loaded with merchandise. Contrary to many of the chains, the product which they sell is not a necessity in the strict sense of the word. A buyers' strike will hold up sales indefinitely and this is exactly what happened. Where the Penney company came through the period of storm and stress with comparatively small losses, some of these chain furnishings shops had large reserves of merchandise and also had commitments a long way ahead. Because of the nature of their trade, their stock proved unwieldy. Sixty per cent. of their business was in shirts and the public was absolutely indifferent to shirts.

Buying far enough ahead to ensure supply in adequate quantity is necessary. Buying ahead too far is dangerous. There is a proper middle distance which experience will determine with a fair amount of exactitude.

One grocery chain, the purchasing policy of which is typical of many of the medium-sized chains, says, "We buy canned peas, corn, tomatoes, etc., in large enough quantities to last us through most of the year. Dry groceries, like beans, flour, corn meal, sugar, etc., are bought just from week to week. We probably make a couple of turnovers a month on some of these items, whereas with certain canned goods we have to carry them in stock a whole year before they sell. Canned red pie cherries, rhubarb, and spinach, for instance, are packed in the early summer but do not sell in any big quantity until the following spring, when people get a touch of spring fever and want these three spring-like items."

This brings up another point—seasonal purchases. It is true that, in certain lines of merchandise, it is possible to predict in normal times a particular month or months when the price will be especially low. In canned goods, for example, the price will be low right after the canning season, and if the chain wishes to purchase the output and store it away, it is possible to reckon out approximately whether this policy will prove profitable or not. This problem, however, is not confined exclusively to the chain store but is merely one of the general rules of purchasing— to buy when the article is cheapest.

The Buyer.—The buyer in any organization is an important individual, but in the chain his position is particularly prominent. But whereas in a small organization a buyer often has to turn his attention to many dissimilar articles, in the larger chains the buyer is an expert in a particular line. He knows the manufacturers of that article, he knows the sources of supply, the channels of trade, and the market trends. That is, by a careful study of the market, connected with a study of business conditions in general, he knows fairly well what the market will do. He usually belongs to local and national organizations of purchasing agents, and subscribes for publications devoted to purchasing as well as trade papers of the industries from which he gets his supplies. He has a wide range of acquaintances and is an exceedingly wide-awake business man. Good buyers are always in demand.

All purchases in the chain are made by the buyer or purchasing agent, as a general rule. Local managers, however, are often given an opportunity to pick up perishable goods from local sources and sell them. Grocery chains often do this.

To return to the buyer, he has, depending on the size of the chain, several assistant buyers under him who are all experts in different lines. The five and ten-cent chains, for example, have large staffs of buyers, each experienced in a particular line.

The main buying office of the J. C. Penney Co. is in New York, with branches at St. Louis and St. Paul. The whole idea is to provide a pipe line from the sources of supply direct to the distributing stations. As New York is the center of so much of the buying activity, many chains, like the Penney organization, maintain offices there for purchasing purposes.

It may be necessary to maintain buyers at distant points. Clothing chains, for example, might have buyers in New York and Chicago, the centers of the garment trade. They might even have buyers in London or Paris. Shoe chains that do not manufacture their own product would probably have a buyer stationed in some shoe-manufacturing center.

At all events, the chain store buyer goes out to buy and does not remain at home waiting for salesmen to visit him.

Buying Policies.—How far may the buyer act on his own judgment and to what extent must he follow the policy of the store? There are many variations. In general, however, some such policy as the following is used:

· 1. For staple sellers a certain rate of turnover has been established. By keeping records it is known just about what quantity of the article is needed of a given quality and a given style. Therefore, the buyer is authorized to keep a comfortable margin ahead of requirements.

2. In the case of novelties and new products, the store manager is often given a certain amount and told to feature it. As results come in, the buyer is informed and from these results he makes corresponding purchases.

Some buyers may have more authority, some less. If a buyer could prove to the management of a chain that he had an opportunity to buy up the product of an entire plant for a year and also could show how that product could be moved, in all probability he would be authorized to go ahead and make the purchase.

Some of the larger chains permit local purchasing in some cases, as has been mentioned before. In the big cities where there is more than one store, an assistant buyer may be sent out to pick up articles out of stock to tide the stores over until shipments arrive from the company. One company is known to allow its store managers to buy from traveling men. The store manager may be allowed to purchase any extraordinary bargains, provided he is sure he can dispose of the merchandise thus procured.

Branded Goods vs. **Private Brands.**—The question of private brands is discussed elsewhere, but a few words are necessary here in relation to the buying policy. The purchases of a chain are made strictly according to the criterion of what goods it is going to be able to sell, and at what prices. That is, the needs and desires of the community to which it caters are paramount. If there is a call for advertised goods, the chains endeavor to satisfy this call. At one time there was much substituting in chains, but this policy, when found unprofitable, was abandoned, and instead the policy was adopted of selling the customer what he wants.

Some communities demand advertised brands; others prefer the larger quantities possible to obtain from the chain's private brands.

The buyer of a five and ten-cent chain is said to divide his purchases more or less as follows:

1. *Advertised lines.* Such articles catch the eye of the consumer immediately on entering the store and make prestige for the five and ten-cent company. More and more advertised articles are finding their way to their counters, owing to the profitable results obtained by manufacturers from this easy method of sampling (discussed in the following section).

2. *Articles which will give impression of a great deal for the money.* These have been purchased by the chain at bargain prices with this end in view.

3. *Special feature articles made to draw trade.*

Buyers should constantly look for good prices but it is a mistake to imagine that quality should be sacrificed. A chain store ordinarily has to maintain a certain standard. In fact, a great part of its trade is obtained by a recognition of that standard of quality. The buyers must keep this point in mind all the time, whether they are purchasing branded or unbranded goods.

Some chains, such as the Piggly Wiggly, confine their purchases entirely to branded goods. They prefer to let the manufacturers assume the selling effort. Other firms, such as Penney, buy only staples—no fancy or unusual goods. Their appeal is directed to the middle class, and they do not care to deviate from the policy of carrying only goods in ordinary demand. In shoes, for example, they do not carry "Double A."

In a great many chains, we have the policy of selling branded goods and private brands as well. In fact, this seems to be the modern trend—to allow the customer to decide what the store shall sell. This policy, of course, is directly reflected in the purchasing department.

The Buyer and the Manufacturer.—Some buyers have found it to their advantage to get in extremely close touch with the manufacturers. They have been able to contribute towards the more efficient handling of the manufacturers' own problems. Manufacturers, as the F. W. Woolworth Co. says, are not necessarily merchandisers. Many times they cannot see the possibilities of an item until they are shown. Our buyers have gone far enough many times actually to show manufacturers how they could revise their methods so as to increase their efficiency and make a larger output possible. The buyers know that unless they can make it possible for the manufacturer to get a fair profit, their source of supply is bound to be curtailed. Therefore, they work in the closest coöperation with the maker.

As an example of this, they quote celluloid dolls which the war had made impossible to get in America, simply because no one over here knew how to make them. But the buyer who had previously purchased toys in Europe before the war had made

6

such a close study of the subject that he was able to show American manufacturers how to produce celluloid dolls which would retail at ten cents.

Christmas tree ornaments were scarcely to be found anywhere the first years of the war. Again, the Woolworth buyer induced a manufacturer to try some experiments and as a result the Woolworth organization sold millions of Christmas tree ornaments.

Woolworth has been given as an example of the good results which can be obtained by close contact of the buyer with the manufacturer. But, as a matter of fact, the buyer of any chain has the same advantages open to him. He, too, can become acquainted with the manufacturers and, knowing as he does or should the demands of the public to which his organization caters, he can often make valuable suggestions to the manufacturer. The buyer should remember that anything which helps the manufacturer to make more money will in the end result in a more satisfactory price to him.

The Manufacturer and the Buyer.—We have shown how the buyer can work with the manufacturer with benefit to both. Now, in some cases the manufacturer can use the buyer to his advantage, that is, for sampling purposes. This is comparatively a new development and is confined to the five and ten cent stores.

The manufacturer's object, as was mentioned previously, is to obtain as much publicity as possible for his product. The more he gets it before the public, the more publicity he will get and consequently his sales volume will mount up proportionately, always assuming his product is a good one.

At one time, all manufacturers frowned upon the five and ten cent store. The latter's counters were bare of advertised goods. There has been, however, a marked change in the attitude of the manufacturers, and many of them are now as anxious as they were previously reluctant to do business with the chain stores.

The reason is obvious. The large variety chains sell in all parts of the country. They purchase in large quantities and as long as the article sells their patronage is steady. Of course, all articles cannot be used as samples, but it is surprising how many articles can be disposed of in this way, even at a profit.

Before the war, Colgate & Co. sent a trial tube of their tooth paste for six cents in stamps and kept a large force busy. They did, however, put out a ten cent size when the government placed a stop on sampling during the war. A great many manufacturers with nationally advertised goods have followed their example.

But the point is this: the buyer for the chain will not purchase articles of this kind unless there is a demand for them. The manufacturer cannot have his sampling done free. He must create a demand. The chain will not sell the article—the article must sell itself.

Conclusions.—In the chapter on Purchasing Records, the reader will find a full discussion of procedure and practice in a typical purchasing problem. In the following chapter on the warehouse he will find a discussion of a subject which is so closely connected with the purchasing problem in most chains as to be almost inseparable.

This chapter has described the general aspects of the purchasing problem in their broader phases. The constant trend of the chains towards a more direct purchasing contact with the manufacturer or other source of supply has been emphasized. This purchasing economy is effectually summed up in the phrase "Centralized purchasing department and quantity buying." Coöperative buying associations have attempted to do the same thing and their failure to secure the desired results leads to the conclusion that not so much of the chain's efficiency as had been supposed was due to the purchasing. Purchasing is one of the essentials, but it is not the only one.

CHAPTER VI

THE WAREHOUSE

OUTLINE

Its location.
1. To form the hub of chain wheel of retail stores.
2. Location with reference to probable future development.
3. On transportation routes.
   (a) Rail.
   (b) Water.
   (c) Truck.
4. Ease of access for deliveries.

Size.
1. Large enough to carry stock comfortably.
2. Designed so that additions can be made easily.

Construction.
1. Number of floors.
2. System of conveying articles.
3. Miscellaneous considerations.

The stock.
1. Methods of arranging.
   (a) According to frequency of demand.
   (b) Weight.
   (c) Group class.
   (d) Alphabetical.
2. Need for room.
   (a) In order to take frequent inventories.
   (b) To facilitate moving of stock.
3. Desirability of putting old goods in front.
   (a) To avoid old goods.
4. Desirability of placing heavy, bulky articles near exit.
5. Importance of having regular place for all stock.
   (a) Facilitates handling by porters.

The warehouse superintendent.
1. Position.
   (a) Subordinate to purchasing agent.
2. Duties.
   (a) Keep stock up-to-date.
   (b) Keep adequate reserve.
      1. Notify purchasing agent when stocks are low.

84

    (c) Charge of personnel.
        1. Must see that orders are filled promptly.
    (d) In charge of goods in storage.
        1. Responsible for theft.
        2. Must see goods are checked properly.

Deliveries.
    1. Medium of delivery.
        (a) Truck.
            1. Expense.
            2. Speed of delivery.
        (b) *H*orse.
        (c) Care of delivery trucks or wagons.
    2. Frequency of deliveries.
        (a) Dependent on
            1. Distance from member stores.
            2. Frequency of turnover in member stores.
            3. Storage capacity of member stores.
        (b) Desirability of having regular deliveries.
    3. Routing of deliveries.
        (a) Certain number of stores to each driver.
        (b) Should know time necessary to deliver for each truck.

Filling requisitions.
    1. Requisites of warehouse clerk.
        (a) Knowledge of stock.
        (b) Knowledge of brands or sizes.
        (c) Knowledge of code numbers if employed.
        (d) Accuracy.
        (e) Speed.

CHAPTER VI

THE WAREHOUSE

In the previous chapter we discussed the purchasing function, and in this chapter we treat the warehousing function. All goods purchased must ordinarily be stored at some central point preparatory to being distributed to the various retail outlets. For the ordinary retailer, this function is fulfilled by the jobber, but the chain, for various reasons, such as price economy, adequate deliveries, etc., takes this function upon itself. Thus, the warehouse becomes the focal center of the distributing system. Large national chains have several warehouses located at central points.

Warehouses are in charge of an experienced warehouseman who sees to it that supplies are received, that lots are broken when necessary, graded, assembled, and shipped at appointed times or as soon after orders are received as possible.

Warehouses operate on a maximum and minimum basis, inventory being kept by a modification or amplification of any one of the methods indicated elsewhere in the chapter. On the accuracy of these inventories and the manner in which they are kept up, not only does the efficiency of the purchasing depend, but also the ability to fill orders promptly as they come in from branch stores.

The warehouse function may be divided as follows:

1. It maintains an adequate and fresh stock of goods on hand at all times.
2. It is so arranged that orders from stores can be filled and shipped out at maximum speed and with maximum accuracy.
3. It must do this with the minimum expense for overhead.

The Warehouse Location.—There is a right place and a wrong place, just as there is in the case of the retail store, to locate the warehouse. But the problem varies a great deal more in relation to the individual peculiarities of the chain. There are some general rules in this as in the other phases of chain store operation.

1. The warehouse should form the hub of the chain circle.

That is, a chain is not really a chain in the sense that each branch store forms a link. It is more like a wheel with the warehouse at the center. This holds true whether the chain is national or local. A chain organized in the East may have to have warehouses in San Francisco, Denver, Omaha, Minneapolis, Kansas City, New Orleans, Chicago, Atlanta, Detroit, Cincinnati, Cleveland, Buffalo, and Baltimore, as well as in New York and Philadelphia. In other words, there is a series of wheels scattered over the country. If the chain is local, the warehouse should be located as nearly as possible in the center of the member stores. This saves time and expense in deliveries to member stores.

2. A chain warehouse should be located with an eye to the future. Where are the new stores going to be? Which way is population growing? These are only two of many of the questions which, in consideration, form a complex problem in commercial research.

3. The warehouse must be located, if possible, on a railroad siding, where goods can be transferred directly from cars to the warehouse.

4. The warehouse can be located to suit its own convenience and with a view to reducing overhead. It can be located, in other words, where rent is cheap. It must, however, be easy of access by road, so that trucks will find no interference going to and fro.

The Size of the **Warehouse.**—The best plan in building a warehouse is to have a building large enough for all immediate needs and for requirements in the immediate future, and to have it designed so that additions can be put on inexpensively and rapidly. This will avoid waste and, at the same time, provide for future developments. If possible, the experience of the following chain should be avoided.

The warehouse of the company in question, when built, ten years ago, was much too large, but at present it is too small. Consequently, various lines of canned goods have to be stored in the basements of some of the larger stores. This, as is readily seen, causes extra trouble. It is necessary to keep a storage record of these lots, and whenever anything is removed from any store basement, a requisition has to be filled out in the office, given to the truck driver who is to get the goods, and have the store manager check the goods and O.K. the requisition. Some goods, such as canned peas, may be left untouched until spring, when the carload that was originally put into the main warehouse has been sold off. Then they begin to draw in from the basements, a hundred cases at a time.

It is a question whether the extra trouble involved in finding extra storage space does not offset, in great measure the economies effected by buying goods ahead in large quantities.

Of course, the size of the warehouse depends a great deal on the goods sold by the chain and the number of stores supplied. A grocery warehouse would have to be much larger than a shoe warehouse or a haberdashery warehouse, and much more specialized in the first and the last case.

Arrangement of Stock in Warehouse.—There are several methods of arranging stock, according to frequency of demand, according to weight, according to group classification, etc. This is a matter for the warehouse superintendent to determine in accordance with the nature of the product. There are a few hints which it would be advisable to heed:

1. Do not overcrowd the goods. They must be easy of access both for counting—necessary when goods are repriced and at other stated intervals—and for adding to or removal.
2. Old goods should be in the front so that these may be used up first, thus ensuring a fresh supply of goods at all times.
3. Heavy goods should be as near as possible to the place of loading to save effort in moving.
4. Each article stocked should have a regular place, so that all confusion may be avoided.
5. Goods must be checked on arriving and on leaving. For this reason, the checking desk should be near the loading platform. In some cases, where warehouses contain several floors, checking is done separately for each floor.

Orderly arrangement of stock and efficient handling of it will reduce overhead and carrying charges. It will also guard against confusion in filling orders and in speeding up operations generally.

The Warehouse Manager.—The man in charge of the warehouse may be a rather important individual, or he may be a mere subordinate of the purchasing agent. In the smaller chains, the purchasing agent has his office in the warehouse, and the control of warehousing problems is placed directly in his hands.

But where the warehouse is placed at a distance, the warehouse manager has much responsibility. He must see that his stocks are kept up to date, and in sufficient reserve to fill all ordinary requirements. He must see that the central purchasing office is informed daily of the exact book inventory of the business, and he must see that orders for branch stores are filled promptly. It may be that some of the buying is done from the branch warehouse, such objects, for example, as are staple and the only saving in which comes from quantity purchases.

The warehouse manager is responsible for checking goods as they come in and as they go out. His system should be made such that it would be practically impossible for employees to destroy or break open goods without the knowledge of the auditing department. He is also, of course, in charge of the warehouse personnel, porters, checking clerks, billing clerks, and probably the delivery personnel, truck drivers, helpers, etc.

Deliveries to Member Stores.—The problem of delivery comes down to three factors: the medium of delivery, the frequency of deliveries necessary to stores, and the efficient routing of delivery service.

The first question, whether delivery shall be made by truck or horse, is a matter of cost to be decided by the chain management. Some firms maintain horse delivery is cheaper for short hauls and motor trucks for longer distances. The majority, however, use motor trucks.

The second factor, that of the frequency of deliveries to stores, depends on the turnover in the store, plus the storage capacity in that store. This will naturally vary among the several chain branches. Some stores will require replenishing of stocks daily, some semi-weekly, and some weekly. This frequency can be determined very quickly after short experience.

The routing is merely a matter of traffic, but it is claimed scientific management of truck deliveries will save considerable time and money. The traffic manager can ordinarily tell about how long it will take to deliver at a certain distance from the warehouse, and can arrange his routes accordingly.

Filling Requisitions.—When an order comes in to the warehouse, it must be filled as quickly as possible and with absolute accuracy. The man performing this task must have complete knowledge of the stock, the sizes, the code numbers, the prices, etc. It is easy to imagine how accurate his knowledge must be in warehouses stocking a great variety of articles. In some cases it may be desirable to have the order pass through several departments, in each of which a special clerk picks out the goods.

In one haberdashery chain, a special conveyor on wheels is used which has been designed to carry the merchandise to and from all parts of the wareroom. It eliminates repeated handling of the goods, and allows the order from one store to be filled at one time and prevents any confusion of goods ordered for another store. These conveyors are wheeled to the charge desk, where goods are packed for shipment to the stores. In this chain, after a shipment is charged and rechecked, it is passed along to a marker who weighs, addresses, and marks out whatever receipts are necessary, such as, in the case of this chain, bills of lading and express receipts, while in the case of other chains it might simply be a driver's receipt. In this haberdashery chain there is a billing clerk who decides just what sort of case to use for each shipment. Using a case too large for the shipments sometimes make a difference of forty cents in transportation charges.

Requisition Blanks and Price Codes.—Requisition blanks may, if desired, be designed according to arrangement of stock in warehouse to make it easier to fill orders. It is most important, however, that they be so simple as to avoid all possibility of misconstruction. The requisition blank on which the store manager merely writes down a list of what he wants is not ordinarily efficient.

If the warehouse is divided into several distinct departments, the store manager should be instructed to make out individual orders on each department of the central organization from which he is ordering supplies. This question is treated at length in a later chapter. It is only desired to show here that a simple fool-proof requisition blank is important from the warehouse end of the business.

Some chains find it desirable to use codes for simplicity in ordering. Where there is a great variety of stock, this practice has much to recommend it, or where there is some arrangement according to departments. The following is a description of a code used in a men's furnishing chain:

"The code book is divided into sixteen departments, numbered consecutively from 1 to 16. The derivation of the sequence of these numbers is the order in which they appear across the top of the daily report. That is: Silk shirts department No. 1; cotton shirts department No. 2, etc. In making up a number for an article, the first part of the number is the number of the department in which the article belongs, the second is an initial or two initials designating the article, and if there is more than one price for an article having the same initial it is designated by a numeral following the initial. That is, '1' indicates first price '2' second price, etc. As an example, let us take knitted neckwear. Neckwear is department 3. 'K' is used to indicate 'knitted' and '1-2-3-4' etc. to carry the price. In this case '1' means 50c, '2' means 65c '3' $1.00, and '4' $1.50, and it follows that knitted neckwear selling at $1.50 will be coded simply '3K4.'

It goes without saying that code variations are numberless. Convenience and efficiency should be the sole criteria in determining the use of such a short cut to ordering.

The Perpetual Inventory.—Different plans may be used to keep inventory of stock in warehouses, but there is no disagreement on the fundamental point, that the inventory is the keynote of the whole structure. On it depends a large part of the efficiency of the purchasing organization. The organization must know when it is getting low on this or that item, and how to avoid buying too much of something else. In a following chapter, an account is given of a model purchasing and inventory process. In this chapter, it is merely intended to indicate some of the various methods of keeping inventory.

The stock record card is the simplest form and the one ordinarily most in use. For an illustration of such a card, see Fig. 30. This plan can be used for almost any type of chain. Cards may vary in size from 3 × 5 inches to 5 × 8 inches, according to the nature of the information which it is desired to include. Ordinarily, a separate card is used for each item. At the top of the card is listed the article, the manufacturer, and any other general information necessary. The body of the card is arranged in accordance with the illustration, although any additional information desired may be added in extra columns. It is most important in all cases that these stock record cards be kept up to date, and for that purpose a special clerk should be delegated to enter receipts and withdrawals on the card.

Some drug chains, handling from 60,000 to 90,000 articles, keep a book account for each article. Suppose this book is opened at random and we come to the statement for Amolin, 2-oz. size. The page would appear as follows:

STOCK RECORD BOOK
1922

Article	January		February		March		April		May	
	Date	Am't	Date	Am't	Date	Am't	Date	Am't	Date	Am't
Amolin 2-oz.	1	450	1	153						
	8	137								
		323								
	10	500								
		823								
	16	320								
		503								
	28	200								
		303								
	31	150								
	–	153								

On the first of January there were 450 bottles on hand. The eighth of January, 137 bottles were withdrawn for distribution to retail outlets, leaving 323 in stock. On the tenth, an order of 500 bottles came in, bringing the stock up to 823 bottles. On the sixteenth, the twenty-eighth, and the thirty-first, there were withdrawals, leaving the stock on hand at the end of the month, according to the book balance, 153 bottles.

At the end of each month a physical inventory is taken. In this case, the physical inventory corresponded with the book inventory, for there were, by actual count, 153 bottles on hand in the warehouse, on February first. Since there were 450 bottles in stock the first of January, and 500 bottles added during the month, sales for the month are obtained by subtracting the inventory for the first of February, that is, 153 from 950, leaving total sales of Amolin for the month of January at 797.

Supplies are ordered, as mentioned before, in accordance with a maximum and minimum scale, that is, an amount is determined under which it is unadvisable to go. In the same way, a maximum amount is determined. These warehouse maximums and minimums are constantly varying as the chain adds more units, or as seasonal variations affect sales of various products.

A Special System.—Because of the special features which it contains and its adaptability to a chain warehouse holding any kind of product, a brief description of an inventory system patented by Carl O. Williams, of the Acme Cash Basket Stores, Akron, Ohio, is included.

For example, this system includes the following features:

1. It allows one man to keep stock for an entire warehouse representing about 1,200 to 1,500 items.

2. The management can know by 5 p.m. each evening just how much stock is left of any and all items.

3. No matter how many orders go out during the day, only one entry is made in the stock record book. This saves time and work in fingering the pages, saves paper, and avoids the danger of error. Since but one entry and one subtraction is made daily, there is less chance of error than if thirty or fifty entries and subtractions were made. In spite of the apparently large duties of the stock clerk, he has no need of hurrying or rushing through his work.

Briefly, there is a stock record book for each floor of the warehouse. On each floor is an arrangement like a postoffice file, containing as many pigeon holes as there are items on the floor. These holes are narrow, about ⅝ of an inch being wide enough. They are arranged in the same alphabetical order as the pages in the stock record book.

Figure 8 shows a page from the stock record book, arranged for a grocery warehouse. The arrangement can be altered to suit any type of business which requires a warehouse. Entries are made on this page but once daily as will be explained.

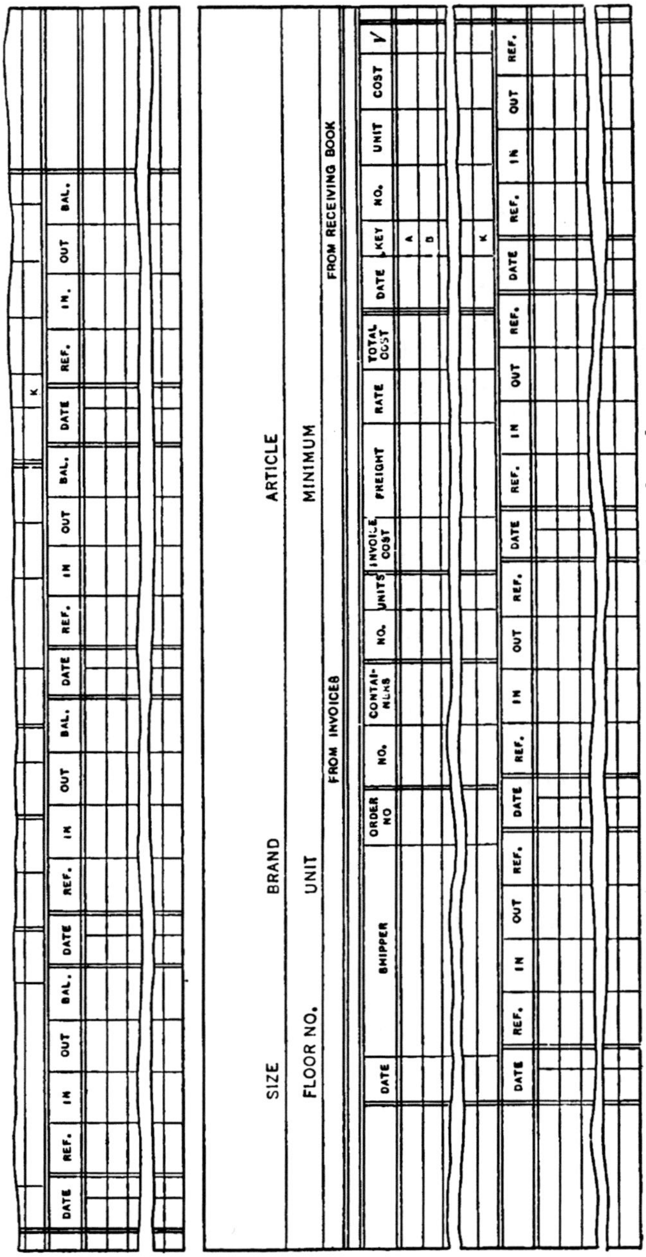

FIG. 8.—Warehouse stock record card.

All outgoing orders are recorded by the stock record clerk. Suppose he sent out

> 1 Case Capstan Peas
> 3 20-oz. mop heads
> 1 half barrel glucose
> 20 lbs. lentils

He picks up a "one case" card and slides it into the slot under Capstan Peas. There is another color card for one or two of any special item, and he inserts the color card for "3" in the 20-oz. mop head slot. A similar card with a "1" on it goes into the half-barrel glucose slot. There is another color for "pounds" and the lentils are taken care of by a card of that color and bearing the number 20.

At the close of the day the stock clerk runs through his file of cards for the day. In the Capstan Pea slot, for example, are a number of colored cards which total 24 ½ dozen cases for the day. The clerk turns to the Capstan Pea page and records down 24 ½ dozen cases, subtracting this from the total in stock and bringing down the balance.

The stock clerk notifies the buyer when any item in stock is nearing the minimum. He makes up a little card containing the following information.

> Name of item
> From whom purchased
> Date and amount of last purchase
> Price of last purchase
> Average monthly consumption
> Stock on hand

Every day the stock clerk verifies about ten items on one floor of the warehouse and corrects the figures in the book. A perpetual inventory needs constant checking up, no matter how good it is, as mistakes are bound to occur.

Conclusions.—We have by no means exhausted the variety of inventory systems which various chains employ. Nothing has been said about the replica of the main store, counter for counter, which is maintained by some five and ten cent stores as a store warehouse. All these variations require different handling of records and routine. It is appreciated that wherever records are concerned, it is exceedingly difficult to obtain an accurate idea of order and sequence unless one particular system is taken, and the process followed through from beginning to end. For this reason, Chap. XVI is devoted to purchasing and warehousing records as employed in one chain.

The theory of warehousing can be readily summed up:

1. A warehouse building large enough to contain sufficient stock and conveniently located in relation to retail outlets.

2. A system of records which will keep the buyer constantly and accurately informed of stock on hand at any moment.

THE SALES PROBLEM

OUTLINE

Seasonal.
1. Stimulus to retail selling by
    (a) Holidays.
        1. Christmas.
        2. Easter.
2. Necessity of preparations
    (a) To distribute sales.
3. Sales records as bases of predicting seasonal volume
    (a) For entire organization.
    (b) For individual stores.

Daily.
1. Importance of Saturday.
2. Influence of weather.
    (a) Rain.
    (b) Excessive heat or cold.

Business conditions.
1. Ability of chain stores to weather financial stress.
2. Business of chains dealing in necessities actually better in periods of economic depression.

The product.
1. Characteristics.
    (a) A necessity or semi-necessity.
    (b) Turns over rapidly.
    (c) Portable.
2. Number.
    (a) Large variety.
    (b) Standard sizes only.
        1. Extra large and extra small avoided.
        2. Sizes most commonly required.
    (c) Standard styles.
3. Quality.
    (a) Necessity of uniformity.
4. Trend towards packaged goods.

Merchandising policies.
1. Display.
    (a) Window trims.

    (*b*) Counter displays.

    (*c*) Shelf displays.

2. Cut price sales.

    (*a*) Loss leaders or weekly-specials.

    (*b*) One cent sales.

3. Seasonal sales.

    (*a*) Small necessity of

4. Novelty sales or selling ideas.

    (*a*) Coöperative merchandising campaigns.

5. Premiums and trading stamps.

CHAPTER VII

THE SALES PROBLEM

All chain store problems are affected by the question of sales, for a chain store organization is essentially a highly organized retail selling machine. The purchasing agent, before any purchasing is done, must know the rate at which goods can be sold. Furthermore, the nature of his purchases must be regulated by the buying desires of the public. The personnel, the store managers, the clerks, the supervisors, etc., are all people who have been trained in the art of selling. All efforts made to maintain morale have been made with the intent of increasing sales.

In this chapter three phases of the sales problem are discussed:

1. Causes which lead to fluctuations in sales, either regular or irregular, over periods of time.
2. The general nature of products sold in chain stores.
3. Various merchandising plans and policies.

In general, the laws of merchandising which apply to any retail selling organization apply to chain stores, with the exception that national chains have a great many problems due to their broad distribution that do not come up in handling an independent business or even a small local chain. For example, it is quite evident that the tastes of one community will not coincide exactly with the tastes of another, nor can any efforts on the part of the clerks offset this community antagonism to particular products. On this point the standardized policy of the chain must give way.

As far as possible, conditions applying to the majority of chains are used. But each chain has to face these conditions in different ways.

Seasonal Fluctuations.—Chain store organizations, as almost every other merchandising activity, are affected by seasonal trends. Christmas is an almost universal stimulant to every business. The summer is apt to mark a falling off in most lines.

Every different product has its off seasons. Seasonal activities are regular in occurrence as differentiated from periods of prosperity and depression which alternate at infrequent intervals.

For purposes of illustration the monthly sales of the F. W. Woolworth Co. for 1918–1921 have been taken. The sales of this company serve well as an example because the five and ten

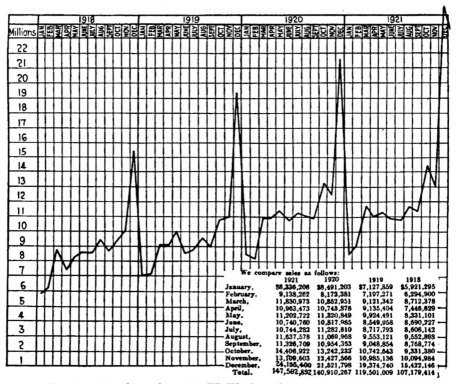

Fig. 9.—Monthly sales of F. W. Woolworth Company, 1918–1921.

cent store business is not one primarily affected by good times or hard times. This factor has but slight significance in determining volume of sales.

Glancing at Fig. 9, it is apparent immediately that each Christmas brings a great peak of business activity. The month of December alone doubles the average sale of any of the preceding 11 months. One point of value is at once evident. The company must prepare in advance for this inrush of business, and from its records it can forecast with fair certainty the volume of sales in each particular store.

Looking further, another peak is seen in March or in April, a much lesser peak but still appreciable, and this can be attributed to Easter sales. There is a drop in late summer reflecting vacation times, and thereafter business is fairly good until the Christmas rush suddenly doubles sales. January and February bring the lowest ebb of the year's business. The experience of the Woolworth chain is not unique. The other five and ten cent store chains experience the same seasonal trends.

What is shown so clearly by the Woolworth case is applied more generally in Fig. 10, comparing a number of chain stores with each other and with department stores, apparel stores, and mail order houses. Chain groceries show

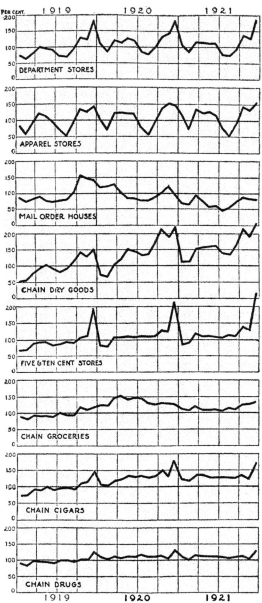

FIG. 10.—Comparison of seasonal trends (chart prepared by Federal Reserve Bank of New York).

the least seasonal peaks with chain drugs reflecting only Christmas activity. Chain cigar stores and chain dry goods have decided seasonal peaks. In the case of the drygoods chains there is a distinct mid-summer reaction.

Figure 11 is a composite chart of retail activities averaged over 1919, 1920 and 1921. This shows plainly the falling off in January and February, the recovery lasting until the end of

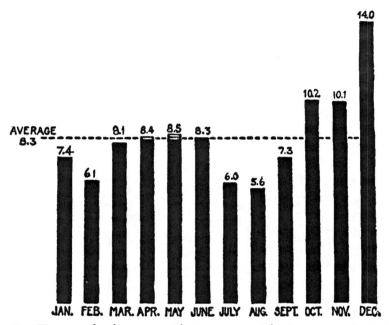

Fig. 11.—How retail sales vary with the seasons (chart prepared by Federal Reserve Bank of New York).

June, the summer apathy and the fall rise culminating at Christmas time.

The United Cigar Stores Co. has spent a great deal of time and thought on the seasonal problem and has done much towards distributing the seasonal peaks. For example, its executives realized that in the holiday season the stores would be overcrowded and many sales lost, unless some means were taken to spread the sales out over a few weeks prior to the actual event. As it is against the policy of the chain to feature cut-price sales, unusual offers are made, such as including extra articles for the same price, and these offers are made some time before Christmas.

In January and February tobacco sales are poor. In addition to the post-holiday apathy, there is the fact that smokers do not enjoy smoking out-of-doors in very cold weather. Also, many are consuming the cigars given them for Christmas. Thus special sales are again resorted to. One year every purchaser of a pipe was given one half the amount of his purchase in anything in the store. The company figured that these special sales gave enough news value in advertising to pay the actual falling-off in profits.

What has been done by this company can also be done elsewhere. With the records of sales for previous years as a basis, some scheme can be worked out for distributing seasonal congestion, and perhaps bringing up sales in off-seasons.

Daily Fluctuations.—It is not only possible to forecast monthly sales by a careful study of records, but daily sales as well. Some days in the week are far better for business purposes than others. For example, the Great Atlantic & Pacific Tea Co. does half the total business of the company on Fridays and Saturdays. To a great extent the same is true of the five- and ten-cent store chains. Officials of F. W. Woolworth Co. point out that sales on Saturday are usually $800,000, or equal to the business of two days during the week.

Daily sales cannot, however, be forecasted with such accuracy as monthly sales, because other factors enter the equation. For example, few people shop in very stormy weather, or very hot or very cold weather. Weather extremes discourage retail sales activity.

Where a chain deals in perishable goods this element of uncertainty is important. Mort Hamburger, Sales Promotion and Advertising Manager of the Federal System of Bakeries of America, Inc., says: "In any retail bakery business there is always the element of what we have termed 'day-old bread.' The ideal situation in the Federal Bakery is to sell out the day's output of bread. Certain kinds of pastries can be carried over without losing their flavor or taste and are just as palatable the second day as the first. Practically every Federal Bakery has an unusually heavy bake Friday nights in order to have sufficient supply of merchandise saleable for Saturday, and hence it is necessary to carry not only cakes and pastries, but extra bread."

As far as regulating the production of baked goods in Federal shops is concerned, this is left entirely to the judgment of the manager. In the cash-and-carry business it is difficult to judge to the very loaf just how large a quantity should be baked. After all is said and done, the element of production is the one problem in the bakery business that cannot be solved accurately.

A sudden down-pour of rain, or an unusually cold or warm day, will have a marked effect on the cash-and-carry business, and managers are at all times on the lookout for these hazardous days. Every manager in the Federal System gets a daily report on the weather and is guided accordingly when ordering his bake. If, for instance, on a Friday night the manager gets a report from the Weather Bureau to the effect that Saturday will be a cold, rainy day, he will cut down his production a little bit so as to avoid the possibility of discards.

Although the weather may be the cause of decreasing some sales, the chain drug store which carries umbrellas will find a sudden increase in sales, the chain shoe store will double its sales of rubbers, etc.

Business Conditions.—Apart from any seasonal, daily, or climatic influences on sales, chain store organizations are subject to the general effects of business prosperity and depression. This is very unequally distributed in its action, largely due to the nature of the product, the successful purchasing policy of the chain, the wisdom of the management in foreseeing conditions, etc.

The five- and ten-cent store suffers little from business depression. The Woolworth sales chart readily shows that the business depression of 1920–1921 failed to retard to any marked degree the healthy growth of the chain. In fact, it is true that in hard times more people patronize the five- and ten-cent stores than in good times. In a grocery chain, normally dealing in low-priced staple articles, business depression also has but a slight hold.

The Product.—What sort of goods can be sold in chain stores? At first thought it would seem almost everything. It is not limited to tangible products but can be extended to intangible products such as a chain of theatres, hotels, and shoe repair shops. Now, are there are rules which can be applied to the choice of products possible to sell through retail chains? Theoretically the answer would be "No," but no system has yet been evolved which makes possible a successful chain for retailing some products There may be isolated examples of small chains, but there are no great chains of jewelry stores or furniture stores. Thus there must be some general principles which govern the products sold in chain stores.

1. The more rapid the turnover, the more adapted the product is for chain store retailing. A well-known brand of cigarettes, turning once a week, is better than a line of cut glass turning once a year. Slow turnover means large overhead expenses which means failure in efficient chain store operation.

2. The product should preferably be a necessity or a semi-necessity. The chain store must have constant patronage. It must be able to predict its purchasing requirements. Demand for luxuries is uncertain and the larger profit cannot offset this uncertainty.

3. The article should be portable. Since most chain stores are cash-and-carry retail outlets, the easier the article is to wrap up and take away, the more sales can be made.

4. The product should be such as to permit centralized and standardized executive control.

The fact that a product is merchandised successfully through chain stores without fulfilling all these requirements does not prevent these rules from general application.

The Number of Products.—A chain store may carry a larger variety or a smaller variety of goods than its independent competitor. In a grocery chain the number is usually smaller. The Kroger Grocery & Baking Co. usually carries not more than 400 brands in place of 900 to 1,000 carried by the independent grocery. The reason here is that the chain store carries only groceries which turn over rapidly. No brands of questionable reputation are stocked. No goods for which there is little call are allowed to take up valuable space on the shelves. The Piggly Wiggly Co.'s stores are necessarily, because of the self-service idea, restricted in products to the best known brands. This policy allows concentration on a few lines.

The case of the drug store is the reverse. The large chain store is likely to have a much larger variety of products, due to its great merchandising power. The chain drug store, usually located in very advantageous city sites, can often stage a special sale and complete it in one day by means of newspaper advertising, a proceeding outside the reach of the independent druggist.

The stock problem of the five- and ten-cent store is a difficult one. Professor Duncan in his book "Marketing, Its Problems and Methods," states that 92 per cent. of the stock of such a store is made up of every day necessities, four per cent. luxuries, candy and jewelry novelties two per cent., and fads and souvenirs two per cent. more. In addition there is always an opportunity for trying out experimental goods. Some five- and ten-cent stores take on as many as 48 different lines of goods, including groceries, automotive parts, etc., and with such appurtenances as a flower department, a photograph gallery, a soda fountain, and a restaurant. It is claimed that the limit of expansion has been reached in the variety field, and that further extension of lines carried must be reached by raising the price limit. In support of this argument, it is noteworthy that, with the exception of Woolworth, the other five- and ten-cent store chains have raised their price limit while retaining the selling advantage contained in the name five- and ten-cent store.

The United Cigar Stores Co. claims to have deviated in but two respects from its original policy, and one of these deviations was to take on the retailing of sundry merchandise such as candy, chewing gum, safety razors, playing cards, etc. Several members of the organization were averse to taking on lines which would, in their opinion, detract from the individuality of the store and render a clerk trained to sell only tobacco products less efficient when he had other things to sell as well. As a compromise, at first only goods were taken on which did not require to be sold, but only put on display. Then other articles were tried out. Pencils, handkerchiefs, and books were not particularly successful, but chewing gum was an immediate success. Candy was sold in packaged form. At one time a bulky glass jar was introduced for use at home for holding cigars and sales surpassed all expectations, the jars being carried off in thousands.

When the United Retail Candy Stores Co. started in business, it was feared that sales of candy in the cigar stores would immediately fall off, but, on the contrary, no effect has been observed. A cigar store is an excellent place for retailing candy as a side line, because approximately 80 per cent. of all candy sales are made to men.

Number of Lines.—The policy of pleasing the public extends logically to the number of lines carried, and even to the sizes in particular lines. The manufacturer's great problem in selling the chain stores is to create a demand for his product among the public. If any missionary work is to be done by the chains, they do it in behalf of their own products and private brands. Manufacturer's goods must sell themselves.

Grocery stores ordinarily limit the number of sizes of a particular line in stock. Extra large packages are avoided both because of the difficulty in carrying away and because there is comparatively little demand for them. A customer will usually take two of the smaller size if she desires a considerable quantity.

The Dotson-Kerwin stores, in Iowa, have an ingenious method whereby a stock of odd sizes sufficient for one store is made to do for five, and by this method makes it possible to secure a large enough turnover of these odd lines to warrant carrying them. The company has five stores, in Waterloo, Independence, Oelwein, Vinton, and Cedar Falls. Although Waterloo is about four times the size of the other towns, all stores are stocked uniformly as to variety and grade. The size of the stock varies, of course, with the demand. "Off sizes," says an article in the Chicago Apparel Gazette, "are carried by each store, and each store keeps a list of odd sizes and patterns carried by the other stores." As the stores are all within a radius of 30 miles, whenever a customer asks for an odd size and it is not in stock, the clerk looks it up in the card file and in a few moments has telephoned and is assuring the customer he can get it that afternoon.

As a general rule, however, chain stores do not and should not attempt to carry anything but standard sizes and lines.

Quality.—It is a peculiarity of human nature that, whatever price is charged for an article, the customer expects good quality. No chain store can afford to sell inferior goods. Like the attitude of the clerk, the quality of the articles offered reacts on sales in all the other stores of the chain. Grocery chains ordinarily make a practice of inspecting all goods at the warehouse and exercising the most careful supervision over standardization of quality under brand names.

Enough has already been said about the necessity for turnover and fresh stock, under the head of purchasing. Quality goods are necessarily fresh and not left-overs. No chain store organization should try experiments with the quality of its products. The best for the price is none too good.

Packaged Goods.—Wherever possible, chain stores prefer to sell packaged goods. The grocery chains and the drug chains are the outstanding examples of this tendency. At one time the grocer measured out ten pounds of sugar and five pounds of corn meal, etc. Now he simply hands over the counter a neat package all done up. Packaged goods are another move towards efficiency since they eliminate a great deal of time spent in preparing bulk articles for a customer. In many cases, a clerk could wait on two or three customers while measuring and doing up parcels of bulk articles for one customer. Recently one large chain store grocery did away with all its coffee-grinders, confining sales of coffee to packaged goods.

Where chain stores do carry bulk articles, it is a wise practice to have clerks get standard weights wrapped up and ready in their spare moments, so that no time will be lost in making sales.

The Place of the Product in Chain Store Merchandising.— The product plays a larger part in chain store merchandising than in the merchandising policies of a single, independent store, because chain stores depend so much on display, on the appeal of the article to the eye of the consumer. In the five- and ten-cent store the product must virtually sell itself. The policy of substitution has almost died out and the chain store customer may be sure of getting what he wants.

The merchandising plans and policies of chain store organizations are not build around service, nor exclusiveness of trade, but solely around the product. In many cases it may be the price of the product. Probably in the majority of cases price will be the basis upon which the merchandising policies are formulated. But some chains emphasize the quality of the product. The more necessary an article to the consumer, the less sales effort is required to dispose of it. It becomes a question of selling a number of staple articles to the consumer by efficient display, seconded by other selling methods.

Chain store organizations have certain settled merchandising policies, some of which are inseparably connected with the chain idea, and other of which are elaborations of ordinary retail selling methods. For example

1. Efficient display.
   (a) Window trims.
   (b) Counter displays.
   (c) Shelf display of product.
2. Cut price sales.
   (a) Loss leaders.
   (b) One-cent sales.
3. Seasonal sales.
4. Special novelty sales.
5. Premiums and trading stamps, etc.

The first point has been treated at length in the chapter on the member store.

The theory of pricing will be discussed in the following chapter. The point to be brought up here is the effect of pricing as a sales appeal. "All people want to make a good bargain. Let them!" said Frank W. Woolworth, and he proceeded to base his whole merchandising campaign on a display of goods at the lowest possible prices.

Many chains have a fixed policy of featuring each week a so-called "loss leader." That is, some well known article, the price of which is usually standard and known to the majority of purchasers, is put on sale at actual cost to the chain or even at a slight loss. This is done on the theory, which works out in practice, that people will be attracted to this bargain and will buy other goods as well.

Loss leaders are often termed "weekly specials." One chain says: "Our business was built up on the idea of weekly specials. Every week we cut the price of about twenty items in the store and sell them, for that week only, at what amounts to almost a wholesale price. "Many other chain stores follow this idea with their own variations.

The "One-cent" sale, so highly and successively featured by the Liggett stores, is one of the variations of this loss leader idea, very ingeniously carried out. At first glance, it actually appears as if the drug store were taking a terrific loss. The explanation, however, is simple.

The person in charge of organizing the sale makes a list of long-price articles, that is articles the cost to the store of which is quite low compared with the selling price. Suppose, for example, that an article cost 10 cents and retailed for 25 cents. This leaves a gross profit to the store of 60 per cent. Now suppose a 1 cent sale is announced, that is, a purchaser can obtain two of these articles for the price of one. By paying 26 cents, the customer can procure two packages of the 25-cent size. One article is sold for 25 cents and the other for one cent. If the average cost of doing business is 20 per cent. no money is actually lost on the sale. By increasing the turnover, the expense of operation is reduced.

Seasonal Sales.—Generally speaking, the chain stores make much less use of the season as an excuse for staging special sales than regular independent organizations. The reasons are obvious. The chain store, with its larger turnover, its more efficient purchasing organizations, and its wide distribution, is able to sell its goods as they come in. Chains, like Penney, which make a rule never to buy ahead, naturally never have seasonal cut-price sales.

Grocery chains often have a canned goods sale, but these are rather in the nature of loss leaders than genuine seasonal clearing out of stock. Chain shoe stores, like any other shoe store, have seasonal sales, but often this is due to the large number of manufacturers' chains included among the chain shoe retailers.

The average chain considers it more profitable to estimate seasonal demands closely enough so that there will be no large surplus of left-overs, with overhead expenses of storage and sales losses.

Special Novelty Sales.—Originality in selling methods always attracts the public. Feature sales are always popular with firms which advertise. It gives them something to talk about and explain. Novelty in window display is another method. But new selling ideas pay better than any other method.

President Ralph B. Wattley of the National Drug Stores says his ideas were founded on what he himself would like to find on entering a chain store. One of the first things he did was to bring the prescription counters out in plain sight instead of keeping them in the rear according to traditional drug store practice. (See Fig. 12.) Then he formulated the policy of selling all prescriptions at cost, the company even going so far as to carry part of the cost. This was like offering the public something in the nature of a perpetual loss leader with a reduction of something like 50 per cent. to the public. This was a new idea and quite opposite to the trend in some drug chains to minimize the prescription business or even concentrate it in a few stores.

One day he observed a man who was rushing from one counter to another in the endeavor to make up a list of purchases. This man was evidently in a great hurry and was much inconvenienced by the fact that he had to go from counter to counter to make his purchases. President Wattley immediately conceived the idea of a men's department, carrying all the small articles a man would be likely to purchase. It would contain everything from razor blades to poker chips.

The Federal System of Bakeries occasionally features a novelty product. They originated a name for a slightly different product such as Priscilla Cake, Oliver Twist, the Longfellow Loaf, Tokio, and Honey Boys. Generally speaking, these names convey little of the nature of the product. To each product one solid week of selling effort is devoted and to this end all merchandising policies are bent. In Tokio week, for example, the following merchandising plan was followed:

1. The product—a poppy seed loaf of bread with slightly different shape.
2. The advance window paster "teaser."
3. The window displays.
4. The inside store displays.
5. Advertising and publicity.
6. Sales caps for the sales girls.

It should be stated that previous to putting on the complete sales campaign, the detail had been carefully worked out in several cities on a test-campaign basis.

During the Tokio week, sales of Tokio bread averaged 4.2 per cent. of total sales, two stores going over 11 per cent. As a method of stimulating sales and gaining publicity it was a distinct success because of the carefully planned campaign.

Coöperative Mechandising Campaigns.—There has been a movement of recent years by manufacturers to coöperate with retailers in staging sales campaigns. This is but another phase of the trend towards more direct distribution, but it deserves close watching in the future.

The Sun-Maid Raisin Co., which recently ceased distribution through jobbers, coöperated with the Federal System of Bakeries in putting on a Sun-Maid raisin week. Since many of the bakery's products were naturally made with raisins, any increased sales would accrue both to the benefit of the manufacturer and the chain. The following analysis of results accomplished by retail units during the Sun-Maid week is interesting as showing what such coöperation will effect.

Average sale for raisin bread three weeks prior to
Raisin Week.................................. $19.66
Average sale raisin bread during Raisin Week....... 26.03
Average sale two weeks following................. 20.94

This meant that, during Raisin Week, sales of raisin bread increased 32½ per cent. Although sales afterwards fell off, there was a net gain of 6½ per cent.

Chain organizations with manufactured products of their own normally prefer to feature such products, but there are undoubtedly possibilities in the idea which have not yet been fully exploited.

Premiums and Trading Stamps.—The premium department of the United Cigar Stores Company is one of the features of the company. The policy of giving premiums was initiated when this company first started in business. A special company was formed to take hold and expand the premium end of the business. Originally the list of articles given away in return for premiums was chiefly made up of articles which men ordinarily liked, but it was soon found that silk stockings and other articles for women assumed marked importance and the premium list was accordingly enlarged.

The clerk is instructed to place the certificate in the consumer's hand. Otherwise not half of them would be taken. The premium department buys all merchandise at half the price the consumer would have to pay and it gives these premiums as

s

an inducement for the customer's trade. By buying at the United Cigar Stores, in other words, and saving up the coupons, the customer can redeem these coupons for articles at virtually wholesale prices.

Cost is figured on a 100 per cent. redemption basis, and is taken care of by profits from increased sales. Of course, there is never a 100 per cent. redemption. In one year the United Cigar Stores had 86¾ per cent. of its premiums redeemed, a figure remarkably high. When redemption percentage is low, profits are left with which to start new premium stations, pay clerks, etc.

Some chains use trading stamps as a drawing card for customers, but the practice has never become very wide spread. Premiums and trading stamps are both forms of service which, in particular cases, it is found profitable to give because of the increased sales resulting from them, and the consequently increased profits to take care of the increased cost.

Conclusions.—The sales problem is the great problem in chain store retailing. All others are subordinated. Without volume of sales there can be no success, because the narrow margin of profit absolutely demands this volume. Thus the first principle of sales is to find out what the public wants. The owner of one small drug chain installed a want book and noted down everything asked for in his drug stores, from hair nets to piano strings. In this way he was led to stock tennis and golf supplies, fishing tackle, baseball goods, bathing suits, fountain pens, alarm clocks, and scissors. He was able to sell this heterogeneous collection of goods because his public wanted them.

Public taste changes rapidly. One grocery chain noticed that sales of black tea were increasing. Several lines of green tea were immediately dropped and the black tea pushed. The result was that in three months sales of black tea were exactly doubled.

Control of sales lies naturally through careful records and accounting, but the increase of sales comes from careful watching of these records, plus sales ideas. When these sales ideas are embodied in merchandising plans, tested in advance for their practicality, increased sales must result.

CHAPTER VIII

COMPETITION

Bases of chain store competition.
1. Accounting.
2. Display.
3. Goodwill
    (a) Of public.
    (b) Of employees.
4. Location.
5. Management.
6. Personnel.
7. Price.
8. Purchasing.
9. Sales policies.
10. Turnover.

CHAPTER VIII

COMPETITION

Competition in the chain store field is definitely divided into two sections, first that between the chain store and the independent store, and second, that between the chain store and the chain store. The first type of competition is the one most talked of, while the second is the one that matters most to the chain organization. A chain expert on locations can tell after an analysis whether the community can support one of his stores, and the chain store will be sure of a certain amount of trade based on its location and its price appeal.

There has been very little unpartisan discussion of the question of chain store competition. In the months just prior to the war there was much talk and some outcry against chain policies by those independents who were unable to meet chain prices. When the war brought almost universal business prosperity, money was made so easily that the phenomenal strides made by the chains in expansion programs passed almost unnoticed. The result is that now the lines are fairly drawn. Each town and city supports a certain quota of chain grocery stores. Other chains are close behind. These chains obtain a certain percentage of the trade, namely that percentage which is willing to pay cash and do without deliveries. Although for some years past the trend has been towards "cash-and-carry" chains, it is quite likely that in the sharper competition of the future some chains may offer delivery as a special inducement. Several grocery chains, in fact, are offering this service at present.

Many independent retailers have held the chain in such dread that they have been willing to sell out on the mere invasion of the chain store in their territory. Others are so narrow-minded as to close their eyes or turn them the other way when they pass a competing chain store. This deep-seated antagonism on the part of the independent retailer has done him great harm. He has indulged his natural tendency of avoiding pushing branded

117

goods which chain stores carry in order to avoid the almost inevitable price comparison.

The present situation is that the chains take a certain class of trade and the independents another, namely, the class of trade with money which prefers the personal service and trouble which only the independent retailer can give. In return this class is willing to pay an extra amount.

The Position of the Independent Retailer.—Will the small retailer ever go out of business?

As far as any definite answer can be given, it is "No!" The small retailer can obtain a hold on a certain section of the public through forms of service, square dealing, courtesy, handling low-turnover goods in small demand which some of his customers wish, and by carrying an extra good line of something else as an added attraction.

Many people who go to a grocery store do not like to experiment and they wish someone to choose for them. If they know a certain retailer will send them good fresh lettuce, fruits, and vegetables, they will buy there and pay the extra price. It is the same point which nationally advertised goods are hammering home all the time. "Don't experiment! Our goods are always the same. The other fellow may be all right but you can always rely on us."

One grocery chain expert who has studied the question of independent competition has noted the following methods by which independent chain store retailers were trying to hold their business and even increase it:

1. Several retailers have installed a window bakery and feature fresh baked bread, cakes, etc.
2. Others have joined a corporation which enables them to buy groceries direct and save the jobbers' profit.
3. A few have opened confectioneries in connection with their grocery stores, so they can stay open Sundays.
4. A few have combined groceries and meat markets with good success.
5. Many little grocers have gone into market houses, where a small stall can be rented and where a comfortable retail business can be built up without much risk or high rent.

It is well worth quoting the opinion of an official of one grocery chain in regard to the status of the independent grocer.

He predicts a "war" between the various distributors of

foodstuffs, because the cost of living must be reduced, and that means eliminating the bad accounts, the inefficiency of small grocers, and the other unnecessary expenses incidental to the old-style method of conducting a grocery business.

There are more failures in the grocery business every year, according to this authority, than in any other line of business. Ne'er-do-wells and dreamers who have a few hundred dollars to spare start a grocery store and settle back for a long lifetime of easy profits. Others start stores and let their wives and daughters run them while they keep on with their regular jobs. Such 'grocers' are easily stampeded into buying too much, they have no grounding in the rudiments of business, and have not the stamina to carry them through when business is a little slow. Most of them just choose the grocery business because 'if we can't make it go, we can eat our stock ourselves.'

The small retailers, like the poor, will be always with us. And as long as we have small retail grocers, we shall need wholesale grocers.

Chain Competition with Other Chains.—There has been much debate, more in the past than at present, about the possibility of gigantic chains monopolizing the retail trade of the country. The United Retail Stores Company is frequently quoted as an example.

The best safeguard of the public against high prices is in most cases the chain. In communities where the local dealers frequently charged all the traffic could bear, the advent of the chain store revolutionized prices. When two chains or more share the territory in a city and cover the same ground, there is a certainty of low prices. For example, the chain grocery business is not in one set of hands. New chains are constantly springing up and taking their place by the side of old ones.

The most potent argument against the chain store's being able to monopolize the retail trade is that the average chain deals in products made from the most ordinary materials, things which no one could possibly corner. In the grocery chain, for example, what individual could hope to control the supply of sugar, coffee, beans, tea, cocoa, wheat, corn, etc.? The moment a chain tried to charge more than a fair price, the field would be flooded with retailers anxious to undersell him.

It is a strange fact, but many times corroborated, that if,

by the side of an old-established chain branch, a new branch of another chain comes, the old chain store shows no diminution in sales, perhaps even an increase. In the majority of cases, the new branch builds up a satisfactory trade for itself. It is not recognized by many retailers that the coming of a chain store will mean increased business for the whole locality. People will buy in suburbs who had previously purchased in town. The price appeal of the chain store is a universal attraction.

Private Brands.—Just as unfair competition, secret discounts, etc., have been the slogans of the independent retailers in their denunciation of chain stores, the cry of the manufacturer has been against the private brand of the chain store.

It was found very early in chain store development that it was possible to make products and put them on sale in the chain's own stores at a much lower price than a nationally advertised, well-known product could be put out. These private brands became a bone of contention and remained so for many years. Both sides went too far and lost money by it. At one time, Mr. Hartford, the founder of the Great Atlantic & Pacific Tea Co., leaned heavily to private brands, but his keen business sense finally taught him that the public will eventually have what it wants, and if it prefers nationally-advertised goods, it is more profitable to sell them than to allow the customer to go elsewhere. As far as substitution is concerned, the chain store clerk or manager has no time to spend in pushing private brands. In fact, he is compelled to spend nearly all his time in disposing of articles called for by customers. The manufacturer of branded goods can be sure, at this date, of having his goods stocked, provided he creates a large enough demand for them.

There is frequently a problem to meet in the grocery business when the policy is to simplify the stock yet at the same time satisfy the majority. This is the frequent cause of a cry of substitution on the part of the manufacturer. The chain store side of the question is rarely heard. Here is what one chain store has to say:

"We don't handle Gold Dust, Grandma's Washing Powder, Rub-No-More and a dozen other soap powders. Instead of these, we standardize on Sea Foam soap powder, buy it in car-loads and push it hard. If a woman comes into one of our stores and asks for Gold Dust, the clerk (if he is any good) will tell her why we do not handle it and that Sea Foam will do anything that any other ordinary soap powder will do. Maybe he sells her a five cent package of Sea Foam and, if she likes it, we have made a new customer. Frequently, of course, she will not listen or refuses to try a substitute. But a chain store has to cater to the majority, and we have so many advantages in simplifying our stock that we do not worry about the occasional customer that wants something else.

"Most retail and wholesale grocers get loaded up with a lot of dead goods that nobody wants. We take on new items, now and then, but generally drop an old item when we do. Recently, at one of our managers' meetings, there was considerable desire shown for us to stock a certain baking powder, an advertising campaign being then in full force on this item. We called for a vote and found that more stores wanted Rumford's (which we already handled) than this other brand. We chose, therefore to stay with Rumford. We do not wish to divide our business between too many items, because that means we should have to buy in lesser quantities, lose our quantity discounts, and also not be able to turn over our stock so frequently."

The main reasons why chain stores push private brands of their own are:

1. Possibilities of making extra profits.
2. The advertising value of the brand to the store.
3. Avoidance of trouble with manufacturers on price disputes.

Naturally, the first consideration carries the most weight but chain stores realize that sales resistance eats up profits and they will never succeed in trying to stand out against an overwhelmingly strong popular brand.

The manufacturers' private brands are nationally advertised and must be so if the chain stores are to stock them. But the chain's own private brands as a rule are unadvertised in any way other than by display, and by price comparisons indicated by means of tags. The United Drug Co. has advertised its private brands in many cases. It advertises nationally, locally, and by means of dealer helps. It has made its trade name "Rexall" known all over the country. Ordinarily, this company pursues a policy of concentrating on one brand and pushing it.

Substitution.—What is meant by substitution? There is a difference of opinion on this point. Some maintain that it is limited to wilful delivery of one package in place of another.

Others contend that it is the sales effort of the clerk to induce the customer to "take something just as good." The chain store organizations claimed that it was a fundamental rule never to substitute, but always to give the customer what he wanted if it was in stock and never attempt a sale until after the customer had made his choice. The manufacturers claimed that the bonus which many chains give to their clerks as a reward for selling their own goods made it impossible for the chain to stop substitution even though it desired to do so.

In view of this difference of opinion, the report of an investigation of the Liggett stores in Greater New York, made by J. A. Murphy, representative of Printers' Ink, and by the president of a large pharmaceutical company which manufactures and distributes some 2,000 items, is informative. Report had come from checkers that the Liggett stores were flagrantly practicing substitution, and, in the case of the company in question, substitution was fairly easy because the company had stopped advertising.

All but five or six of the 72 Liggett stores on the list were covered. Mr. Murphy asked either for Baume Analgesique Bengué or Scott's Emulsion. To make matters doubly sure, he often wrote the name of the former product on a slip of paper. The president of the pharmaceutical company asked for his own products. Both men pretended not to know each other.

In the first half-dozen stores requests were made in a brisk and businesslike manner. There was absolutely no attempt to substitute or to sell additional merchandise.

In the next group of stores visited, the requests were put in a less positive fashion, asomething like the following: " A small bottle of Scott's Emulsion. Scott's is the best, isn't it?" The answers varied from "It is a very good brand," "It is the best known," to "We carry several."

The president finally asked a girl why she didn't take advantage of such a good chance to push the brands of the company. She said it was against the rules of the company, and customers must be given what they ask for.

The conclusion is that the only way for the manufacturer to sell his goods in chain stores in competition with the private brands of the chain organization is to get the public to ask for them. The chain store will sell just what its customers want.

Combination.—One problem remains for discussion in connection with competition between various chains, namely, the tendency of the larger chain to absorb the smaller chain. This is, as the "Principles of Marketing," by Ivey, points out, a simple case of cause and effect. The greater the number of stores, the greater the outlets. The greater the outlets, the more competition in purchasing. To be able to purchase in large quantities a chain must have a certain number of outlets, and it may prove far cheaper to purchase or affiliate with another chain already in operation and in this way at one moment secure this purchasing advantage.

In addition, to function properly, a chain must have a certain size. It enables much more efficient standardization of routine management and expenses.

Lastly, there has been an unconscious profiting by one of the chain store principles of growth. The larger the number of member stores, the larger the sales per unit store. We are discussing here the reasons for combination, and this is the most potent one. To go back to our old illustration, the Woolworth stores, which are not affected greatly by prosperity and depression, we find the following facts.

F. W. WOOLWORTH COMPANY

	Number of stores	Total sales	Sales per store
1911	596	$ 52,616,123	$ 88,282
1912	631	60,557,767	95,939
1913	684	66,228,072	96,824
1914	737	69,619,669	94,340
1915	805	75,995,774	94,404
1916	920	87,089,270	94,662
1917	1,000	98,102,857	98,102
1918	1,039	107,179,411	103,156
1919	1,081	119,496,107	110,542
1920	1,111	140,918,981	126,800
1921	1,143	147,644,999	129,181

Nineteen hundred and fourteen was the only year to show a recession over figures of sales per store for the preceding year, and this can perhaps be ascribed to the outbreak of the war and the immediate depressing effect on every type of mercantile activity.

In 1911, sales per store were $88,282, and in 1920 sales per store were $126,800, a difference of $38,518 for the average store.. The Kresge stores, by raising their price limits, were able to increase average sales per store from $150,671 in 1915 to $271,139 in 1920, an increase of over $120,000 in average sales per store, with an increase of fifty store units.

This principle of increased sales with increased number of units applies elsewhere than in the five and ten cent chain field. Take, for example, the Great Atlantic & Pacific Tea Co. which possesses the largest number of retail stores under its own management.   Back in 1915, it had 1,726 stores and gross sales for the year were $44,441,000.   In 1919 there were 4,246 stores and gross sales of $194,646,000.   In 1915 sales per unit store were in the neighborhood of $25,000 and in 1919 were over $45,000, an increase in unit sales of over $20,000.

Thus there is a logical incentive to combination because of the increased economies obtained thereby, and the increased volume of sales per unit in operation.

The Bases of Chain Store Competition.—Every successful line of business can trace its success to certain policies, to the protection of patents perhaps, or the protection of tariffs.   The success of some companies may depend on the personality of the executive.   The reasons for chain store superiority lie not so much in the application of one policy as in the application of the consensus of many policies.

In order to review some of the main reasons which make it extremely difficult for an independent store to maintain itself in competition with a chain store, and which are the bases for the very keen competition in price, service, etc. of one chain store system with another, the following ten headings are arranged alphabetically without any attempt to classify them according to their importance.

1. Accounting
2. Display
3. Goodwill
4. Location
5. Management
6. Personnel
7. Price
8. Purchasing
9. Sales policy
10. Turnover

1. *Accounting.* Many retail stores keep no accounts and some keep partial accounts; but very few keep full accounts. The whole efficiency of the chain store organization is based on careful accounting. Some companies have spent years in standardizing and rearranging their systems of accounts to make them more perfect.

A proper system of accounting allows the chain executive to know at any moment the state of affairs in his business as a whole and in any particular store. Accounting is a necessity to a chain organization but to the independent retailer is a luxury which he feels unable to afford. On this head the chain has marked advantages.

2. *Display.* A chain organization sells its goods through display which, it has found, is the easiest and least expensive form of advertising. Each member store is in itself an individual and typical display. Each interior helps to carry out the standard plan. The window trims are arranged by experts who know how to design displays that will make sales.

Lastly, the goods are shown in the best possible fashion, with prices tagged plainly. Contrasted with the independent store, the comparison is all in favor of the chain. When compared with each other, the displays of two chains dealing in the same line of goods often show little difference. But this is a very real item in competition, and one in which the independent retailer can profitably take lessons from the chain.

3. *Goodwill.* Can a chain store exercise so strong an appeal to its customers that they will return regularly? Some say it can, and some say it cannot. A great deal depends on the location and the character of the clientele passing the store. More depends on the personality of the store as interpreted by the sales force and the general appearance of the premises.

The great value of goodwill lies in the regular customer. This ability to get and hold regular trade is what piles up sales in a store. It has normally been considered that the independent retailer has a monopoly on this goodwill, that by his services and his attentions he can secure and hold a certain percentage of trade. Experience has proved and is proving that the manager of the chain store has at his disposal exactly the same means of pleasing the customer. For example, one of the large grocery chains has just installed a delivery service delivering for customers on the payment of ten cents extra. Thus, the customer can very often make her purchases at the chain store, have them delivered, and still find her bill less than if she had gone to the independent store.

4. *Location.* "There is a right place and a wrong place to locate a store," said F. W. Woolworth. "Put your stores where the dollars stick out," says B. H. Kroger, president of the Kroger Grocery and Baking Company. The ability of the chain organizations to pick and choose the spots which make failure next to impossible has been one of their strongest assets in retail competition. It is frequently possible to see three or four chain stores in the same block, all dealing in groceries and all apparently successful. The independent retailer as a rule does not know how to locate. He may even shun the good locations because of the proximity of a chain store, anxious as he is to avoid all price comparisons.

5. *Management.* Chain stores have brains to direct them. This naturally gives them an enormous advantage. They can afford to pay an executive to see that no mistakes are made in policy. The independent retailer has to find this out for himself.

Good management is more than seeing the stores open at eight and close at six. It is more than seeing that all links are functioning properly and that there is no friction. Good management means careful business prediction, the faculty of seeing ahead. It means a thorough grasp of business principles. Business is no longer an empirical enterprise which anyone with a small amount of money may enter. It has become a science, and each phase of business overlaps another phase. Thus the independent retailer, encompassed as he is in a very narrow sphere, is at a marked disadvantage.

6. *Personnel.* The store managers and the clerks have always been cited as the chain organization's weakest point, and probably this is true. Human nature is very difficult to standardize, especially at a distance. It is even more difficult to keep it interested unless there is some strong incentive. Personal profit inspires the interest in the independent retailer. And the chain has borrowed this incentive for its own use. It adds a security against failure which the independent owner can never feel.

If the personnel is the chain's weakest point, everything that can be done towards making it as strong as the rest of the organization is being tried out in different ways by different chains. It seems generally agreed that the manager and possibly the subordinate clerk should participate in earnings. That is, a premium is placed upon the good salesmanship of the clerk and the good management of the store manager.

7. *Price.* The independent store cannot sell at the same price as the chain store. For many people, this constitutes the strongest reason for the strength of the chain. Why should people pay more at the individual store when they can get the same thing for less money next door?

As time goes on, this question of price will grow even more important than it is now. When competition between chains becomes keener, as it inevitably will, practically the ultimate point of differentiation will be in price. The costs of two chains of approximately the same size will vary little. Whatever economies good management can make will be reflected in the price.

8. *Purchasing.* The economies of purchasing are all on the side of the chain. The history of the chain movement has been one long rebellion against the middleman's discount and an effort to buy nearer the source. After a long struggle, the combat seems to be settled and most manufacturers agree to sell the chains direct. They cannot afford not to do so.

The independent retailer cannot, as a rule, buy in quantities. He has no place to store away surplus supplies, and, even if he did have, they would be too old by the time he was ready to sell them. The jobber, therefore, is a necessity as long as the small retailer lasts.

Savings in purchases can generally be passed along to the public. The quantity discount is the independent's chief reason for being unable to meet chain store prices.

9. *Sales policies.* The chain organization picks the products that will sell themselves rather than those which have to be sold. It devotes itself to a few lines of goods, rather than to a great many. The goods which are sold are generally staple articles. Every article must prove itself before being allowed a permanent place on the shelves.

10. *Turnover*. The chain store has found that profits from selling are derived from turning goods quickly at a low profit rather than seldom at a high profit. The independent retailer in many cases has not discovered this. It is, or should be, a rule in the chain store that no goods should be allowed to stay on the shelves beyond a certain time, varying, of course, with the nature of the product. If they do not sell, they must be moved at any price. Perhaps some other store can sell them. If not, reduce the price until they go.

Conclusions.—All the phases of competition have not been exhausted in this chapter. Only those have been discussed which have seemed to refer most specifically to the chain store and its sales problems. The point which appears from an analysis of the essentials of chain store competition is that there is nothing phenomenal about it. It is, in the last analysis, nothing more than the scientific application of business principles to the problems of retailing. The remarkable fact is that the rise of the chain store came so late. The extent and rapidity of its growth have shown the economic need which existed in the community at large.

The analysis of competition is both an executive and a local function. The executive must measure the strength of his competition collectively in the territory in which his chain operates. The local manager must analyze the character of the particular specific competition which he must confront. In every case the result aimed at and, in the majority of cases attained by the chain store, is "The public be pleased." The chain store exercises a retailing function and its success must be measured finally by the degree of public approbation of its executive and its merchandising policies.

CHAPTER IX

PRICING AND TURNOVER

OUTLINE

Theory of pricing.
1. Fallacy of old theory of charging all product will bring.
2. Proper pricing.
    (a) Determination of by
        1. Purchase price paid by chain.
        2. Share of overhead expense.
        3. Share of selling expense.
    (b) Possible to obtain by
        1. Economic purchasing.
        2. Minimum overhead expense.
        3. Efficient retail store management and accounting.
3. Methods of pricing in vogue.
    (a) Cost of goods plus share of overhead and selling expense plus necessary percentage of profit.
    (b) Price maintained on main stock but loss leaders offered.
    (c) Cut prices.
Price range.
1. Normally low.
2. Policy of decreasing unit size in periods of increasing prices.
3. Prices standardized throughout chain.
    (a) Exceptions.
4. Putting price changes into effect.
    (a) Regular intervals or immediately.
Principles of turnover.
1. Keep stock turning.
2. Keep every line turning.
3. Make profit on every line.
Increasing turnover.
1. Increasing rate of sales while stock remains same.
2. Price cutting.
3. Shifting goods.
Rate of turnover necessary.
1. Dependent on
    (a) Keeping quality of product.
    (b) Capacity of store.
    (c) Price at which sold.

2. Setting turnover quota for managers.
    (*a*) Supplying managers with past records in their stores.
    (*b*) Importance of turnover in
        1. Seasonal goods.
        2. Style lines.

Securing adequate turnover.
    1. Careful purchasing of goods.
    2. Efficient merchandising policy.
    3. Coöperation of the personnel.
    4. Careful inventory system.

CHAPTER IX

PRICING AND TURNOVER

Profits in chain store retailing are largely determined by the selling price and the rate of turnover. In the careful adjustment of these two factors lies one of the secrets of chain store success.

The price at which a product can be sold is or should be determined automatically by

1. The purchase price paid by the chain.
2. The share of overhead expense.
3. The share of selling expense.

It is evident, therefore, that a low selling price can be reached only by

1. Economical purchasing.
2. Minimum overhead expenses.
3. Efficient retail store management and accounting.

But the rate of turnover exercises a modifying influence on all the above factors. By turnover is meant stock turnover, that is, the number of times the money invested in merchandise is liquidated and reinvested during the term of a year. Obviously, the larger the turnover, the more profits, and consequently the lower the selling price, which can be set.

A large turnover is secured by:

1. Careful purchasing of goods and products that will sell readily.
2. An efficient merchandising policy.
3. The coöperation of the personnel.
4. A careful inventory system.

A large turnover, however, will not bring large profits unless the selling price is high enough to carry the overhead and other charges against it. Thus, in a cut-price war, an enormous turnover may bring enormous losses. But it is obvious that, the larger the turnover, the less profit it is necessary to make on each sale to obtain an aggregate profit satisfactory to everyone.

The Theory of Pricing.—In the old days, and even now among many retailers, the custom is to mark goods at whatever prices it is thought they will bring. Probably everyone has gone into a store, priced an article, found it too high, and been on the point of leaving the store, when the proprietor said: "Well, I guess I can let you have it for a little less." Charging the public what it will pay, or, in other words, profiteering, is a crime that can be laid at the doors of very few chain stores. The chain store policy is to deal only in those products which can be sold at a profit, no matter how small. Loss leaders, which in the majority of cases are not losses, result in increased profits because they increase turnover.

R. C. Swanton, General Auditor of the Winchester Repeating Arms Co , has explained the theory of marking up goods from cost price so plainly that the following is paraphrased from an article of his in the Winchester Herald, the house organ of that company.

Mark-up, he says, is the amount added to the cost of merchandise to cover operating expenses and a profit. It is controlled in its upward trend by competition, and may be controlled in its downward trend by the use of accounting figures. The expense of doing business, which is the largest outlay of money outside of the actual purchase cost of the goods, must be covered in setting the sales price, before a profit can be taken. Capital invested in stock is entitled to a net profit on every sales transaction.

Figure 13 is an analysis of departmental reports. The average mark-up for the total sales of all departments, to obtain an average net profit of 13 per cent., must be 56.7 per cent., while the average mark-up to obtain a net profit of 9.6 per cent. on the Tool Department must be 47.4 per cent. This does not mean that each item in the tool classification is so marked-up. Some may be marked up 75 per cent. but a study of this statement shows that if the merchant marked up at this lower figure he would sustain a loss on each article, and that he would sustain a loss on each sale marked up at less than 33 per cent., because the ratio of the store's operating expense is higher than the mark-up;

STATEMENT

OF BUSINESS CONDITION AND NET WORTH - MONTH ENDING *February* 19 *20*

		Dept. Name	Sales: Cost	Sales: Retail	% Depts. to Total	% Mark up Cost	Gross Profit: Amount	Gross Profit: % Depts.	Expense: Amount	Net Profit: Amount	Net Profit: % to ...	Avge. Invent.: Amt. at Cost	Turnover: Do by Depts.
THIS MONTH	F	TOOLS	514 27	758 03	14.2	47.4	243 76	32	159 15	84 58	11.1	1250 00	.411
	H	CUTLERY	146 31	222 97	4.2	52.4	76 66	34	46 82	29 84	13.3	95 00	.154
	J	GENERAL	675 80	1063 03	20.0	57.3	387 23	36	223 23	164 00	15.5	2400 00	.281
	L	BUILDERS	562 98	886 13	16.7	57.4	323 15	36	186 08	137 07	15.6	2200 00	.255
	M	HOUSEHOLD	428 27	690 37	13.7	61.2	262 10	38	144 97	117 13	16.9	560 20	.764
	N	PAINTS, ETC	215 03	295 23	5.6	37.3	80 20	27	61 99	18 21	6.2	480 00	.448
	P	SPORTING	315 41	473 11	8.9	50.	157 70	33	99 39	58 31	12.3	390 50	.807
	V	SPECIALTIES	493 21	889 25	16.7	80.3	396 04	44.5	186 74	209 30	23.5	750 00	.657
		TOTAL BUSINESS	3351 28	5278 12	100.	57.3	1926 84	36.5	1108 40	818 44	15.5	8125 70	.412
		EXPENSE % TO SALES 21%											
		EXPENSE % TO COST OF SALES 33%											
YEAR TO DATE	F	TOOLS	814 54	1200 91	16.2	47.4	386 37	32.3	270 98	115 39	9.6	1140 40	.714
	H	CUTLERY	192 62	293 67	4.1	52.4	101 05	34	64 64	36 41	12.3	213 36	.902
	J	GENERAL	1131 77	1780 22	24.1	57.3	648 45	36	404 72	243 73	13.5	2720 36	.416
	L	BUILDERS	794 86	1254 19	17.	57.4	459 33	36.5	279 52	179 81	14.3	1698 14	.467
	M	HOUSEHOLD	559 54	902 09	12.2	61.2	342 55	38	198 44	144 11	15.9	370 90	1.50
	N	PAINTS, ETC	328 04	450 46	6.1	37.3	122 42	27	101 42	21 00	4.6	461 10	.71
	P	SPORTING	329 83	494 83	6.7	50.	165 00	33	105 33	59 67	12.1	283 35	1.17
	V	SPECIALTIES	556 45	1003 15	13.6	80.3	446 70	44.5	215 37	231 33	23.0	429 54	1.29
		TOTAL BUSINESS	4707 65	7379 52	100.	56.7	2671 87	35.1	1640 42	1031 45	13.8	7317 15	1.43
		EXPENSE % TO SALES 22%											
		EXPENSE % TO COST OF SALES 35%											

BALANCE SHEET	$	$	%
ASSETS			
CURRENT			
CASH ON HAND & IN BANK	1016 31		9.8
NOTES RECEIVABLE			
ACCOUNTS RECEIVABLE	2140 50		21.3
MERCHANDISE INVENTORY	6785 92		65.0
TOTAL CURRENT ASSETS		9942 73	
FIXED			
LAND			
BUILDINGS			
STORE & OFFICE FIXT. & EQUIP.	438 00		
DELIVERY EQUIPMENT			
TOTAL	438 00		
LESS: - DEP. ON BUILDINGS			
" DEP. ON STORE FIXT.	24 50		
" DEP. ON DELIVERY			
TOTAL FIXED ASSETS		413 50	3.9
TOTAL ASSETS		10356 23	
LIABILITIES AND CAPITAL			
NOTES PAYABLE	600 00		5.8
ACCOUNTS PAYABLE	1200 00		11.6
OTHER LIABILITIES			
TOTAL LIABILITIES		1800 00	
PROPRIETORS CAPITAL ACCT.		8556 23	82.6
TOTAL LIABILITIES AND CAPITAL		10356 23	

NET INVESTMENT 8556 23 RATIO OF TURNOVER TO INVESTMENT 3.89

ACCOUNTS RECEIVABLE 2140.50 RATIO TO INVESTED CAPITAL 23.7

FIG. 13.—Monthly statement showing control of pricing and mark-up. (*Winchester Herald*, April, 1920.)

therefore, if the merchant decides, and trade conditions are favorable, to take a net profit of ten per cent., his safe low limit of mark-up on all merchandise in this class would be 47 per cent.

Mark-up is based on cost of goods, and gross profit on returns from sales. Gross profit is the difference between cost of goods sold and the mark-up price obtained. This amount, in ratio to the sales price, gives the gross profit percentage. Noting the illustration, Goods in the Tool Department took an average mark-up of 47 per cent. and obtained an average gross profit of 32 per cent. For instance, let us assume an item in the tool classification:

```
Cost to the merchant....................  $1.00
Plus. ..................................         47% mark-up
Equals.................................  $1.47 sales price
```

The difference between the cost and the sales price is $.47 which, divided by the sales price of $1.47, leaves a gross profit of 32 per cent. Assuming that the overhead expense of making a sale is 21 per cent. this deducted from the gross profit leaves a net profit, or an income on capital invested in the article, of 11 per cent. on the sale. Much trouble is encountered because of the confusing of mark-up with gross profits. Remember that gross profit is based on sales; mark-up is based on and added to cost.

Methods of Pricing.—Goods may be charged to retail stores at either wholesale or retail prices. In the great majority of cases goods are charged at retail so that the member store will have but one price to consider, and that price the one at which the goods are to be sold to customers. It also simplifies accounting methods.

Where a chain conducts a wholesale business or sells to agencies, it frequently bills goods to its own stores at wholesale prices. If they were to bill their goods to their own store at retail prices and to agencies at wholesale prices, it would mean keeping up two systems, and would cause much confusion.

There are several methods of retail pricing in vogue:

1. The logical and ordinary method of fixing the price of all goods at a certain percentage over the purchase price and the overhead and selling expenses.

2. Maintaining prices according to the first system, but each week running a list of loss leaders at cost or fractional profit.

3. Selling at competitors' prices, or below them, a practice which leads to cut price wars and elimination of the weakest competitors.

Where operating and selling expenses are standardized down to the last degree, there is not much difference in the price at which the various chains can afford to sell the majority of their products. Some merchandising expedient, some quirk of efficiency, may pull them ahead for a moment, but the rest of the field gradually draws abreast again, since chain competition is essentially a competition of price.

The Price Range.—The chain stores, as has been mentioned before, generally concentrate on staple, low, and medium-priced merchandise, because it is in this class of products that the largest turnover is obtainable, and these products are sold to the class of people to whom the price of the article makes a great deal of difference.

The war brought about very interesting conditions in the chain store field. Before that time, when biscuits, chewing gum, cigars, hats, shirts, and innumerable articles could be featured at a standard price, it gave chain shops something upon which to build a reputation. A dollar watch or a dollar shirt or a five-cent cigar gave the customer something to remember.

In the short history of the chain store movement, the war was the first major economic upheaval which upset this standard price. Nowhere was this more evident than in the five and ten-cent store field. For some time previous to the war, the merchandise assortment of the five- and ten-cent stores had begun to narrow. The days when Butler Brothers had been able to offer more than 120,000 separate articles to be retailed at five- and ten-cents were past. When the war came, it caused a break-away from the old, five, ten, twenty-five cent limit. Most variety chains found they could not offer a large enough assortment to get the required turnover. Woolworth clung to the old policy by decreasing the units. The size was made smaller, less candy was sold for ten cents, matches which had been one cent a box were five cents; things were sold separately, one stocking for ten cents, the pail ten cents and the cover ten. To the amazement of its competitors and the public, the Woolworth chain was able to come through without changing its traditional ten-cent limit.

Those variety chains which have broken away show as yet no tendency to revert to the old system. While keeping their lower-priced lines as intact as possible, variety of stock was increased. It was known that a large part of any department store's sales were under $1, and the Kresge chain acted on that theory with great success. Tinware, crockery, and household lines gave way to drygoods, with a tendency, however, to keep away from piece goods.

Generally, the prices of goods in all stores in one chain are standardized, except that some chains make a difference for stores west of the Mississippi. The United Cigar Stores have only one price, and this price is the same for one cigar or a hundred of the same brand.

Managers may be allowed to make their own prices on local purchases. One grocery chain management says: "All our prices are standardized throughout the chain. The only exception to this rule is in the case of green vegetables, dried meats, cottage cheese, and other items which each store manager buys for himself and on which he bases his own prices. A store three miles away from the markets naturally is entitled to a little longer price on lettuce and celery than a store downtown which can restock its green-goods counter at any time during the day. Also, in the three-mile-away store, the manager runs a larger risk of not selling out all his vegetables. He has to add enough margin of profit to insure himself against loss."

The question of cutting prices is a matter of individual policy. Some stores never cut. The Penney practice is to put the price on an article and never mark it down. The American Stores Co. cuts prices on its goods when it deems it sound merchandising policy to do so.

Turnover.—How many times must I turn my merchandise to make a profit? If this question could be answered specifically, much worry would be saved retailers. But, as a matter of fact, turnover differs very widely. It is generally larger in the chain store than in the independent store, and larger in the grocery, tobacco, and drug chains than in the dry goods and "five and tens."

Just what do we mean by turnover? Ordinarily speaking, turnover to the manager of a chain store means the number of times the money invested in stock can be liquidated and reinvested during the year. "One of the common mistakes," says Mr. Swanton, of the Winchester Stores, "in figuring turnover is this: you will hear many merchants say: 'My sales are $200,000 this year. My inventory is $50,000. I have turned over four times, because $200,000 is four times my inventory figures.' Turnover must be figured as the cost of goods sold to the cost value of inventory. Take the case just quoted. If this merchant should sell $200,000 worth of merchandise in all departments of his business, and his average mark-up was 57 per cent., his cost of goods sold would be $200,000, less mark-up figure, which would be $127,000. This amount, divided by his average inventory, say $50,000, would equal two and one-half times turnover and not four times turnover."

The value of turnover analysis to the chain is that it keeps constant check on the articles which show profit and those which do not. The great secret of success in chain stores is to keep the stock turning, to keep every line selling, and to make a profit on every line. A chain would rather be out of a certain product, and permit the customer to go somewhere else, than to carry it if it is losing money. This explains, according to Mr. F. J. Arkins, of the Alexander Hamilton Institute, the reason that in order not to lose money, as soon as it is discovered that a particular line is moving too slowly, prices are reduced and bargains featured. If the first reduction in price does not attract attention the reductions continue until a market is found for the articles. The whole effort is to move that particular line out of stock as rapidly as possible, and, if it is necessary to take a loss, to get the loss behind the chain at the earliest possible moment. The idea is not new or untried. It was a principle established by A. T. Stewart, in the merchandising of dry goods in New York, in the early part of the last century.

It was the strict pursuance of this policy of keeping up turnover that allowed the great majority of chain organizations to liquidate without the enormous losses which many retailers experienced in the post-war deflationary period through holding on to their stocks rather than cutting prices before it was too late.

Analysis of **Turnover.**—A slow turnover involves waste and expense. In some cases the damage is apparent at first sight, but in others it lies deeper and must be analyzed. The Chamber of Commerce of the United States has divided the elements of waste due to slow turnover into the following classes:

1. Investment.
2. Interest.
3. Mark-down.
4. Salaries and wages.
5. Shelf or storage room.
6. Prestige and reputation.
7. Inefficiency.

Taking them up individually:

1. The amount of goods in stock and the amount of time these goods must be carried before they are sold determines the profit, assuming mark-up is the same. Naturally, the more frequent the turnover, the larger the profit on the same investment.

2. As few chain stores are borrowers, the interest charges would rarely enter the turnover equation. With many independent retailers, however, interest becomes of great importance.

3. The necessity of marking goods down is ordinarily a sign of poor turnover, which, in turn, might have been due to overbuying, too high a price, or lack of demand.

4. Naturally, sales expense is increased with slow turnovers, since the same sales force, more efficiently managed, could sell in six months what actually sells in a year.

5. Shelf or storage room is too valuable to be taken up by slow-moving goods.

6. The reputation of the store suffers if it is known to have a large stock of old goods.

7. Over-buying is ordinarily a dangerous policy. Except when there are extraordinary conditions, fresh supplies can be obtained at short notice; but an oversupply of goods cannot be so easily disposed of. Hence the whole chain of evils arising from slow turnover will occur.

Figure 14 shows graphically two ways of illustrating the profits due to more frequent turnovers:

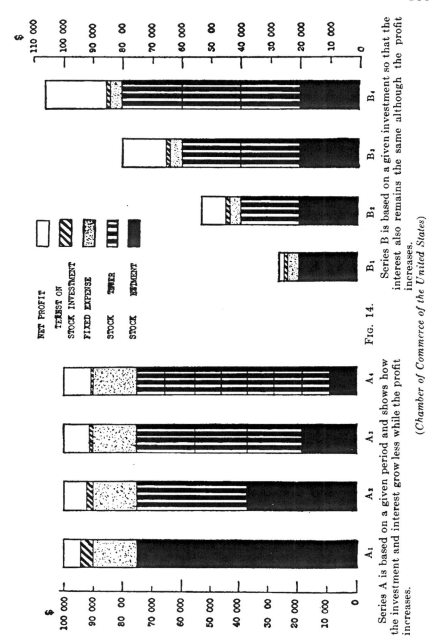

Fig. 14.

Series A is based on a given period and shows how the investment and interest grow less while the profit increases.

Series B is based on a given investment so that the interest also remains the same although the profit increases.

(*Chamber of Commerce of the United States*)

Each of the columns in series A represents sales amounting to $100,000, but the number of turnovers increases from 1 in A–1 to 8 in A–4, and it will be observed that, with each increase in turnover, the stock investment as well as the interest are cut in two while the amount of profit increases.

Series B shows uniform stock investments and costs of interest throughout, while the amount of profit increases with the number of turnovers.

Series A proves the decreased investment needed to perform a given amount of business while Series B proves the increased business and profits which accrue to the same investment upon a multiplied turnover.

Increasing Turnover.—It is possible to increase stock turnover in two ways:

1. Sales may be increased while amount of stock remains practically the same or increases at a rate below that at which sales are increasing. This method is the ordinary one and is perfectly safe, since it is based on sound merchandising principles.

2. The second method is to cut the price. As one authority on the subject points out, by reducing the price more people are included in the group of purchasers, since more people are able to purchase an article at $1.00 than at $2.00.

Price-cutting, however, is a dangerous operation.

If everybody cuts prices, total sales may not be appreciably increased while profits will fall off dangerously.

Price-cutting of staples rarely does any good except as a loss leader. People buy staples—sugar, flour, coal—even though the price is high; and a reduction in price will not increase their consumption proportionately. Some merchants keep very close track of sales on these non-profit items, such as sugar. In the Sam Seelig stores in California, the average proportion of sugar sales to gross sales is 10 per cent. If one of the stores shows sales of 12 per cent. 15 per cent. or even 18 per cent. there is manifestly something wrong. That is, sales are not merely dollars and cents. If two stores each sell $1,000 worth of goods, it is quite possible for one to earn a great deal more than the other, given the same overhead. One store may sell too large a proportion of non-profit staples.

Staples are essentially inert. The profit comes in selling

articles for which demand is not steady, but can be created. The most reliable business is that which is neither too elastic nor too inelastic, and it is precisely this class of goods in which the chain store deals.

Rate of **Turnover.**—There is no standard rate of turnover. Each store is slightly different, and some stores, even in the same chain, vary a great deal. The turnover may vary with the different years, the stock carried, the local manager, etc. Some of the Penney stores turn their stock ten times a year, but the

Fig. 15.—Average turnover in various lines of merchandise.

average is between four and six. Some of the United Cigar stores are said to turn their stocks 50 times a year. A five- and ten-cent store must secure at least six turnovers a year to be successful, and the large chains do better than this.

Figure 15 shows minimum turnovers for some types of goods, the jewelry turnover being so low that no chains have ever been organized successfully in this field. These figures should not be taken as the approximate rate of turnover only, in any of these fields. They are intended merely to give some comparative idea of turnover in the various lines.

Coming down to turnover in a particular line of business, we find that articles generally have a relation to each other in rate of sales, and that these can be computed with fair accuracy.

One of the large drug chains, for example, has set certain turnover requirements:

```
Soda............................................. 52
Candy............................................ 20
Cigars........................................... 15
Merchandise....................................   8
Total turnover. .................................. 10
```

It endeavors to keep the store managers constantly alive to their stock turnover proposition and make them see how important it is that when the inventory is taken, it should closely agree with the yearly turnover desired.

Turnover is especially necessary in candy and cigars because proper turnover in those lines has a large influence on sales. People like candy and cigars fresh. Patent medicines allow a more rapid turnover than drugs. Rubber goods need exceptional care. In the case of rubber goods, although overbuying is harmful, underbuying and lost sales are even more harmful to the gross profit average because goods of this nature bring an exceptionally good return. The Liggett chain tries to steer a middle course and not lose sight of the fact that annual turnover in the store must show ten times or better. Toilet articles, perfumes, and novelties more often defeat plans for a proper turnover than any other class of drug merchandise. Managers are cautioned to use extreme care in stocking these lines.

According to Mr. Beckmann, of the National Chain Store Grocery Association, the turnover figures in grocery lines are startling in their differences. The average retail grocer turns his goods perhaps twelve times a year, while the chain store turns them from 36 to 50 times, according to actual record. The wholesaling end of the chain store—that is, the department analogous to the grocery jobber—shows a turnover of form 14 to 18, while the turnover of the ordinary wholesale grocer is from six to eight times.

Securing Turnover in All Lines.—The average independent retailers constantly bring down their turnover averages because of the large amount of goods on their shelves which either do not sell at all, or sell so rarely as to make it unprofitable to carry them.

Chain stores go on the principle that all goods carried must sell. If reductions in price do not dispose of them, the chain makes use of its distribution and concentrates the articles where they do sell. It is a fact that some store in the chain can generally be found which will sell a product which no inducement to the public can move from another store in the chain.

If a drop in price is known to be coming, or because it is near the end of the season, chain groceries hold off from purchasing, and transfer goods from the stores that cannot sell them to the stores that can. In this way they make sure that no "shelf-warmers" will be in the way at any store when the anticipated change takes place.

To stimulate the store manager, quotas are often made up from the records at the central office and sent out to him, showing what his total sales for the month should be and perhaps indicating turnover in various lines. Thus the store manager knows at all times exactly where he stands and whether he is improving or running behind previous averages. The merchandise turnover of the chain as a whole depends more or less on the purchasing policy, but in many chains the store manager has it in his power to regulate turnover to a great extent. That is, he selects from the lists sent him those articles he can sell.

The United Cigar Stores Co. ships its stores every week a quota of supplies which must be sold. Turnover is especially important in seasonal goods and style lines. Failure to turn these goods promptly may change profits into losses.

Turnover and Business Conditions.—It is difficult to resist the temptation of purchasing in advance of a rising market. Yet time and again the soundness of the principle of selling at cost-plus has been demonstrated, and the folly of purchasing far in advance of actual requirements. Sharp lifts in price may be met by a grumbling purchaser, but he will remember this in the future. The chain stores consistently build up a background of goodwill by their price policy until the public feels confident that it is not being cheated.

As an example of the soundness of chain policies, the prices of merchandise in the United States declined from 25 per cent. to 40 per cent. in the United States during 1921, while the value of sales in the chain grocery stores declined only 16 per cent. This shows the actual sales volume must have increased. But, as groceries belonging to chains deal mainly in staple articles, the increased turnover must have taken place directly at the expense of independent grocers whose hold on the goodwill of the public was not strong enough to withstand a period of depression.

Charles E. Merrill, of Merrill, Lynch & Co., a banking firm which has financed six of the large chain systems, says: "During the first half of 1921, the decrease in sales prices was so rapid that the problem was to take in enough for operating expenses. This was accomplished by great economies. As a result, the chain stores are making more money than they were a year ago when high prices prevailed.

"The price declines in the five- and ten-cent stores have been nearly as drastic as in the grocery stores. By an increase in the rapidity of turnover, however, the five- and ten-cent chains have been able to side-step losses which occurred to others during the price decline."

The remarkable point about this situation is that, by increasing turnover in a period of unprecedented deflation, chains like Woolworth and Kresge were able to make as much money as in previous years. It illustrates forcefully the practical advantages of turnover and the irresistible attraction of price as a basis of competition in hard times.

Conclusions.—"Small profits on an article will become big if you sell enough of the article" was one of Frank W. Woolworth's maxims. In these few words he has summed up the principles of pricing and turnover. The chain of stores which he founded has steadily carried out the policy which he commenced, and was the only chain to remain proof against the difficult problems which had to be met in the period of war and in the post-war deflation.

It is only necessary to add to the above statement that turnover must be distributed among all the stock and the fundamental statement is complete. One of the greatest, if not the greatest, reasons for the chain store's pre-eminence in the retail field is the careful observance of this policy of pricing and turnover. In a way, the necessity of securing turnover ensures a reasonable price to the consumer, but it is only by the proper correlation of these two factors that the most efficient results are obtained.

CHAPTER X

EXPENSES AND PROFITS

OUTLINE

Cost of doing business.
1. Dependent on
    (a) Policy.
    (b) Size.
    (c) Product.
    (d) Location.
2. Detailed expenses.
    (a) Salary largest.
    (b) Rent next.
3. Savings in expense.
    (a) Elimination of deliveries.
    (b) Cash-and-carry policy.
    (c) Standardization of method.
    (d) Elimination of waste.
4. Overhead.
    (a) Decreased by
        1. Increased volume of sales.
        2. Addition of new retail links.
        3. Efficient management.

The "cash-and-carry" policy.
1. Eliminates bad debts.
2. Enables chain to discount purchases immediately.
3. Simplifies accounting.
4. Saves time verifying accounts, making out charge slips, etc.

Gross profits.
1. Increase normally.
    (a) Through addition of new links.
    (b) Through increased sales in old links.
    (c) Through improved merchandising methods.
        1. Further standardization.

Store profits
1. Dependent on
    (a) Location of store.
    (b) Ability of manager.
    (c) Turnover of products.
    (d) Efficient supervision by headquarters.

    2. Advisability of abandoning unprofitable sites.

Increasing profits.

    1. Increasing turnover.

    2. Increasing average sale.

        (a) Interdependence of cost of product and average sale.

    3. Odd-cent profits.

    4. Profits made by local managers.

CHAPTER XI

EXPENSES AND PROFITS

In spite of large overhead expenses for highly paid executives, specialists in window trimming, merchandising ideas, purchasing, etc., the chain stores manage to do business at an average cost less than the majority of their independent competitors. "Why is this so?" is the constant query of the independent retailer, and he is told to imitate the chain, whereupon he seems to be no better off than before. He is told to standardize his accounting methods, increase his turnover, cut out credit and deliveries, move to another part of town where the location is better, sell only stock the public wishes, etc. And because he cannot do these things he sets up a clamor about unfair competition and secret discounts. The truth of the matter is that the chain is an organization of individuals whose combined intellects form a far more powerful force than the average single individual running an independent store can command. The store manager is the personal representative of an impersonal organization; the independent store owner is the personal representative of a personal business.

Probably the greatest factor in keeping down chain expenses is a careful accounting system. Every dollar that comes in bears a certain charge against it, determined by long experience and careful records. Policies that do not pay are ruthlessly abandoned on the graphic evidence of their failure to make good. If a chain finds some particular location does not bring in enough business to carry the overhead and earn a profit, that store is promptly discontinued. Losses are minimized. No old goods are allowed to remain in stock, taking up room and eating up profits. It is a combination of business initiative and system which keeps down chain store expenses and enlarges net profits.

The Cost of Doing Business.—The variations in the actual cost of doing business are wide. They are dependent on so many factors of policy, of size, of line of goods carried, of location of stores, etc., so that the matter can be treated only suggestively, by stating a few of the general principles, and supporting them by concrete examples from stores in several lines.

The following table is made up from a number of sources, and is not intended to be authoritative or complete, but merely illustrative of the effect of the product on costs.

Cost of Doing Business

Druggists	22–30%
Tobacco	8–20
Dry goods	10–25
Groceries	4–15
Variety	18–25
Shoes	18–25

Groceries and tobacco, where the turnover is very rapid, can usually bring operating expenses farthest down. The Penney organization, with a 10 to 12 per cent. operating expense, is unique in the dry goods line when compared with 20 per cent. for independent retailers in direct competition with them.

Detailed Expenses.—The merchandising department of the *New York World* supplies the following average figures on chain store costs.

Average rental	8%
Average help	15
Average loss and depreciation	1
Average light, maintenance	2 ½
Average overhead	3
Total	29 ½%

The Piggly Wiggly stores present by far the lowest operating costs of any figures available. In the week ending October 6, 1917, the net sales of nine stores operating in Memphis were $25,429.90. The cost of doing business during that same period was $795.11. The average cost of doing business was 3.12 per cent.

The expense total was made up as follows:

Insurance..	$ 13.70
Salaries...	494.85
Ice...	46.20
Light...	21.74
Rent..	180.92
Sundries..	24.32
Telephone.......................................	11.81
Water...	1.67
Total...	$795.11

Salaries are the largest item of expense, and efforts to econo-
mize along this line generally result disastrously, especially

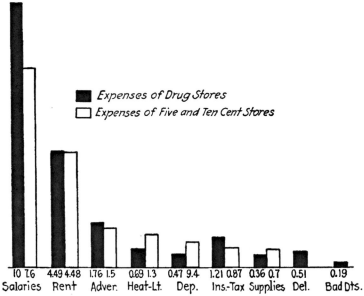

Fig. 16.—Comparison of expenses of five and ten cent stores with those of drug
chain stores.

when it is considered that so much of the chain's prosperity lies
in the hands of the store managers. Rent is generally the next
item. This must be carefully watched. For example, in the
United Cigar Stores, where every item is figured in percentages,
it is immediately possible to point to a store paying too much rent.
If Kansas City were paying eight per cent. for rent, there would
be an immediate investigation.

Elimination of delivery and credit accounts, together with

small amount of advertising, are the largest factors in decreasing chain store expenses, as compared with independent retailers. The salary percentage, as a rule, is higher. From two to five per cent. is saved on deliveries and perhaps ½ of 1 per cent. on bad debts.

Figure 16 shows a comparison of expenses between the five and ten cent store and the drug store. The first three items, salaries, rent, and advertising in both cases follow the same order. Heat and light in a five and ten cent store, owing to the larger unit size, would naturally be double that of a drug store.

Few chains are willing to disclose their operating costs from a just reluctance to discuss their particular methods of effecting operating economy. It must not be supposed, however, that profits are determined by the cost of doing business. This figure with its components is merely the index number which points out to the executive how this one factor in profits, control of operating expense, stands at the moment.

Overhead.—Overhead shows broad variations. In periods of prosperity, when sales are large, overhead goes down. When sales fall off, overhead increases. Overhead is inelastic in most of its items, and is slow to react to business conditions generally. Where all buying is done at headquarters, overhead is apt to be larger than where local managers have some buying responsibility.

George H. Bushnell, Vice President and Comptroller of the J. C. Penney Co., once stated that each store was charged a fixed percentage on sales each month for the maintenance of the central offices. This takes care of rent, salaries, traveling expenses for officials, etc. In 1918, this percentage was one and two-fifths per cent. which included cost of accounting for 197 stores operated at that time. Accounting was only two-fifths of one per cent. This percentage for 1918 absorbed all the corporation taxes assessed against the stores.

Again, the vice-president of a large drug company said: "We aim to keep overhead at four per cent. of gross volume, including salaries of general officers, rent, traveling, auditors, sales managers, etc." The executive of another chain of 250 stores claimed his overhead expenses had been going down every year. For the first year or two it ran up to ten per cent. and since then had declined at the rate of about one per cent. annually. In 1918 it was only three per cent.

Overhead decreases with the number of member stores operated. A new retail link in the chain requires little addition to the chain overhead. Thus small chains normally have larger overhead expenses than the larger ones. The whole matter, of course, is dependent on efficient management. Large salaries paid to executives do not necessarily mean great overhead, because the expense is so broadly distributed, and the profits accruing from the benefits of having these high-salaried executives at the head of the business are so large that the entire sum appears small.

Keeping Expenses Down.—Ask the proprietor of an ordinary retail store what his expenses are and he may be able to tell you, but probably he will not. The executive of a chain can tell almost instantly just what the expenses of the chain as a whole are and the expenses of each his stores. Expenses are kept down and should be kept down by unceasing supervision. The variations in expense between stores of the same size that have obtained their normal volume of business is not as a rule very great. In the case of a new store, of course, which has no definite clientele, and is not known, etc., there is a high initial overhead which comes down to normal as the store becomes established.

In one drug chain all the store managers are given a bonus of $25 a month if they can succeed in holding their expenses, outside of rent and advertising, down to 15 per cent. of their sales. Rent and advertising are eliminated because the selection of the location and the rent paid are not controlled by the store manager. This, of course, is true in almost all chains.

All percentages used in making up the bonus are computed according to the sales volume of the store.

Salaries and commissions	10%
Light, heat, water	1½
Contingent, renewal, expenses	1½
Supplies	2
Total	15%

A great many of the store managers earn the bonus every

month, since this 15 per cent. is computed on the average of all stores, and many managers find it possible to surpass this average. It can be done by getting more volume of sales and turnover, or actually decreasing some of their expenses. The store managers, in addition to the actual cash bonus, are glad to have their store make a better showing than the other stores, and it makes them feel as though they were on the road to promotion.

This example has been given because the majority of chains base their bonus to store managers on the volume of business or the net profits of the store.

Albert I. Stewart, Manager of the Sam Seelig Stores in California, says the average cost of doing business for a grocery store is 13 per cent. A curious system of giving a bonus to managers is in vogue in this organization. Every manager who at the end of the month shows an actual inventory in excess of his book balance gets a bonus of $\frac{1}{2}$ of 1 per cent. of his sales for the month. The basis is not volume of business but store managing efficiency. The manager who constantly earns this bonus has his pay raised.

The bonus is reckoned not on expense but on inventory. Every month the inventory man comes around. Suppose one month he finds stock worth $3,809.05 and the following month $3,824.04, as in the example quoted in "Business" for November, 1921. Then headquarters draws up this recapitulation.

Inventory at beginning of month	$ 3,809.05
Purchases through month	6,444.08
Total charged	$10,253.13
Sales for month	6,497.06
Book balance	$ 3,756.07
Retail inventory	3,809.05
Book balance	3,756.07
Gain	$ 52.98

The reason for this gain is that many articles are invoiced to the store at group prices, that is, two bars of soap for 15 cents, three cans of soup for a quarter, etc. Thus if the store is properly managed the manager should have no difficulty in showing a profit.

Eliminated Expenses.—The majority of chain stores are "cash-and-carry." In the last 20 years this idea has become thoroughly fixed as one of the principles of chain store operation. It has several great advantages:

1. It eliminates bad debts.

2. It enables chain organizations to discount their purchases immediately, and this alone is a saving not generally recognized. For example, 2 per cent. payable in a month is 36 per cent. in a year.

SAVINGS EFFECTED THROUGH TAKING DISCOUNTS

	NET	PER CENT. PER ANNUM
1 per cent. 10 days	30 days	18
2 per cent. 10 days	30 days	36
3 per cent. 10 days	30 days	54
3 per cent. cash	30 days	36
5 per cent. 10 days	30 days	90
8 per cent. 10 days	30 days	144
2 per cent. 10 days	60 days	14.4
3 per cent. 10 days	60 days	21.6
2 per cent. 30 days	60 days	24
5 per cent. 30 days	4 months	20
5 per cent. 30 days	60 days	60

3. It simplifies accounting, which otherwise would assume great proportions.

4. It saves time verifying accounts and making out charge slips, bills, etc.

Another great expense which has been done away with by chain organizations is delivery. In the case of grocery stores this expense often mounts up to four and five per cent. of gross sales, while a department store pays around $1\frac{1}{2}$ per cent. for deliveries.

The Piggly Wiggly stores by their self-service idea have cut down the largest item of expense, that is, labor, but it has yet to be proved how far the self-service dea can be extended.

After all, the greatest universal saving effected in chain store operations is the efficient standardization of all processes connected with running the business from the top to the bottom. The greatest saving is the elimination of waste.

Profits.—The ultimate proof of the success of any business is the ability to pay regular dividends to stockholders. Capital is

invested in the business for the sole purpose of having it return
net profits.   Net profits on sales are not the same as net profits

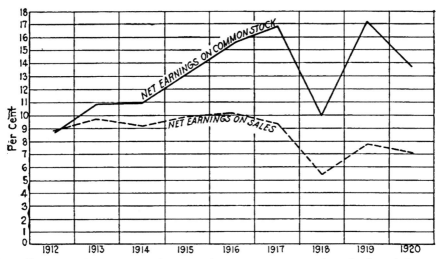

FIG. 17.—Comparison of net earnings on common stock and sales of the
F. W. Woolworth Co.

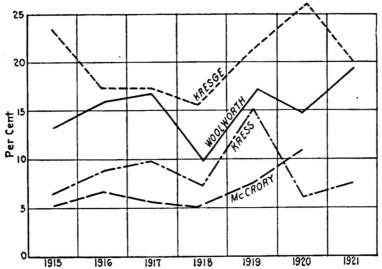

FIG. 18.—Comparison of earnings per share of common stock of the four
largest five and ten cent store chains.

on the invested capital.   They are higher or lower in accordance
with the number of times the inventory can be turned over and
the percentage of net profit realized.   Figure 17, showing the net

earnings on sales of the Woolworth Co., compared with net earnings on common stock, shows how wide the variation between the two may become. With the exception of 1912, the year of the Woolworth reorganization, net earnings on the common stock have been larger than net earnings on sales each year.

Figure 18 shows a comparison of the earnings per share of common of each of the four largest five- and ten-cent store organization during the past five years. Woolworth, as mentioned before, was the only one of these chains to keep the price limit at ten cents, while the other chains went up above this. The point which this chart clearly brings out is that a chain store dealing in the cheapest kind of commodities, as the five and ten cent

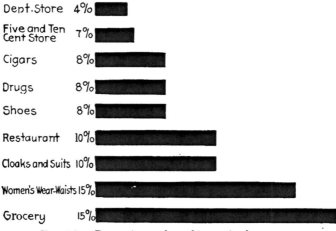

FIG. 19.—Percentage of profit required on gross.

store, can make profits in times of high prices as well as in those of low prices.

The ideal of the United Cigar Stores for a long time was to cut gross profits one per cent. each year and by selling the consumer more at a lower price make larger net profits. Ordinarily a chain store is satisfied with a far smaller profit on gross than the independent, and the secret of its willingness to accept this lies in turnover more than in any other cause. It pays to sell Uneeda Biscuit a shade less than independent grocers when the chain can turn it 52 times in the year and the independent grocery not half so often. The average grocer would like to get

25 per cent. gross profit on a sale, and this he feels he must do if he is going to make a profit. The chain grocery in many cases is satisfied with half this. The grocer may get five to eight per cent. net, but a chain grocery with a turnover from three to four times as large can be satisfied with two per cent. net.

Figure 19 shows the percentage of profit on gross which chains in various lines of retailing plan to obtain. These figures, of course, are mere approximations, and it is perfectly possible for an organization to operate successfully with a larger or smaller profit on gross. Generally, the older the company, the smaller profit needed to obtain on gross. This is due to the standardization of method which comes only with long practice.

Store Profits.—Profits from each individual store depend on all the factors we have been discussing—on the ability of the manager, on the location of the store, on the pricing of the products, on the turnover, on the efficient supervision by the central office, etc. Notwithstanding all these attentions, some stores make more money than others, because of the predominance of some particular advantage. Stores that do not make profits should in most cases be abandoned, and actually are. If there has been a mistake in judgment, the easiest way to remedy it is to take immediately whatever loss has been incurred and start another store somewhere else.

Some chains find it desirable to operate several links at a nominal profit rather than sacrifice the advantages to be gained in the way of publicity and advertising. A show store which barely pays for itself as an individual unit may serve as a drawing card for all the others.

Store profits, like everything else, and more than anything else, are scrutinized by the management. If profits fall off in a particular store, there is immediate inquiry. There is no waiting to see what will happen next month. There is an investigation to find out what really happened to cause this sudden fluctuation. A sudden profit causes a similar investigation to find out whether the cause for profit in that store cannot be applied equally well to other stores. The chain organization is constantly profiting by the mistakes and by the constructive plans of its store managers.

It is to the advantage of nearly every individual in the chain to increase profits. It is possible, therefore, to teach the personnel methods of increasing profits. One method which has been found successful is to increase the size of the average sale.

Law of the Average Sale.—An increase in volume, in itself, does not necessarily mean an increase in profits, but an increase in the average sale per customer does mean an increase in profits. The following figures and comments are adapted from an article by K. G. MacDonald, General Manager of the Federal System of Bakeries of the South:

The law of the average sale is briefly as follows: "The cost of the product sold, the average sale per customer, and the net profit are interdependent—fluctuations in one are reflected in the other two, and by increasing the average sale, the profit is also increased."

The following figures were taken from six different stores in four different states, chosen at random. In the case of these stores, the cost of the products fluctuated with the change in price of the raw materials from which they were made. In the average store this factor would show far less fluctuation, since in normal times the cost on the average varies but little.

Following are the figures on store A:

"A"	Raw material used %	Ave. sale	Profit %	Increase or decrease from previous month		
				Raw material	Ave. sale	Profit
June (sales, $4,043.26)...	42.5	24.0	11.1			
July (sales, $3,783.57)....	45.1	24.9	12.5	+2.6	+0.9	+1.4
Aug. (sales, $3,667.52)....	45.0	23.8	7.9	−0.1	−1.1	−4.6
Sept. (sales, $3,614.60)..	40.8	24.9	12.0	−4.2	+1.1	+4.1

In July, this store earned more profit than in June, although the July sales were nearly $300 less than the June figures. Although the material cost increased in July, the profit also increased. As an explanation of this, the average sale was increased by nearly one cent per customer. Comparing July with August, although material cost was lower, the profit was considerably less for the average sale fell off more than one cent per customer in August. That is, material cost down, and average sale up makes increased profits.

"B"	Raw material used %	Ave. sale	Profit %	Increase or decrease from previous month		
				Raw material	Ave. sale	Profit
June (sales, $3,847.19)...	44.5	20.9	2.4			
July (sales, $4,015.81)...	51.0	21.7	5.2	+6.5	+0.8	+2.8
Aug. (sales, $4,248.52)...	43.3	20.9	16.3	−7.7	−0.8	+11.1
Sept. (sales, $4,699.54)..	42.8	21.7	18.3	−0.5	+0.8	+2.0

In store B there is an increase in volume and increase in average sale in July as compared with June which makes increased profits even although material cost was higher in July. Comparing August with September, although material cost was practically the same, the profit was increased because the average sale was increased by almost one cent per customer.

"C"	Raw material used %	Ave. sale	Profit %	Increase or decrease from previous month		
				Raw material	Ave. sale	Profit
June (sales, $5,562.56)...	37.8	17.8	16.9			
July (sales, $6,044.49)...	37.4	18.5	24.5	−0.4	+0.7	+7.6
Aug. (sales, $6,597.96)...	37.6	19.1	26.7	+0.2	+0.6	+2.2
Sept. (sales, $5,962.16)..	36.9	18.9	23.3	−0.7	−0.2	−3.4

The figures for store C show how fluctuations in the amount of the average sale affect a store doing a large volume of business. In four months, material cost varied less than one per cent. but the percentage of profit went up as the average sale went up, and the profit came down as the average sale dropped. The volume being large, a slight falling off in the average sale resulted in a serious decrease in the percentage of profit.

"D"	Raw material used %	Ave. sale	Profit %	Increase or decrease from previous month		
				Raw material	Ave. sale	Profit
June (sales, $4,491.65)...	47.3	21.3	9.3			
July (sales, $4,420.66)..	37.8	21.9	18.7	−9.5	+0.6	+9.4
Aug. (sales, $4,221.57)...	38.5	21.6	15.3	+0.7	−0.3	−3.4
Sept. (sales, $4,198.49)...	38.9	23.2	16.0	+0.4	+1.6	+0.7

June and July was a period of reorganization at store D. It resulted in an improved system of operation and consequent conservation of materials. Comparing July with August, there is a falling off in profit due to lower average sale. In September profit for the month increased in spite of advanced material cost because average sale was more than 1½ cents more per customer than in August.

"E"	Raw material used %	Ave. sale	Profit %	Increase or decrease from previous month		
				Raw material	Ave. sale	Profit
June (sales, $1,827.55)...	48.3	16.2	−6.9			
July (sales, $1,762.00) ..	41.4	16.9	1.9	−6.9	+0.7	+8.8
Aug. (sales, $1,872.28)...	46.7	15.2	−0.5	+5.3	−1.7	−2.4
Sept. (sales, $1,730.60)..	46.4	15.0	−3.8	−0.3	−0.2	−3.3

In three of the four months store E lost money. The low average sale is significant.

"F"	Raw material used %	Ave. sale	Profit %	Increase or decrease from previous month		
				Raw material	Ave. sale	Profit
June (sales, $4,551.21)...	38.8	16.3	2.5			
July (sales, $4,832.72)...	39.5	18.5	6.3	+0.7	+2.2	+3.8
Aug. (sales, $5,116.39)...	40.3	19.3	7.7	+0.8	+0.8	+1.4
Sept. (sales, $4,541.60)..	42.2	17.6	1.6	+1.9	−1.7	−6.1

Store F belongs to the class of store where a certain minimum volume of business must absolutely be done each month to permit any profit at all being earned. This is chiefly on account of the heavy fixed overhead in the way of rent and amortization charges which stores of this class must carry. Below a certain point in sales, no profit at all is possible, no matter how well controllable expenses are held down and no matter how high the average sale may be. The law still holds, however.

In the case of this store, $4,500 per month is about the minimum on which any profit can reasonably be expected. Comparing June with July, a small increase in the material cost was far more than offset by a marked increase in the average sale which resulted in an increase in profit. In August, although material cost was slightly higher, as the average sale increased nearly one cent per customer, the profit also showed a fair increase. In September, the material cost advanced again, while average sales fell off nearly two cents per customer, with a consequent sharp falling off in profits.

This condition has been examined at length because of the lucid explanation of the subject and the evident bearing of the point in question, namely, the effect of increased average sale on profits. We have already seen in another connection how the Liggett one-cent sales, by increasing average sales, allow the store to make this enormous reduction in selling price and still make a nominal profit.

Miscellaneous Profits.—A member store in a grocery chain frequently turns in more profits than was to be expected by an examination of goods shipped to that store. Many items sell for nine cents, three for a quarter, or so much a case of one hundred. Now these are usually charged out to the store at the group price, and consequently there is a steady but uncertain source of profit from these odd cents.

Then many member stores are allowed to buy milk, green vegetables, cottage cheese, and other articles by themselves. This forms another source of profit not generally counted on.

Chains go on the theory that "a penny saved is a penny earned." Thus often a careful check is kept on how much paper and string each store uses. In many chains a penalty is put on waste. That is, a manager is allowed a variation of $\frac{1}{2}$ of 1 per cent. on bulk goods. He is allowed ½ pound out of one hundred pounds of sugar and if the difference runs over this, he is charged for it.

Conclusions.—In regard to expenses, the chain organization expenses should be no more proportionately than those of independent stores in the same locality or neighborhood. As a matter of fact, they should be materially less due to the various economies and savings possible for the chain store to effect, which have been mentioned and discussed in this chapter. That is, the elimination of credit accounts, the abolition of deliveries, and the speeding up of turnover will decrease expenses and consequently increase net profits.

In comparison with other retailing ventures, the chain organizations are remarkable for consistent steady profits. By carefully pursuing a policy of increasing sales, increasing turnover, and standardizing of method and routine, they offer an almost impregnable front to periods of prosperity and depression.

CHAPTER XI

ADVERTISING

    (*b*) Character of copy.
        1. To create interest.
        2. Attractive and artistic.
  2. Price advertising.
    (*a*) Featuring loss leaders.
        1. Most common form of chain advertising.
The advertising agency and the chain.
  1. The difficulty of the agency in handling local advertising.
  2. Necessity for contact man.

CHAPTER XI

ADVERTISING

Chain organizations have always prided themselves upon being in the forefront of retail progress as far as selling methods are concerned. Yet in advertising they have lagged behind, not from ignorance, but from choice. The inception of the chain store movement occurred prior to the great development in advertising. Chain merchandising relied on location rather than advertising, all unconsciously choosing the most primitive and most effective form of advertising, namely, that of showing the product directly to the consumer.

It is only recently that chain stores began to realize that after all the appeal of their products to the public might not be entirely based on price. A certain class of people will always be drawn by the price appeal, but there are other classes to whom the price appeal means little. The chain advertising policy is showing signs of breaking away from the traditional price-list advertising. What the future has in store is by no means clear as yet, but the following tendencies in advertising are at work:

1. Increased competition between chain and chain, both selling at approximately the same price. For one chain to attract the balance of the trade it is necessary to find a new appeal. Hence, the rise of institutional advertising by some chains, the coöperation of manufacturers and chains in merchandising campaigns which include advertising, etc.

2. Merchandising and sales policies fully developed. The attention of the chains is being turn on publicity.

3. The very rapid growth of the chain store movement in the past ten years. This has made it possible for many chains to advertise which before had to confine themselves to handbills and "dodgers." After all, a chain must have a certain minimum distribution to make advertising effective.

4. The growth of the science of advertising, and its natural

extension to the chain store field as a logical opening for applied modern advertising.

The real reason why the chains have never advertised to any extent is that they never had to advertise. The customers came anyhow. It was like the early days of the automobile industry when cars could not be made fast enough to supply the demand.

The Advertising Department.—The advertising of the chain organization is rarely done by agencies. The chain is closely organized and is composed of men who thoroughly understand their business. In some chains the advertising department is separate from the other departments, while in others it is attached to the merchandising department. This depends a great deal on the size of the chain and the policy adopted in regard to advertising. In some chains advertising is under the direct control of the general sales manager who takes care of sales in all the branch stores. In smaller chains the sales manager frequently handles the advertising himself.

The window dressers may or may not be attached to the advertising department. They may be part of the sales department or of the merchandising department. But in any event the closest coöperation must exist between the advertising and the other departments.

The personnel of the advertising department may vary from where one man does everything, to the large chains where there is a manager, an assistant who looks after the copy, a research department, an artist, several photographers, copywriters, and perhaps the window trim experts. Some chains find it profitable to operate their own printing plant to get out placards, notices, hand bills, price lists, circulars, and all the other printed matter necessary in the routine work of a large chain.

Where newspaper advertising is done, the ordinary practice is to prepare copy at headquarters and send electrotypes to local managers for insertion in the local papers. Full instructions are sent at the same time about the position of the advertisement, the days it is to run, etc. Naturally this newspaper advertising is closely coördinated with the weekly sales specials or whatever products the company wishes to feature at the time.

The branch manager is responsible for inserting the copy in the local papers. In some instances, branch managers are allowed to write their own copy and arrange for space. In other chains the branch managers are allowed a certain percentage for advertising. In the Penney chain this is two per cent. Many chains employ a specialist whose duty it is to buy space in papers. They do not care to leave this to the branch manager. whose experience in this line is likely to be limited.

Counter cards, window display cards, signs, circulars, hand bills, price lists, pamphlets, etc., are prepared by the advertising department as a rule although they may be decided upon with the sales or the merchandising departments. As a rule they are sent to all stores simultaneously. The managers of the Federal Bakeries have an opportunity to order what they wish of sales promotion matter prepared by the merchandising department.

When advertising is decided on at the central office, it is usually done by conference. Various plans are submitted and the best one chosen. One of the determining factors in this, as in so many other chain matters, is the records of what happened in previous years under certain conditions. The records tell not only the kind and character of the advertising, but also the products advertised and the actual results obtained.

It is an excellent plan to call into this conference members of the sales and merchandising departments. Their suggestions can frequently be used to advantage and objections are much easier to rectify when they come at the beginning than after everything has been settled upon.

It is important to have new ideas, not only because the public expects them, but because of the stimulating effect on the whole organization. Not only the public but the personnel also feels the benefit of a distinctive sales policy.

Does Advertising Pay the Chain Store?—"Of the firms which fail each year, 84 per cent. are among the non-advertisers," said A. C. Pearson, president of the Associated Business Papers. That chain stores have not done what is technically known as advertising does not mean that they have not kept themselves before the public. Quite the contrary. Each member store of a chain organization is an advertisement in itself. The old customer, wherever he is, seeks the familiar store front.

The United Cigar Stores say they have never been able to tell whether advertising paid or not. On the books it has been thc custom to set it down as a total loss becausc it cannot bc traced. The Childs Company stated that as a result of advertising conducted by them, the average check was brought up from twenty-five cents to forty-five cents. Each chain will have its own problem to face but the issue in each case will be the same. "Good advertising consists in presenting your message to as many prospective customers as possible at the most reasonable cost, and in a way that will attract their attention and bring them to your store."

There have been costly mistakes made in advertising in the past; At one time advertising was considered as a panacea for all ills. But the chain store has been reluctant to put faith in it until after it has proved itself. Consequently the movement on the part of the chain stores towards advertising is very significant. Even the very conservative non-advertising Singer Sewing Machine Co. has announced an advertising programme, with emphasis placed on the individual store. The Piggly Wiggly Stores have always shown pronounced ingenuity in their advertising campaigns.

Chain store advertising is yet in its infancy. It is too early to make any definite statement about the future. What little advertising has been done in newspapers and, in a few cases, in national media, has been encouraging in its results. Properly handled, advertising will help the chain in the following ways:

1. Increase turnover by increasing demand while stocks remain stationary.
2. Enlarge clientele.
3. Increase confidence in the chain and its products—an inevitable result of the right kind of publicity. Goodwill is an invaluable asset for the chain organization as well as for any other business.

The Media of Advertising.—This brings us directly to the question of where the chain should advertise to obtain direct benefits. There are, of course, two main alternatives open to it. The first is national advertising and the second is the local papers. As the chain advertises to the consumer the choice is limited. As far as national advertising is concerned, the field is immediately narrowed down to the few chains with national distribution, that is, with branches extending over enough of the territory of the United States to make it profitable for them to use such a medium of publicity as a national magazine. The Douglas Shoe Co. is a consistent advertiser in national periodicals. The United Drug Co. has also experimented in this field. But when the benefits are analyzed, the results in proportion are seen to be small, even for a company with branches all over the country. A large number of the readers will not be in a locality where it is possible to patronize the chain. Therefore a large percentage of this advertising is bound to be lost. In the second place a magazine will not cover the local field in the way the local paper can.

The local newspaper offers the logical medium of publicity for most chain organizations. Even here, the results are likely to benefit no particular link in the chain but rather the whole local organization. One chain executive says: "The question of advertising is very important. Chain stores render less service to their customers than old-time stores do: how are they going to overcome that fact? We do it by making our prices lower and then by telling everybody about it. We operate many stores, some one of which is sure to be not more than a few blocks from your house, no matter where you may live. But because a chain store gets part of everybody's business probably at least once a year, and because a customer of No. 5 feels perfectly free to stop in at No. 45 if she is out that way and has time to buy, we have no actual personal acquaintanceship with our customers, such as a small retailer has. We have to shoot our advertising in the air and make it cover the whole town.

"We use the local newspapers. Some chains use handbills or dodgers. Recently some chains have been issuing a weekly paper, containing advertisements of the week's 'specials' and containing jokes, cartoons and reading matter so that the children will take the paper home. This is a new development in the business and merits consideration."

The People's Drug Stores, operating a chain of twelve stores in Washington, D. C., used fourteen pages, a complete advertising section, in one of the daily papers as a means of bringing home to the public that it was the chain's sixteenth anniversary. The president of the company, M. G. Gibbs, stated that for ten days after the advertising appeared the company did the largest business in its history. This is an instance of an extraordinary use of newspaper space, but, as a general rule, chains use newspaper space in varying quantity. Some advertise every week; some only on special occasions. It is possible the day may come when the chain stores will be as lavish users of newspaper space as are the department stores today. Drug stores frequently take page advertisements for special sales. Grocery stores, with a few exceptions, do price advertising. As we shall see later, there is some institutional advertising done.

Preliminary Advertising.—When any retailer starts a new store he wants as many people to know about it as possible. He may offer special inducements to get people to come to the store. He may distribute handbills from house to house. He may do nothing at all beyond choosing a good location and relying on the name over the door and the price display in the window. Without doubt the latter method is the cheapest but it will not reach all the people who might be considered as potential customers. It is a logical policy to put an advance notice of the opening in the local paper.

When the Metropolitan Stores, Inc. opened in Philadelphia, on the first business day it made 69,000 sales to 40,000 customers. It is one of a chain of five- to fifty-cent stores, stocking about 10,000 different items. The method used to attract customers was the insertion of the following advertisement in the local papers:

".The merchandise is all new. It has been personally selected by expert buyers. Many of the articles have never before been obtainable at these prices or offered on the counters of chain stores.

"The merchandise must be seen to be appreciated. Come to our opening. You will be under no obligation to purchase. We want you to see the remarkable stocks as they stand complete—to see what is possible for a merchandise organization such as ours, buying in large quantities, to offer within a selling range of from five to fifty cents.

"We guarantee satisfaction to all purchasers."

Advertising is a short cut. In a comparatively brief time it does what otherwise might take and has taken years to accomplish. The fact that the Great Atlantic & Pacific Tea Co. did not advertise does not mean that another store, with a location equally good and a stock equally low-priced and a manager with equally good personality could do the same thing. A store which retails to the public must have goodwill. A large chain has a fund of goodwill already prepared to draw upon. A chain which enters a locality for the first time must create its goodwill. The success of the Metropolitan Stores advertising was directly mirrored in the number of people who came to the store the first day.

The method pursued by the United Retail Candy Stores when they started in New York deserves re-telling. This company, a subsidiary of the United Retail Stores Corporation, and amply backed with capital, planned to start several stores in New York at once and after these were running, go on to another large city. The story is told by George A. Nichols in "Confectionery Merchandising" for August, 1920.

In New York the company secured leases for its various store buildings and then began alterations upon them all at the same time. The yellow fences were built around the front of the stores. Upon these for some time there was no wording whatever. Then one morning on every fence there appeared the slogan "Happiness in Every Box." Thereupon ensued a guessing contest. Everybody wondered what would be in the box. The guesses ran all the way from face powder to cigarettes.

The fact of the matter was that the candy chain saw in those fences a wonderful opportunity for some real outdoor advertising. They might have followed the stereotyped plan and have put on the boards an announcement to the effect that the United Cigar Stores were now going into the candy business on a large scale and that in a short time a store would be opened in that location. But this was an unusual undertaking and the ordinary methods of advertising would not answer. Something was needed to keep the interest up until the time for the store to open.

The slogan was presented in various guises for two or three weeks and, then, the billboards one morning contained a big announcement telling what it was all about. A candy store was to be opened there on a certain date. "Happiness in Every Box" meant happiness for everybody in the family. The billboard, therefore, contained pictures of happy smiling faces of people from babies up to old age. It was explained that the store would be part of a nation-wide system of fine candy stores and candy factories planned to being candy quality, candy purity and candy goodness direct to the consumer without extravagance or high prices. This was followed up with advertisements in the newspapers.

To conclude, when a chain store decides to enter a new locality, it has the following possibilities of publicity to choose from:

(*a*) Location
(*b*) Window trims
(*c*) Window pasters
(*d*) Outdoor advertising, cards, etc.
(*e*) Moving pictures
(*f*) Advertising in local newspapers
(*g*) Distribution of hand bills, pamphlets, etc.

The first methods are dependent for their efficacy upon customers passing by the store. Thus the value of passive forms of advertising is almost wholly dependent, apart from the intrinsic merit of the display, on the number of people passing the spot. Outdoor signs, of course, do not have to be placed directly on the site of the chain store, and there is no limitation on number, beyond expense and local ordinances governing their erection. The non-advertising chains usually have excellent locations and feel that they can do without this extra expense.

The active forms of advertising, that is, local newspapers and house-to-house distribution of sales and advertising literature, brings us directly to the following section, namely, the appeal and purpose of the advertising. The chain itself must decide by actual experience which forms are the best to use. Probably it will be best to combine several. The window trim may be regarded as essential in any case. The Piggly Wiggly arrangement whereby customers look directly into the store is, in effect, a novel method of window trimming. Newspaper advertising should pay for itself, especially where the store is a new one and people not in the habit of going there.

The Advertising Appeal.—Chain store advertising falls naturally into two classes: Institutional advertising and merchandise advertising.

1. *Institutional Advertising* tells about the chain organization, its methods, etc.

Figure 20 shows one of a series of advertisements of the Waldorf System, Incorporated, operating a chain of self-service lunch rooms, which was run in the newspapers. The advertisement appeared in a different Boston paper each day during the week, that is the same advertisement came out in a different paper daily.   Two weeks after the insertion of an advertisement in the Boston papers, the same advertisements were started in

FIG. 20.—A good example of institutional chain advertising.

fifteen outside cities.   The idea behind this is that many people outside Boston read the Boston papers, and that these people will see the advertising when it appears in these papers.   Two weeks later they would see the advertisement in their own home town paper and by force of repetition the advertising appeal would be so much the stronger.

This is strictly institutional advertising.   It does not aim to sell any goods or increase the sales of any one store. It is designed to present to the public the idea of the system. It will serve eventually as a background on which merchandising advertising to increase the sales of some of its products can be done.

There is nothing cheap about the make-up of this advertisement, as is the case with so much newspaper advertising. This goes as far towards quality advertising as is possible in a newspaper. The eye is instantly attracted by the decorative border and the novel introduction of a column of reading matter by the side of the regular advertisement.

The Piggly Wiggly Co. has set out to sell the public the chain store idea and more specifically the Piggly Wiggly Co.'s own methods of self-service operation. Too many people believe the sole advantage of the chain is its lower price.

The following is an example of Piggly Wiggly advertising:

"Piggly Wiggly is a system of merchandising that provides every housekeeper with a well-ordered pantry that she can go to any time between 7 a.m. and 6 p.m., Saturdays until 10 p.m., and there select with her own hands those articles of food that she may of her own mind want to select. More than one thousand different items are to be found in every Piggly Wiggly store.

"Money. You save from 10 to 20 per cent on every article purchased at Piggly Wiggly. A regular patron will save from $8 to $30 a month without sacrificing either quantity or quality.

"Time. You save time, energy, and patience as you wait on yourself and don't have to ask the price of any article, as a swinging price tag indicates the price. You don't have to ask about any article, as only nationally known products are to be found on Piggly Wiggly shelves. You don't have to listen to Mrs. *H*ard-To-Please or Mrs. *H*aggler, as they have no one to argue with.

"*H*ealth. The most precious thing in the world. You can see with your own eyes that the goods are clean, that the surroundings are clean. Some of the goods are in air-tight cartons, others are weighed and sealed in packages of different weights by automatic machines without a human hand touching them."

The above is a good example of what a live chain can do in the way of advertising. It aims to make permanent customers rather than transient customers attracted merely by the price feature of the week.

· Some of the headlines from the Piggly Wiggly advertising are interesting as showing the continued stress on novelty and arousing the interest of the public—so contrary to ordinary chain advertising policies.   Some of them read as follows:

*H*allelujah—Triplets at Last.
A Royal Princess is to be Born.
1492—A Memorable Day it Was.
The Piggly Wiggly Price List.
Music, Flowers, and Women.
The Piggly Wiggly Beauty Contest.
Something is Going to *H*appen.

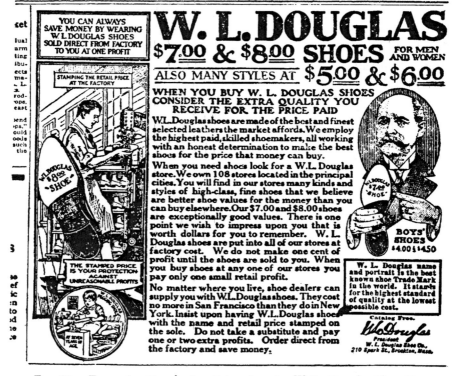

Fig. 21.—Type of national advertising done by W. L. Douglas Shoe Co.

Each of these headlines is designed to attract interest.   Only one of them mentions price.   All of them are selected to attract the attention of the reader.

2. *Merchandise Advertising.*—This is confined mainly to emphasis on price.   Figure 21 shows the form of advertising used by the W. L. Douglas Shoe Co., a form which has

FIG. 22.—Common form of local newspaper price advertising.

been used by them for many years both nationally and in local papers. The price appeal is stressed, with quality and durability slightly second.

Figure 22 shows the most common form of chain advertising, namely a price list. This particular advertisement is arranged so that certain items stand out more than others.

When it is a case of institutional advertising, the same copy may be used in many cities, in fact everywhere. The appeal of the copy is universal. But when it comes to merchandise advertising a new element enters the equation. Conditions are frequently not the same in different cities. For example, take the case of a cigar store chain. In some cities it has to compete with local cigars which prove very strong competition. The character of the local advertising must take this into consideration. Again the wants of the community vary. The stock of a store in New York would be different than that of one in California or Florida. Thus, the character of the merchandise advertising depends a great deal on the size and distribution of the chain branches, and also on the policy of the company.

One shoe chain standardizes all its advertising while one of its direct competitors allows the local manager to spend a certain amount. The result is that the former concern has a great deal to show for its advertising while the latter concern has never been able to teach its salesmen to be successful advertising copy writers.

Advertising Policies.—The advertising agency has taken a definite place in the merchandising program of the average manufacturer, but its place in the chain field is not yet clearly marked. Most agencies show a tendency to keep away from local copy and much of the chain store advertising is necessarily local copy. The advertising should always be governed to a great extent by the particular facts as they exist in the various communities. Institutional advertising for chain stores has been handled and is handled in excellent fashion. But when it comes to merchandise advertising, the chain management seems to prefer someone directly connected with the organization and its conditions to do the work.

If the appeal of the advertising can be universal, the agency can be used to advantage. If it is necessary to watch local conditions, it would hardly be economical to use an agency, on account of the money expenditure which would be required to ascertain the exact local conditions. The chain itself is in a far better position to do this.

The chain may find it advisable to employ a contact man to look after local conditions and to keep traveling constantly with this purpose in view. By means of sales records, the management is in a good position to judge the strength of the competition, and the contact man verifies the opinions of the local managers and analyzes the situation.

The chain is constantly facing the following problem in its publicity: it wishes to find a basis of publicity common to all stores, yet it must take into consideration the status of affairs in the various cities and towns where the stores of the company are located. Each local manager doubtless knows best what conditions are, but that local manager is not an advertising man and never will be. He is hired as a salesman and unless he is a salesman first, last, and always, he is not going to make good on his job. But for the very reason that he knows local conditions so well, he may not be able to analyze them so well as an outsider. Hence, the value of the advertising agency as a specialist in advertising problems as contrasted with selling problems.

Some chains have tried a scheme whereby the advertising is blocked out at headquarters and space left for the local manager to insert local copy. At best this is dangerous policy because the local manager may or may not be competent to do this. Some chains have a number of advertising men attending to districts. If competition is particularly strong in some city, they have authority to run advertising more frequently. They take care of all space buying and positions in the papers.

Coöperative Advertising.—With the closer contact between the chain store, as a retail outlet, and the manufacturer has come the question of coöperative advertising. Both the chain and the manufacturer stand to benefit by this. Figure 23 shows the method in which the manufacturer's product and the chain's product were tied up together in a window trim. This was a direct outcome of the growing policy of manufacturers to spend thousands of dollars to get retailers to coöperate and concentrate in a selling campaign.

12

One progressive chain, and the same facts hold true in other cases, gets a special discount from some manufacturers, especially

Fig. 23.—Form of coöperative window advertising.

of a hitherto unknown item, to cover part of the cost of the advertising. "Every week," says this chain, "we have a full page in the three local papers and two columns in the paper of each of the towns in which we have a store. Part of this space is, of

OUR BIG FALL CANNED GOODS SALE
35% OFF!

BIG stocks—BEST goods—LOWEST prices. *First-choice* of the *new* 1921 pack—at 35% off 1920 costs.

These prices make Early Buying PAY!

Corn Maine Style Dozen $1.18	can 10c	Tomatoes Standard $1.73 No. 3 Can	15c
Corn "Golden Rose" Extra Fancy Maine Pack Dozen $1.89	can 16c	Tomatoes Doz. $2.69 No. 3 Can	23c
Corn Golden Bantam Dozen $2.35	can 20c	String Beans Cut, Wax or Green Doz. $1.95	17c
Peas Fancy Sweet Wisconsin Dozen $1.63	can 14c	String Beans "Golden Rose" Whole Ref. Dozen $2.95	25c
Peas "Golden Rose" Sweet Sifted Dozen $2.69	can 23c	Salmon Pink Alaska Dozen $1.19	tall can 10c
Tomatoes Standard No. 2 Dozen $1.18 Can	10c	Salmon Red Alaska Dozen $2.95	tall can 25c
Tomatoes "Golden Rose" Doz. $1.73 No. 2 Can	15c	Salmon "Golden Rose" 1 lb. Can 6 for $2.35	40c 1-2 lb. can 6 for $1.47 25c
Cond. Milk "Standard" Can	16c	Evap. Milk "Van Camps" or "Borden" 6 for 67c	can 11½c
Peaches Sliced, Heavy Syrup 6 for $1.29	can 22c	Spinach Extra Fancy Pack Dozen $2.35 No. 3 can	20c
Pineapple Finest Hawaiian Sliced. Dozen $2.85 No. 2 can	24c	Asparagus Tips 6 for $2.03 No. 1 Flat Can	35c
Pineapple Finest Hawaiian Grated Dozen $2.43 No. 2 can	21c	Pork & Beans, "Golden Rose" No. 2 Dozen $2.25 Can	19c
Pears Fancy New York 6 for $2.23 can	38c	Pork & Beans, "Golden Rose" No. 3 Dozen $1.29 Can	11c
Sardines Norwegian Smoked Dozen $1.47	can 12½c	Crab Meat ½ lb. can 38c 1 lb. can	75c
Raspberries or Strawberries 6 for $1.75	30c	Sauerkraut, 6 for 88c	can 15c

CHEESE lb. 29c
White or Young America Type

EGGS "Pine Grove" Fancy Selected 45c DZ
"Wm. Elliott" Extra Fancy Fresh, Doz. 69c

NOTE: Owing to the frequent market changes, we cannot guarantee the price of Eggs. All other prices guaranteed for the entire week.

TEAS "Golden Rose" Finest Selection, Delicious Flavor, Air-Tight Packages. OOLONG, MIXED OR ENGLISH BREAKFAST (ORANGE PEKOE CEYLON. Lb. 49c) 45c

Coffee "GOLDEN ROSE" lb. 29c | Coffee "JOHN ALDEN" lb. 39c
A Choice Old Coffee At Popular Price | Perfect Blend Old Crop Coffee

MACAROON SNAPS lb. 19c
A Delightful Biscuit made with Fresh Eggs and flavored with Luscious Cocoanut Sale Price for This Week

PRUNES New Crop, Fancy Santa Claras, Several Cars Just Received 60-70 Size lb. 14c 5 lbs. for 67c

Milk Bread, "Golden Rose" in Wax Paper From Our Own Daylight Bakeshop Large Loaf 1 lb. 5 oz. 12½c

The GINTER Co.
Stores Everywhere--Boston and Suburbs

Watch Ginter Co.'s Newspaper Advertisement in Boston Papers for our Special Weekly Sales

Fig. 24.—Counter leaflet featuring price.

course, given over to whatever the new item may be, to a new brand of canned meat, of a pumpkin flour, or a pancake syrup, etc. Chain stores demand all the discounts they can get and we are close buyers. This saving, small in itself, is of considerable importance when figured over the period of a year."

Although this movement has not attained as yet any wide proportion, it is always worth while watching developments, ready to take advantage of them when favorable opportunity offers itself.

As an example of a possible method of advertising, the handbill has been occasionally tried. This may be distributed from house to house, wrapped up with merchandise, or left on the counter for the customer to pick up. Figure 24 shows an excellent example of such a handbill, in this case got out weekly by a the central office and delivered to the stores.

Conclusions.—Poor as the average advertising of the chain store has been, it has been immeasurably better than the average of its independent competitors. This independent has been at a tremendous disadvantage for, with the exception of very small communities, it did not pay to advertise in the papers. In some cases, it has been attempted to overcome this handicap by a coöperative campaign with a slogan such as "Patronize Your Neighborhood Store." But whatever effect such a campaign may have, it can never become dangerous to the chain until the neighborhood store is able to compete with the chain on its own ground of price.

The future of chain advertising will be directed towards the chain competitor rather than towards the independent. Chain advertising is yet in its infancy. Chains are only just beginning to feel the necessity of advertising. Previously sales have come in without the necessity of spending money on publicity to make them come in. In the same way that chains are extending their services, they are extending their advertising. Customers must be induced to enter the store and if they do not pass the store in sufficient numbers to secure adequate turnover, the advantages offered by the chain must be conveyed through some advertising medium, such as the local newspaper.

CHAPTER XII

ORGANIZATION

The chain store executive.
1. Characteristics.
    (a) Started chain himself.
    (b) Rose from ranks.
    (c) Possesses executive qualifications in high degree.
2. Functions.
    (a) Supervisory.
        1. Follows up store records, sales, etc.
        2. Sees that all parts of machinery function properly.
    (b) Initiatory.
        1. Expansion program.
        2. Merchandising policies.
        3. Miscellaneous.
3. Sources of information.
    (a) Digested records.
    (b) Able assistants.
The district manager.
1. Functions.
    (a) In charge of group of stores.
        1. Travels and visits each at regular intervals.
    (b) Supervises taking of inventories, etc.
    (c) Consults about disposal of stock, etc.
2. Requisites.
    (a) Loyalty and honesty.
    (b) Ability to teach from own experience.
    (c) Thorough knowledge of merchandise and its adaptation.
        1. To needs of community.
        2. To time of year, day of week, etc.
The store manager.
The clerk.
Specialized functions.
1. Buyer.
2. Window trimmer.
3. Realty expert.
4. Advertising manager.
5. Accountant.
6. Merchandiser.

Remuneration of personnel.
1. Executives.
    (*a*) Paid out of profits or gross sales.
2. Managers.
    (*a*) Fixed minimum salary.
    (*b*) Bonus on volume of sales above minimum.
3. Clerks and salespeople.
    (*a*) Flat rate.
        1. Poorest results.
    (*b*) Some form of commissions payment.
        1. Immediate improvement.
Methods of payment.
1. From home office.
2. By local manager.
    (*a*) From contingent fund.

CHAPTER XII

ORGANIZATION

The greatest strength of the chain store and its greatest weakness lie in the character of the personnel. Few executives have shown greater foresight, greater financial ability, or greater merchandising sense than the executives of the great chain systems. Woolworth, Kresge, Whelan, and Penney are names to conjure with in the business world. If it is true that the success of their respective chains is due to system, it was also true that they created the system, and that without their guidance, the phenomenal growth of these particular chains would not have taken place.

But the weakness of the chain is equally apparent when the last links in the chain store are reached, that is, the clerks. Where, in the majority of cases, goods are sold which require no sales effort on the part of the clerk, it has seemed superfluous to expect intelligent coöperation along sales lines from these people. Yet this assumption has always proved mistaken.

However little attention on the part of the clerk is required to sell the goods, courtesy and service have been found to exert a tremendous influence. And it is undeniably difficult to handle these clerks from a central office, perhaps hundreds of miles away, even through the medium of a store manager, and the supervision of a district manager.

The sharper the competition, and the greater the price appeal, the stronger becomes the tendency to lay stress on methods and not men. If all the initiative is mobilized at headquarters, and managers and clerks become mere automatons, ambition, personality, and the progress of the chain through its branches is retarded, if not stopped altogether.

The Executive Functions.—There are some very definite points which appear at first sight in regard to chain store executives:

1. They have risen from the ranks. They started behind the counter and learned the business from the ground up.

2. They rarely shift positions, except perhaps to start in for themselves.

3. The road to promotion is clearly marked.

In the United Cigar Stores, a man starts in as clerk, becomes store manager, then district sales manager, superintendent, and finally assistant vice-president with membership in the directorate and title of vice-president. This company follows a conscious policy of building up executive ability. For example, the directorate is composed of the chairman of the board, the president, the acting president, and fourteen associate directors, each one of whom is at the head of a department. According to President Wise, their fundamental need is capable executives, and he says this is especially true of an organization divided into such a large number of units, each of which functions as an individual entity. Thus this company finds proper management possible only when the board functions directly through the heads of the departments.

The United States is divided by the company into five districts and each district is put in charge of an assistant vice-president who is traveling constantly. Directly under them are the district sales managers who are in much closer touch with local stores and conditions.

The number of necessary links between the executive and the retail store ordinarily varies directly with the size of the chain. As long as it is possible, the chief executive keeps in touch with member stores, but as soon as the stores multiply his information concerning them must be gathered by intermediate links who, in addition to performing policing functions, sift information and deliver it to the central office.

In general, the executive functions of the head of a chain store system are two:

1. He must supervise the machinery which he himself or others have set running. He must see that nothing gets out of order; he must follow up indications on the daily executive report; he must be the court of last resort in case of dispute.

2. He must initiate ideas and sift out the best schemes from all those submitted to him by his subordinates. Ideas count in chain store organizations as everywhere else. The continued

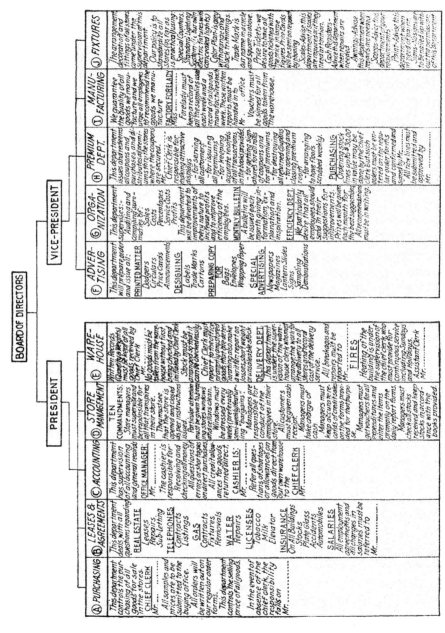

Fig. 25.—Organization chart of Loblaw stores, Toronto, Canada. *(Reprinted from Business Methods, March, 1920.)*

success of a chain store must always be modeled on its ability to keep one step in advance of its independent competitors, and the ultimate responsibility for this rests on the shoulders of the executive.

Owing to the policy of promotion employed in chain systems, namely, that of merit, it is rare to find a chief executive who is not surrounded by a group of able men. Figure 25 shows the apportionment of the various operating functions in a Canadian grocery chain.

The executive of the chain has two methods of getting information, the one supplementing the other:

1. From the daily records, which keep track of stock and sales, allow leaks to be traced, and help train clerks in habits of accuracy and honesty.

2. From the men directly reporting to him and with whom he consults regarding the company's policies. In the days when Mr. Whelan was actively connected with the United Cigar Stores he allowed himself but one vote at the regular weekly board meeting. If he advocated a measure at one meeting, which was adopted, several meetings later he would attack the measure from some other angle.

The executive reports, as illustrated later show how all information is digested in tabloid form for the executive. This is in line with the accepted theory that an executive should not be immersed in detail. His business is to find subordinates who can do the detail work for him. It is an excellent thing, of course, to have the executive deal in percentages but, before leaving this point, it would be well to remind the reader again that only through an infinitesimal knowledge of all the detail connected with the business is it possible for the executive to grasp the true significance of the percentages.

Traveling Superintendents.—As soon as a chain attains moderate size, the executive must delegate some of his functions. He promotes one of his store managers to take active charge of a group of stores, to visit them daily, or at least several times weekly, to advise with them as to their problems, and to see that everything is right. A district manager in the United Cigar Stores is in direct charge of about fifteen stores in one city or an appropriate number in a more scattered locality. Assignment of stores to a manager is made on the basis of traveling facilities and distances between stores. These men are given careful estimates of what sales in each store should be, and it is one of their duties to consult with the store managers as to methods of attaining or exceeding these quotas.

These traveling superintendents often report directly to the chief executive, although in the largest chains this is impossible. George H. Hartford, the founder and creator of the Great Atlantic & Pacific Tea Company, for many years made it a point to see all his traveling superintendents in person. He was not satisfied to accept their reports but often dropped in on the store of the chain nearest the place he happened to be. He always called on the local store where he spent his vacations.

Where the chain is not large enough to hire special inventory men, the traveling superintendent must himself make periodic inventories of the stores in his district. Naturally, a man who is chosen for this position must have certain qualities:

1. He must be loyal. His opportunities for speculation and collusion are naturally broad; but it is to his credit that few cases of dishonesty are recorded.

2. He must be a good salesman. It takes a higher type of salesman to teach others how to sell than it does to sell in person.

3. He must know his merchandise. With his broader knowledge of conditions and wider experience, he should be able to help the store manager with many of his stock problems.

These traveling superintendents, or district managers, or whatever they are called, meet at stated intervals and discuss matters of general importance. They talk over policies which have worked or failed to work, go over sales campaigns, etc.

These men are directly in line for promotion, and have every interest in furthering the progress of the organization. They are the direct links between the managerial and the retailing functions.

The store manager and the clerk have been discussed in separate chapters, but nothing as yet has been said about methods of payment and remuneration for the various grades of employees. Before we take this up in detail there is one further point to discuss in regard to the personnel.

Specialization.—The larger the chain store becomes, the more profitable it is to divide and sub-divide functions among specialists who are experts in their own lines and receive large salaries for the work they do.

For example, the proprietor of a small chain probably does the buying himself, sees to the window trims, prices articles, and, in brief, does most of the work himself. Soon he finds it necessary to have someone do his purchasing for him. He does not have time to look out for it. Next, he has to get a bookkeeper and perhaps an expert accountant. As his chain grows, his staff of experts becomes larger. Someone has to look after the advertising. Finally, he has to have someone to take charge of the real estate.

The number and the functions of the specialists vary with the type of chain. Most chains have traveling auditors who drop in at intervals and audit the individual stores. One large bakery chain employs traveling bakers and traveling merchandisers who operate out of the home office and are not attached to any given district or territory, but make the rounds of the entire country.

The aim is always to keep organization costs down to the lowest possible point, based on experience, which is figured on a general maximum production as against a general minimum payroll. The specialist must demonstrate the worth of his services or he is dropped. That is, the real estate must prove a good investment, the window trims must sell goods, the house organ must instill an *esprit de corps* throughout the organization, etc.

Remunerating the Personnel.—How shall a man be paid what he earns? Few men are satisfied with a fixed salary unless there is opportunity ahead. The chain organizations have probably worked out the most logical and best functioning methods of remunerating employees yet evolved. In general, the following principle is put into effect: After a store attains a certain quota, the manager gets a certain percentage of all sales over this amount. The district managers are rewarded from earnings made by district stores.

To take a specific example, the Woolworth chain pays cash salaries to the founders, the stenographers, and the clerks. Everybody else gets paid on the basis of yearly earnings. The officials in the head office at New York are paid on the basis of earnings made by the entire organization. The district manager of each of the eleven districts is paid on the basis of what his district earns. The manager and the assistant manager take a certain percentage of what their particular store earns. Each man gets his full share of profits. Every employee receives a cash bonus after being with the company for one year, and this is increased by the same amount each year for five years. If a girl leaves to get married after being with the company three years, she is given a cash wedding present.

In the New York Department of Labor investigation of the employment of women in five- and ten-cent stores, it was found that "the manager works on a drawing account and receives a percentage of profits on sales at the end of the year. The percentage of his profits is apparently a matter of individual bargaining between the central or district chain office and the manager himself, although in some cases percentage rates are fixed for certain class stores. Under this system, the manager very naturally has every incentive to put his store on a paying basis, realizing that his own earnings depend upon the number of dollars in profits the store succeeds in making."

The United Cigar Stores never give a share in the profits of the store but base extra payments entirely on sales. This rule is made so that the clerks may not be induced to sell the goods with the most profits in them. Each head clerk receives a certain percentage of receipts for his share of the business, while each clerk receives a salary commensurate with what he sells. The success of this method of payment is plainly demonstrated by the fact that the labor turnover in this concern is small.

In the March, 1921, issue of "Administration," President Wise goes into further detail. Among other things, he says that in paying men for their services, the company does everything possible to increase their earning capacity. The stores work for business on a monthly rating. In addition to fixed minimum salaries, commissions are paid for increased volume. Ratings are so figured that extra compensation is earned as sales increase. In addition, there is a bonus which it is planned to give employees who rank above store managers as an incentive to increase business in stores under their supervision.

The total volume for the year is arbitrarily computed and month by month vouchers are distributed, based on this volume. Vouchers have a money value which increases as the amount aimed at is reached. Mr. Wise believes that this is the most scientific method of profit sharing yet evolved.

The Piggly Wiggly Company's method of paying its employees is interesting. One of its stores employs ordinarily from two to three men, with five men in the big stores. All employees receive regular salaries. In each store there is a salary allowance of three per cent. on gross sales of $2,000 per week and one and one-half per cent. on everything over that. Out of the percentage allowance the salaries must first be paid and then the remainder is distributed equally among the employees.

For example, if one of their stores did a business of $4,000 in one week, the amount available for salaries would be $90, that is, three per cent. on the first $2,000 and 1½ per cent. on the last $2,000. If there were three employees, one receiving $30, the second $25, and the third $20 a week, the pay roll would be $75 a week, leaving $15 to be divided, or $5 for each employee.

A fairly large cash-and-carry grocery chain gives all its men a salary and one half of one per cent. of the gross sales in their stores. Previously the men had been given a bonus at Christmas but this policy was abandoned in favor of the per cent. on sales, paid quarterly. The manager can see with his own eyes just what he is making at any time.

One of the officials of this chain says: "We don't underpay our clerks. It isn't safe. They're handling our money, and if we don't give them enough to live on, it practically forces them to be dishonest. We have very little trouble with dishonesty. Also, our labor turnover is small. Some of our managers have worked for us from ten to fifteen years."

In another grocery chain, managers are paid on a basis of say $30 to $35, with a commission of one per cent. after their salaries at $35 a week equals sales on an agreed percentage basis. In such cases as these, salaries range from $50, which is about the lowest, to whatever amount of business the manager can transact.

Helpers may obtained as high as $17 to $25 a week, depending largely on the report made of them by the manager. Although $25 is high for this class of labor, it attracts an excellent grade of man, who is directly in line for promotion to manager in another store.

The examples given are typical of the majority of chains. Executives and specialists receive high salaries, which is counterbalanced by the comparatively low salaries paid managers and clerks.

The Penney Plan.—J. C. Penney, head of a chain of 313 dry goods stores in the West and Middle West, has a scheme for remunerating his personnel which has received wide publicity and a description of which is well worth reproducing here. We quote from the *Dry Goods Economist* of May 5, 1920:

"The Penney plan may be summarized by calling it an original principle of organization in management, founded upon a real belief in the inherent honesty of human nature and the idea that nothing stimulates a man like the knowledge that hard, intelligent work will bring a certain and substantial reward. This plan results in an intensive coöperation in the passing on of a man's knowledge and qualities of leadership to his helpers in the business, and an endless chain of the development of the individual.

"The plan involves the stimulation of the growth of each new store until its owners are able to start up another, which in turn will send out other branches. The stock of the parent company is classified by stores and a separate set of books is kept for each store.

"Mr. Penney owns all the stock of Store No. 1. In Store No. 2 he owns ⅔ and the manager ⅓. In Store No. 3 he has ⅓, his partner, the manager of Store No. 2 has ⅓ and the manager of No. 3 the other ⅓. Suppose it is decided that Store No. 2 shall start a new branch, in charge of a man who has shown partnership caliber. Mr. Penney retains ⅓ interest. the new partner getting the other ⅓ Mr. Penney held.

"This Store, No. 4, later starts a fifth store in which it is desired that the manager shall have an interest. Then Mr. Penney, as the senior partner drops out, takes none of the new stock, so that the stock in that store is held in equal shares by its manager, the manager of Store No. 4, its parent, and the manager of Store No. 3. Mr. Penney, of course, retains his interest in the other four from which he may start branches in which he will have a share.

"Mr. Penney is constantly training new men for partnership. The men who are admitted to this partnership pay for their interests out of their earnings. There are stores in the chain in which Mr. Penney holds no stock, there being room for but three partners, but it is not his idea to appropriate all of a good thing.   He prefers to have a number of stores in each of which he owns a part interest, rather than a few stores in which he owns all the stock, and, as store after store opens new branches, the number of these part interests increases.

"The men in charge of these stores never fear that someone they are training will come up to supplant them.   They give these men every encouragement and assistance, for the sooner they develop men able to manage a store, the sooner will there be another store in which both will share the profits.   In other words, under the Penney plan it is not a matter of starting a store and then looking for a manager.   The manager is made first and then a store is made for him to operate.

"The common stock is numbered in series according to the number of the store which it represents.   The owners of store No. 10 will hold series No. 10 stock.   Every time a store is opened a man is advanced to partnership, and five other men, all of partnership caliber, are taken into the company.

"The initial salary is small, for a good reason.   When a man must make a small salary stretch a long way, he works all the harder to reach the point where he will become a sharer in dividends.   And the economy he learns while living on little is as useful in handling the income of a store as of a home."

The Penney plan of remunerating employees by making them partners in the business has succeeded in this chain.   How far the same principles could be extended to other chain fields is problematical.   As far as is known, the plan introduced by Mr. Penney goes farther than any other in allowing the employees to obtain a share in the business and active participation in its management.

Remunerating Sales People.—In the very first instance, it is necessary to distinguish between a clerk with no prospects, or at least very faint prospects, of advancement, and a sales clerk in direct line for a local managership.   Some chains find it necessary to employ a great many sales people, mostly girls, who merely work for the salary they obtain.   Other chains find it possible to make the salesmen they employ constantly interested in their work by the knowledge that as soon as they have made good they will be promoted.

The second point to note is the authority of the store manager over his selling personnel.   Ordinarily, the number of clerks employed in a chain store is small compared with other retail stores, because of efficient management, more specialized stock, etc. Stores may be so small that the manager can run them alone with occasional assistance. The five- and ten-cent stores are by far the largest employers of cheap sales help, and have found the labor problem particularly perplexing.

Local managers are ordinarily allowed to hire their own help provided the payroll is kept within certain percentage limits in relation to sales. This percentage figure may come as low as eight per cent. in the larger chains and as high as 14 per cent. in the smaller chains. The payroll, by means of hiring extra workers for Saturdays and holiday seasons, is kept at a fairly constant figure, a deficit during the slack season being made up by a surplus at Christmas.

The old method of remunerating sales girls used by five- and ten-cent store chains has been to pay what the labor market required at the moment, and no more. This, of course, brought with it an exceedingly high labor turnover. The five- and ten-cent store was the last resort when out of work. Naturally this caused a very low degree of efficiency in the sales force.

Conditions are now changing. The progressive chains have come to see that even the policy of "letting the goods sell themselves" can be overdone. In the past, managers have often complained of difficulty in keeping within the percentage limit allowed them for labor. It has been hard to convince the local managers that it pays to teach the clerks better selling methods. The worst temptation the chain manager has to face is the availability of cheap help. One grocery chain found it possible to get men or boys to work from two until six and all day Saturday for $5 a week. An assistant of this sort sweeps the floor, washes the windows, packs away the supplies, and generally reduces store overhead.

But facts and statistics have been tabulated which seem to prove conclusively that higher paid clerks, even in five- and ten-cent stores, are a good investment One chain in particular has conducted a regular campaign to educate its managers in regard to the benefits of better paid clerks. Following is a copy of a notice sent to managers April 1, 1921:

Decreasing Salary Per Cent. by Increasing Efficiency

"The average salary paid salespeople at Store No. X the first three months of 1920 was $15.92 per week. The average number of sales-people employed was 111.

"The average salary for the same period in 1921 is $19.29. Number employed 103.

"Salaries for March, 1920, averaged 10½ per cent, and for March, 1921, 8½ per cent. Is this not conclusive evidence that paying good salaries to efficient salespeople is productive of better results than cutting salaries and employing second-grade help?

"Study your own store on the above basis. It should develop something of real interest."

Efficient sales service cannot be obtained without the coöperation of the central organization and the local managers. It takes time, of course, to effect such a change as the method of paying salespeople. But the trend of the time is in favor of better and more scientific handling of the personnel, and this development in the five and ten cent store field is directly in line.

Wage Rates for **Clerks.**—Sales clerks are ordinarily paid a flat rate. Occasionally there is a wage plus a commission on sales, or a straight commission with no wage guaranteed. It has been found almost universally true that the flat rate gives the poorest returns, as far as sales efforts on the part of the clerks is concerned. Wherever commissions are given, or bonuses for increased sales, the results are almost immediately apparent in the attitude of the clerk and the volume of sales. Some shoe stores follow out a plan by which the clerk is given a bonus only on goods which the company desires to sell. That is, on staple lines, there is no bonus, because there is little selling effort required. On seasonal and special goods there is a large bonus, because the selling effort is correspondingly high.

Generally speaking, the more sales effort is required to sell the goods, the higher salary must be paid to the sales clerk. In many chains, salaries can be kept low because of the prospect for advancement held out to the clerks. In the chain drug stores, a commission is usually paid clerks for selling private brands, or it may be possible for the manufacturer of a nationally advertised article to make some arrangement by which the clerks are given a bonus on what they sell of his goods.

Coming again to the five- and ten-cent stores, it has been stated that in the ordinary five and ten cent store, salesmanship is at a low premium. The tendency at most counters is to make the selling almost automatic. The goods are carefully displayed where they can be examined by the customers and the prices are clearly marked. Some stores are beginning to try out a plan of self-service and the only thing demanded of the salesgirl is wrapping and making small change. At other counters, however, it is still necessary to display goods, to answer questions, and to persuade customers that the goods on hand are exactly those desired. Ribbons, stockings, hats and hat trimmings, underclothes, etc., cannot approach maximum sales without the personal contact between the saleswoman and the customer. It is interesting that in three stores the only salesgirls on a commission basis were those at the music counters, and the difference between the attitude towards customers of these girls with their obvious desire to sell goods, and the attitude of the general salesgirl, who seemed to care little or not at all, was apparent in every case.

Approximately 84 per cent. of the workers in five and ten cent stores belong to the selling force, all women, with few exceptions. In the Department of Labor survey, exactly one-half of the full-time women workers received less than $13.49 a week. Two thirds of them received less than $15 a week. Ordinarily, the smaller the city the lower wage was paid, and this holds true as a rule in all chain stores. An assistant or helper in a city store is sure to obtain larger wages than is paid for the same service in a country store.

Methods of **Payment.**—Ordinarily, checks for wages, bonuses, etc., are mailed direct from the home office. In some cases, however, the local manager pays in cash. It is usual, however, in such cases to obtain a receipt from the employee or have him sign in a book or on a special form which may be forwarded to the central office.

In some chains, checks for employees are delivered or mailed from the central office to reach each branch a day or so before pay day. Then the local manager distributes these checks, cashing them if the employee desires, the endorsed check serving as a receipt.

In some cases, wages·may be paid from a contingent fund. Under any condition, canceled checks or receipts from employees must be turned in to the central office. If any employee is dismissed for any reason, the local manager should be authorized to pay directly and immediately.

Conclusions.—There is a definite form of organization to be found in chain systems. Although the actual duties of the various grades may differ, there is the common requirement that a man start at the bottom and work up. There is also a division of functions at headquarters among specialists in various lines, such as buying, realty, advertising, window trimming, etc.

In regard to remuneration, the aim is and should be to reward each man according to the work he does, and, for better effecting this result, various forms of bonus systems have been introduced. In the average case:

1. The executives receive fairly large remuneration, at least as high as they would probably earn if working for themselves. This policy is profitable because the executives are the brains of the organization, and parsimony in this direction does not pay.

2. Store managers receive some form of payment beyond a fixed weekly or monthly salary.

3. It has been found that even sales people become more efficient if they are given some form of extra recompense for efficient sales service.

CHAPTER XIII

TRAINING MEN FOR PROMOTION

OUTLINE

Promotion policies.
1. Start in at bottom.
   (a) Learn selling first hand.
   (b) Know stock.
2. Fill executive positions within organization.
   (a) Train suitable material.
3. Make promotions on merit.
   (a) Length of service no criterion of efficiency.
   (b) No policy of favoritism.

The road to promotion.
1. Clerk.
2. Manager.
3. District supervisor.
4. Executive position.

Technique of promotion.
1. Controlled by individual records.
2. Dependent on
   (a) Results obtained.
      1. Power to make sales.
3. Shifting men as a form of promotion.

The employment department.
1. Methods of obtaining clerks.

Training clerks.
1. In selling.
   (a) Policy of the chain.
   (b) Store routine.
   (c) Service to customers.
   (d) Knowledge of product sold.
   (e) Miscellaneous.
2. Use of model store.
   (a) Arrangement.
      1. Allowance for variations in stock.
   (b) Arrangement of displays.
   (c) Store conferences.

Desirability of inspectors.
1. To test selling knowledge of clerks.
2. To test following rules and policies established for clerks to follow.
3. To collect new selling ideas.

197

CHAPTER XIII

TRAINING MEN FOR PROMOTION

It is generally agreed that the most difficult problem of the chain is to pick out and train its men. As the chains expand in size, both of number of member stores and territorial extent covered, this problem grows more weighty. A point is finally reached where it is necessary to entrust the choosing and training of the personnel to a separate department. It is difficult to state definitely at exactly what point in its development a chain should institute a personnel department. Roughly speaking, such a department is necessary as soon as the personal touch, which the owner of a small independent store maintains over each of his employees, is lost. As the chain grows larger the functions of the personnel department will increase. Its duties include:

1. Selection of employees.
2. Education and training.
3. Health.
4. Service and maintenance of morale.

Personnel Administration.—"Personnel administration," according to Tead and Metcalf's Personnel Administration, "is the direction and coördination of the human relations of any organization with a view to getting the maximum necessary production with a minimum of effort and friction, and with proper regard for the genuine well-being of the worker."

These questions are treated in this and the following chapters. Personnel administration is comparatively new in its application to the retail field, although for some time it has been used with excellent results in industrial concerns. One large chain organization with headquarters in New York has gone so far as to test its entire personnel for mental alertness. The old process of trying out a man on a job was not furnishing minor executive positions fast enough to fill the demand. The problem was put up to the Bureau of Personnel Research, an organization connected with the Carnegie Institute of Technology. C. S. Yoakum, the director of Personnel Research for that institution, gives the following account of results:

Figure 26 shows the results obtained. The organization has been divided into three groups: Executives, minor executives, and clerks. These groups correspond to distinct divisions within the company. The scores, and the number of individuals making each score, are shown. The highest possible score is 184. Five

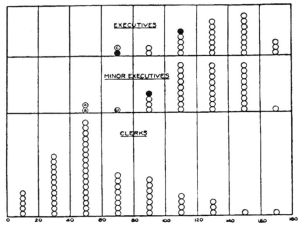

Fig. 26.—Showing the results of a mental test applied to every member of a large chain, from executives to clerks. Each circle represents one member of the organization. Executives of the company all scored above 60, minor executives averaged 119, while in the clerical group average was only 55. (*Forbes Magazine,* Jan. 21, 1922.)

clerks, for example, made scores between 0 and 20, while only two made scores above 140. In plotting the chart not all of the clerks were taken, but only a representative group. If all the the clerks were shown the distribution of scores from low to high would be in just the same proportion as is illustrated. Above the line of the clerks, however, each small circle represents an individual. The chart as a whole represents accurately the distribution of scores of the company's two thousand employees.

The executives of the company all scored above 60 in the test, and only four fell below 100. The average for the group was 127. The minor executives ranged all the way from 45 to 166, while the average was 119. In this group only seven individuals out of thirty-five fell below 100. In the clerical group the range of scores was extremely wide—from 3 to 160—but the average was only 55. Only 15 per cent. scored above 100. The individuals composing this 15 per cent. are just as intelligent, just as mentally alert, and have just as great capacity for acquiring knowledge and skill as have the executives of the company. Comparing the averages of the groups, however, it is clearly shown that different levels of intelligence are represented by the different groups.

The black dots on the chart indicate that one executive and one minor executive left the company because of inefficiency before the results of the test were known. The circle marked A indicates a minor executive who took four years to absorb training usually given in one. Circle B represents a man whose position is due solely to long experience and training but who will probably never go further. C is doubtful but is being given another chance.

As a result of the tests no minor executives were hired unless they scored above 80 and between 80 and 100 only if other qualifications were specially good. After being in operation ten months, Fig. 27 shows results secured.

One hundred and thirty-three applicants have been examined. Eighty-two have been rejected. Twenty-four were automatically rejected because they scored below 80 in the test; twenty others scoring between 80 and 100 were rejected because of low score and the lack of any other specially good qualifications. The remaining thirty-eight were rejected on other than a mental alertness basis. During the same period fifty-one applicants were accepted. Two of this number scored between 80 and 100, and were hired because of very good recommendations. One of these has already been asked to resign because of his inefficiency. Forty-nine of the accepted applicants scored above 100. Of this number only five have proved unsatisfactory, though two others have resigned for outside reasons. Forty-two, or 82 per cent. are making good and will furnish dependable material for the making of future executives. The company considers this a very successful ten months of selection. Hereafter the critical score will be set at 100.

Intelligence, of course, is not the only requisite for an employee of executive calibre, but it is an essential qualification. Tests for other qualifications are being carried out and are being developed. The aim of the intelligence test is, as Mr. Yoakum says "to measure human capacities in observation, in concentration, in simple reasoning, in understanding, and in handling ideas according to instructions. All of these human intellectual powers

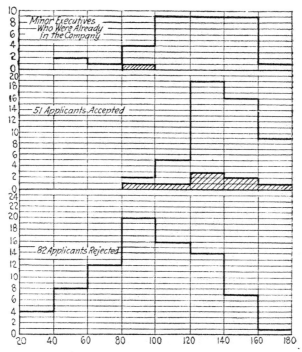

Fig. 27.—Of 133 applicants for minor executive positions examined during a period of 10 months, 82 were rejected and 51 accepted, of whom 42 are making good. The figures at the right represent the number of applicants and the shaded parts resignations. (*Forbes Magazine*, Jan. 21, 1922.)

become of increasing importance as business responsibility increases."

Promotion Policies.—There are certain principles of promotion which can be applied generally to nearly all chains.

1. A man must start in at the bottom and work up. That is, he must first of all learn to sell goods himself, he must become acquainted with his stock, must find out the customers' likes and dislikes. In the Woolworth organization every man, from the store manager up, begins at the bottom. Virtually everybody

in the United Cigar Stores organization has served behind the counter.

2. Higher positions are filled within the organization. It is a fixed policy in all established chains to fill vacancies from men who have actually trained for those positions. The United Cigar Stores Company at their main office never allows a position to remain vacant for a moment, even during vacations. The man below always takes the place of his superior.

3. Promotion is made on merit alone, not because of length of service, influence, or any other reason. Men who do not fit eliminate themselves or are eliminated. No man whose personal views are at variance with the policy of the organization can hope to be promoted.

The United Cigar Stores Co., with a personnel of 6,500, believes there is plenty of executive ability always available. In addition, it recruits the ranks of its buyers from the clerks. In every chain, good clerks are consistently promoted to be managers, and good managers to be supervisors or district managers.

But there is one class in a chain store organization which has little chance for advancement, and this is the girl in the five and ten cent store. Opportunities for her are rare. She may become a bookkeeper, a floor-walker, a window dresser, or in rare cases an assistant manager, but on the whole she has little to look forward to in the organization. This is due to two reasons, one reacting on the other.

1. The girl employed, at the salary paid, usually has inferior intelligence and possesses little sales talent. That is, she is not especially fitted to make herself invaluable to the organization and to put herself in line for promotion.

2. Few five- and ten-cent stores have spent any time or money trying to better the sales talent they have.

But, with this exception, the road to promotion is generally open, and in few other lines of business is it possible for the worker to get a squarer deal from the management.

A Man's Record.—Progressive chains do, and should do, everything possible to increase sales effort on the part of the personnel. Then by their careful system of records, they can watch the progress of a member of their organization from the moment he steps behind the counter. They have a record of the sales in that store prior to the time he stepped into it, and it is an easy matter to compare this old record with the new performance.

In the National Drug Stores organization, the facts about every man are noted on a card. When a vacancy occurs, these cards are consulted, and the man who apparently possesses the most desirable characteristics for the position is sent for and interviewed.

The United Cigar Stores Co. lays especial stress on courtesy. Those who do best to uphold this policy are presented with a gold watch and a testimonial. President Wise says "the power to give service would stand a man in as good stead as anything for promotion. The man who combines honesty of purpose, and loyalty to the company, with active interest in promoting goodwill and satisfying customers, is so valuable to the United Cigar Stores that he is bound to climb rapidly."

Courtesy, without doubt, is a difficult quality to tabulate and put on cards. But it is also true that courtesy almost invariably results in increasing sales, and sales are simple matters to place on record. In addition, the United Cigar Stores relies on a department of inspection, since they have found the average clerk does not like to say "thank you" unless he is prodded. Therefore, a clerk is checked by sales records and personal inspection.

Naturally, a store manager is judged by the results he obtains from his store. It is not always easy to determine just what a manager should sell from a particular store, since volume of sales may be affected by matters outside his control. Thus a store manager should not be judged by what other stores are doing, but rather by what happened in his own store previously. In general, of course, if sales increase in the majority of stores, the rest of the stores should show this same increase unless there are reasons, beyond the control of the manager, to prevent.

Clerks on a commission basis have often complained that at some counters it was possible to make twice as much commission, with half the amount of work, as at other counters. Some managers have tried to equalize this by moving poor selling articles to main traffic channels or having a bargain counter adjoining, etc.

In all chains records should be kept of employees on some

basis which will fairly show the individual merits of every man. In a small chain whoever decides on promotions will probably know the personnel individually, but in larger chains, or chains the links of which are widely scattered, promotion is largely a matter of record, supplemented by personal interview.

Shifting Men.—A man may be shifted for several reasons:

1. To accustom the man to several positions. Some chains habitually shift their organization around to give all concerned a fresh viewpoint. In this way also every position has a number of understudies, ready to take up the regular duties of the position if for any reason it becomes necessary. Some chains find it advisable to shift managers of stores from one city to another temporarily to give them fresh selling ideas, and in their absence the assistant manager takes charge, and is given an opportunity to win his spurs.

2. As a form of promotion. Where a store manager is dependent on the profits or sales of his store for his salary, it is a frequent practice to move a manager who has done well to a bigger or more profitable store. This is equivalent to increasing his pay and promoting him.

There is something to be said against this policy, however. It is not always desirable to break up business acquaintanceships. That is, a manager may be a positive drawing card to a store through the influence of his sales personality. · This is true, of course, only where the manager meets his trade personally and would not apply to a chain department or variety store. But even in those cases, the manager probably has ·a very thorough knowledge of local conditions which benefit both him and the chain directly.

3. As a form of demotion. If a manager fails to make good at a certain store and yet possesses many of the qualities requisite in a manager, it is sometimes possible to move him somewhere else. For example, a manager may succeed wonderfully in a small store where everything was personally attended to by himself, yet fail in a larger store because he lacked the ability to handle other men. The logical move would be to bring this man back to the small store.

Recruiting the Personnel.—Higher positions are filled from the ranks in the manner previously described. We have also seen that a man should start at the bottom. Now, where are the men to be found to fill these initial positions? The somewhat original method used by Mr. Penney in obtaining his men has already been described elsewhere. The success of his method is sufficiently justified by results.

Larger chains have employment departments. There are certain definite qualifications which an applicant is required to meet. There is an unusually large proportion of rejections. Previous selling experience is not a necessity. Some chains regard it as an objection, because they find it far easier to teach a man with no preconceived selling ideas their policies and plans. In the chains that use scientific methods of hiring, there is a small labor turnover. That is, men who are chosen for employees enter the service of the chain with the idea of ultimately becoming store managers, and not merely of working until they tire. Work on the lower rungs of the chain ladder is particularly exacting. Although there are certain closing hours, these are by no means fixed and the clerk may often have to remain after the store is closed to pack away goods received from the warehouse ready for the next day's trade, or for other routine work. But the opportunity which the chain offers to a man without capital of his own to become a store manager insures the average chain an adequate supply of men of the right type.

So far as the woman clerk is concerned, the New York Department of Labor reports that the selection of the girls for the job is governed by what type of girl can be obtained at the particular time she is needed for the lowest wage the market offers. Its finding was that any idea of a permanent, satisfied, well-trained, working force was strangely absent; girls came and went. This was particularly true in factory towns where the girls in good times worked in a factory, and when they were laid off or got tired of factory work, clerked in five and ten cent stores for a while.

There is no accepted practice of hiring or choosing employees, but it is safe to draw the following conclusion: Since the chain organization is dependent on its men as much as on its methods, no effort expended in securing men of the right type can be wasted.

Training the Salesman.—There are two methods of training the salesman, the first before he actually goes behind the counter, and the second training him after he has begun to sell. The educational department ordinarily takes charge of actually training the salesmen. This pre-training period is the direct outcome of the recognition of the value of such training in increasing sales. It enables the chain and the clerk to earn more money.

The chief defect of a chain, and particularly of a large one, is lack of personal touch. If the organization can take its men at the very beginning and teach them just what the organization itself is, the nature of the goods, and in addition give them a brief but thorough course in retail salesmanship, a great deal has been accomplished.

Almost every chain has a particular policy in regard to the conduct of the clerk while making a sale. It is very important that this conduct be standardized. A customer going into one branch of the chain should find exactly the same service that he finds in another branch. Now the only way to standardize service is to teach the man just what is wanted in the first place and then make him hold to that standard. Therefore, one method of training, although a negative one, is keeping inspectors on the road, unknown to the clerks, to see if policies and practices are being carried out.

In large cities or centers of population classes of salesmen are in daily session. An educational director is in charge. In a few weeks he can teach the intelligent salesman facts which experience might not drill into his head for years. The salesman thus trained lacks only experience. Where stores are located at distant points, new salesmen may be trained in district offices. For example, a chain with an educational department in Chicago might refer an applicant in Maine to district offices in Boston. If the application were accepted, the salesman might be trained direct in the Boston district office, and receive his first selling experience under supervision in the district store.

Generally speaking, salesmen are trained along the following lines:

1. Policy of the chain.
2. Knowledge of the product or products sold.
3. Arrangement of the store.
4. Store routine.

5. Service to customers.
    (*a*) Courtesy.
    (*b*) Remembering faces, etc.
6. Miscellaneous points, differing according to the nature of the chain.

In other words, salesmen are taught standardized sales methods applicable to the particular chain.

The Model Store.—When salesmen are trained at a central point, it is advisable to have a model store. This will serve two purposes. It will give the salesmen a practical illustration of what is being taught them, and it will serve the company as a model for window trims, experiments of various kinds in selling,

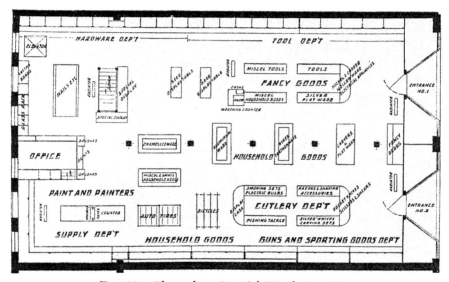

FIG. 28.—Floor plan of model Winchester store.

etc. The model store is virtually a laboratory for the entire chain. It tries out experiments and the result as shown in the model store determines whether they shall be adopted or rejected.

Figure 28 shows the floor plan of a model Winchester store. Contrary to the ordinary hardware store, there is nothing to obstruct the view, no rolling ladders along the wall, nothing cumbersome in the center of the store, and no goods suspended from the ceiling. Goods which display well, specialties, fancy goods, tools, cutlery, or sporting goods are in the front of the store, while more staple lines are in the back or in the basement. No stock is carried above the ledges along the side of the store.

Whether the clerk has to arrange displays in his own store or not, he must be taught at least an understanding of the value of display. The model store is dressed differently every week. Window displays are changed and counter displays of stock are altered. A complete rearrangement takes place to care for seasonal demand. Things in the greatest demand are featured in the windows, on the counters, by floor displays, by displays around pillars or columns in the center of the store, etc.

Let us consider, for example the experience of one chain, as reported by F. J. Arkins, Staff Secretary of the Alexander Hamilton Institute. He states that the work is carried on by professional window dressers, advertising men, experts in the matter of store and stock display. The final display is determined in a conference. All the week, perhaps, these men have been meeting the trade, discussing matters with patrons, and talking with customers regarding their wants. These men have also examined and analyzed the records of all of the branch stores for the corresponding period one year ago, two years back—and the averages over a period of perhaps ten and maybe twenty years or as many years as the chain has been in business. The records give the results from different types of stores, regarding counter and window displays.

These men have before them photographs of all displays for the week under consideration.

Comments from branch managers and customers, complaints, etc., are taken up in conference. Each point is debated. There is certain to be a difference of opinion in the conferences. This is considered fortunate. In this case, it is believed that a decision, when finally made, will meet the objections of everyone present.

After the displays have been decided upon, the windows, the store interiors, and counter displays are photographed and copies of the photographs are sent to every branch manager, who puts up his new display according to the photographs. Thus all store links in the chain will show the same window display, counter display, and floor display at the same time and for the same number of days.

Now assuming that the salesmen have had several lectures on the policy of the organization, its history, its ideals, etc., they are then taught practical retail salesmanship through the model store.

Knowledge of Product.—Chain salesmen should be given a thorough knowledge of the stock they handle, its uses and ingredients, the processes of manufacture, how and why goods are packed in certain ways, the origin of raw materials, and many additional data. They must be ready to answer questions of any kind.

D. C. Keller, directing head of the Dow Drug Co. of Cincinnati, relates some interesting experiences he had while investigating the knowledge of drug clerks in regard to their products. The following is quoted from Drug Store Merchandising for October, 1921:

Mr. Keller went to a drug store in Chicago. He called for a box of sea salt; "bath salt," it is known to the trade. Mr. Keller knew what the particular brand of bath salt brought him by the clerk cost the druggist, and what a fair profit should be. He also knew the prices of certain other, equally popular, bath salts. "How much is this?" he asked the salesman.

The price was given.

"You haven't a cheaper grade of bath salt, have you?" he asked then, as a man who will leave without buying will do, unless he can buy for considerably less, when prices quoted appear high.

The clerk, who had tried to sell the high-priced product first, immediately produced a bath salt selling for much less.

"What's the difference between them?" Keller asked nonchalantly.

The clerk proceeded to expatiate on innate properties of salt derived from water drawn from one portion of the Atlantic ocean as compared with water from some other, taken from the same seaboard, some miles distant.

"But this higher-priced salt was made in Michigan." Keller interjected, reading the label.

The clerk examined the carton, flushed, and said the goods were given him to sell at the prices marked on them. A good salesman always tried to sell his highest-priced wares first.

14

A modern drug store contains so infinitely many items that not even a Solomon could know all a man should know about the goods.

This story goes to show that a clerk may do more harm by ill-advised efforts to sell goods with false information than it would cost the chain to educate him after finding out how little drug clerks really knew about the products they sold. Mr. Keller, now, before every special sale in a Dow drug store, prepares a tabloid essay on the product. This contains information about the raw material; how it is put together; what are the exceptional uses of the product; what are the differences between grades; how goods should be cared for by their buyers, etc.

To quote from Drug Store Merchandising: "One copy goes, by the firm's courier, to every Dow store, and must be receipted for by the manager in charge. It must be posted at once and every employee is responsible for its contents within a reasonable time—a few hours, that is—after posting. There can be no excuse for not having read a bulletin bearing the imprint of the president's office; instant dismissal is the reward of a proof of this charge!"

This policy has proved highly successful in increasing sales. People who dropped in to look around went away with a purchase. They simply couldn't resist the selling argument. Following is a copy of the bulletin sent out on the subject of chamois:

THE PRESIDENT'S SALES PROMOTION BULLETIN NO. 11

CHAMOIS

TO THE DOW SALES FORCE:

As you already know, on the 16th inst. there will go on sale in our stores a big bargain in chamois. This is a special sacrifice price and we probably can't continue these prices after this lot is sold. Chamois will give better service and last longer if they are properly cared for. Water which is too hot, or extreme heat when drying, are injurious. Leaving the skin wet, without wringing it out, when not in use, is also destructive. Strong acids and impure strong soap should not be used on chamois. It is also better to have special chamois for rough, dirty work. After being used, chamois should always be washed thoroughly, in luke-warm, soapy water; using good soap. Then rinse in clear water, wringing the chamois as dry as possible, pulling it out as nearly as possible to its original shape and hanging it up to dry. Do not dry it on a radiator or other hot place. Do not let chamois lie around dirty for a considerable period, but wash as soon as possible after using. Chamois themselves will not scratch the finest of surfaces, but if they are allowed to accumulate dust, grit, and dirt they will not prove satisfactory, unless they are washed thoroughly before using.

All these points should be carefully explained to the customer as a matter of DOW SERVICE. Most of the customers in your store next week are possible purchasers and you should suggest chamois to each of them. These chamois have been retailing anywhere from $4.00 to $5.00 and if the customer already has a chamois don't fail to suggest the purchase of additional ones now as matter of economy, because the price will be higher. Suggest the various household uses—cleaning pianos, furniture, windows, mirrors, interior wood work, and polishing floors, bath tubs, wash stands, pictures, lamps, sewing machines, and all such similar articles, and then, of course, their very general use for automobiles.

These chamois are absolutely "firsts," that is, perfect in every way. Many chamois sold are "seconds," and have in them thin places, hard spots, rough spots, and various blemishes. There is not a second in this lot. These chamois are not racked chamois. A racked chamois is one which has been wet in manufacture and then stretched and tacked to a board, or in other ways held in place until it is dry. It is then much larger, but when it is again wet and dried, it will shrink back to its original size. A racked chamois can frequently be told by small tack holes around the edge. This is good selling talk.

D. C. KELLER,
President and General Mgr.

There are other ways, of course, of instructing the sales force as to the product, but this method has the advantage of novelty and, by concentrating sales effort on the article or product described, the clerk is able to see immediate results. Thus his coöperation is secured. The majority of small chains have to educate their clerks after they are hired. In all chains there must be a constant driving effort to keep clerks up to the mark.

Training in the Right Arrangement of the Store.—The arrangement of branch stores is strictly in accordance with the arrangement of the model store. In fact, arrangement is perfected in the model store. The model allows for variations in stock, due to different localities and their varying tastes, etc. The manner in which the stocks may be alternated is shown. All the changes in stock will take place at one point, or if at more than one point, the salesman is taught exactly where to look. The character and nature of the article in those particular places indicates to him what has been dropped or changed in that store. Methods for adding new counters or tables to handle additional stock during heavy seasonal demands, as in the holidays, are shown.

Figure 29 shows arrangement of stock in the Winchester Model Store. In this store there is not an item carried in stock

Fig. 29.—Section of display panel in Winchester store.

which is not shown in display. Goods are stocked behind the panel doors shown in the illustration.

A thorough knowledge of the arrangement of stock as plotted by the central office allows clerks to be shifted from one store to another in the same chain without the slightest confusion. It is another step in standardizing sales service.

Service.—Although the chain stores have largely cut out what had been known as service—credit, deliveries, returns, etc.,—it is still in their power to render the most important help of all, and that is selling service. Display will sell goods, price will sell goods, but the services of the clerk are needed to make a complete combination. The customer must be treated in such a way that he will come again. And this is the reason the United Cigar Stores Co. insists upon courtesy to the customer and why George J. Whelan says if he wrote a bible for salesmen, the first commandment would be "Thank You." Salesmen are given a specific order, reading as follows:

"THANK YOU"

"Always acknowledge a purchase with a genuine 'Thank you, Sir,' or 'Thank you, Madame,' or some variations of the phrase, as for example 'Many thanks,' or 'Much obliged to you.' Say whatever you say out loud as if you meant it. Under no circumstances must this rule be violated."

Then one day each clerk in the organization received a telegram reading "Did you say 'thank you' to every customer you waited on today?" Some answer had to be made and replies flooded the central office. Mr. Whelan had chosen the "thank you" phrase as the slogan of courtesy for use by the clerk.

In some chains clerks are told to remember the names of customers. All these, of course, are old tricks of salesmanship but the chains have done more towards making a scientific study of retail selling than any other retail organizations in the country, with the possible exception of some department stores.

Other chains dwell on the value of a smile when making a sale, others on an even, well-trained voice. But the point is that the chain organizations train their men to treat customers in such a way that they will become regular patrons.

Service may mean many things, but the chain store definition is service by the salesmen to the customers. For example, the following paragraphs show the idea of service which is taught by the Walgreen Company, which operates 27 candy and drug stores in Chicago and vicinity, (Quoted from Drug Store Merchandising):

1. Employees who are not polite to every customer have little chance of getting on whether in our employ or in the employ of someone else.
2. When the impossible is asked for—be pleasant, that is service.

3. Give each customer your whole attention.

4. Give as much attention to a little buyer as to a big one.

5. Always be circumspect.

6. When an article is not in stock, show a painstaking desire to get it for the customer.

7. Render this service with as much promptness and as little trouble to the customer as possible.

8. See that your floors are always clean, they mean reputation for the company.

9. Service is a matter of attitude as it is of action. You must bear in mind that service without wholeheartedness and simple kindness is useless.

10. Service is advertising that pays. Such advertising is in your power to create.

11. Your ability is judged by your power to coöperate. You progress by your capacity and willingness to coöperate.

12. Executives maintain their positions because they can coöperate with other executives and with their co-workers.

13. Make your coöperation wholehearted and real. It is more than obeying or giving orders. It means working with one's fellows in a spirit of helpfulness and good fellowship. It means avoiding the friction of inattention, deceit, selfishness, egotism. In other words, it means teamwork.

The chain store possesses one enormous advantage over its independent competitor. With the exception of five and ten cent stores and other chains where the mere sales clerk has little or no opportunity for advancement, the chain clerk finds that his service to the customer actually pays him in cash. Where a man's own interest is concerned, there is ordinarily little difficulty in obtaining first class service for the customer.

Inspectors.—But unless the company devises some method of keeping track of the salesman's attitude toward the customer, the high standard which has been set by the educational department will be lowered. Sales bulletins and letters may help, but the only way of actually overseeing the attitude of the clerk is by personal observation. This is comparatively simple where the chain is a small one and the links closely connected. Different members of the organization may take turns inspecting retail service.

But with the larger chains it is necessary to employ inspectors who are unknown to the employees in the different stores. These inspectors ask innumerable questions before purchasing small articles. They may even try to annoy the salesman deliberately with a view to ascertaining his reaction.

It is frequently found that no endeavor to be insulting on the part of the inspector succeeds in ruffling the composure of the salesman. He neither loses his temper nor can he be tempted into making a discourteous retort. He frequently sends away the customer in the best of humor.

It often develops in the course of these inspection trips that points are noted which prove of importance enough to be incorporated in the store manual. This, after all, is the most important part of the inspector's work. Although employees who do not reflect credit on the company's training are eliminated, it is the constructive selling ideas which are of the most benefit.

Their purpose is fourfold:

1. They test the knowledge of the salesman in regard to his stock.
2. They find out whether he is tactful, polite, and considerate even under provocation.
3. They determine whether the salesman seeks to give real service to the patron.
4. They collect new selling ideas which may be applied with profit to the entire organization.

There are, of course, objections to this practice; but in general, it makes for the store's efficiency.

The Saleswoman.—Far less has been done in the line of training women in salesmanship, principally for the reason, as mentioned before, that the chain's efforts were directed towards educating men for store managers and higher positions. But there are signs that executives are beginning to realize the advantage to them of training the salesgirl. The following is taken from a notice to managers:

"Do you realize that the point of contact with the buying public is through your salesgirl? At first thought, some of your managers may be inclined to disagree on this point. A few may think that we are trespassing on their ground. But consider this: A manager's time must necessarily be divided over a great many duties. This does not leave him free to spend his entire time behind the counter. Therefore, he must rely, to a very considerable extent, upon the coöperation and loyalty of his salesgirls.

"Are you managers just paying the salesgirl her weekly wage and dismissing all further responsibility towards her? Or, are you giving her a little insight into your business? Have you convinced her that yours is a Quality store and that she has every reason to be proud of standing behind your counters and selling Quality goods? Have you made her feel that she has a responsibility in the successful operation of your store?"

The New York Department of Labor found in one of the smallest up-state stores a system of giving sales stimulus to the girls by means of an "efficiency rating card." The manager, who was new and young, gave the girl with the highest rating every week a bonus. Rating was apportioned as follows: 10 per cent. for discipline, tidiness, etc.; 10 per cent. for general appearance of counters and shelves; 5 per cent. for having counters and shelves filled; 5 per cent. for having paper and cord on hand; 15 per cent. for having merchandise displayed for selling merits; 15 per cent. for having the under-counters absolutely clean and in order; 15 per cent. for having the price signs in the right places; 10 per cent. for remembering to register money before wrapping; 10 per cent. for care in reducing shrinkage, and 5 per cent. for politeness to customers. The small allowance for politeness is significant in this case as showing the attitude of the five and ten cent store towards the actual manner of making sales.

For a store which, like the five and ten cent store, must keep expenses down to the minimum, such a system offers inducement to the girls for good service and at the same time does not appreciably increase wage expenses. One five and ten cent store chain has a special training force of six women who are constantly on the road opening new stores, selecting employees, and adjusting grievances in stores already opened. Another chain endeavored to get local managers to start classes among the sales girls for training in salesmanship.

Conclusions.—As conclusion to this chapter, one of the general letters sent out by this chain for these training classes shows the type of educational matter best fitted for the salesgirl.

General Letter
Training of Sales Force

The following article is copied from a current magazine:

A Cause and a Cure

Desiring to learn the reason why certain retail customers had discontinued buying goods from them, a large department store made an investigation among 197 different households, as a result of which they compiled the following statistics. *H*ere is what the customers gave as their reason:

1. Indifference of salespeople..........   47
2. Attempts at substitution......................   24
3. Errors...   18
4. Tricky methods...................................   16
5. Slow deliveries.   17
6. Over-insistence of salespeople....................   16
7. Insolence of salespeople   16
8. Unnecessary delays in service....................   13
9. Tactless business policies.........................   11
10. Bad arrangement of store.......................   9
11. Ignorance concerning goods   6
12. Refusal to exchange goods....   4

Total.. 197

The fact which is most forcibly brought out in these statistics is the large percentage of reasons given for which the clerks or salespeople were directly responsible.   There are the ones numbered 1, 2, 6, 7, and 11 in the table shown.

*H*ere are 109, at least, out of the 197 households interviewed, or a little over 55 per cent., who gave such reasons as indifference, insolence, ignorance, and over-insistence on the part of the sales people as the cause of the discontinuance of their patronage.

When it comes down to a final analysis of the situation, the clerks were not so much to blame as the store management.   . . .

In this connection, we cannot over-emphasize the importance of the saleswoman's position in your store, as the connecting link between the management and the customer.

The advantage of training men for promotion has been amply proved by experience.   The advantage of training salesmen and salesgirls in standardized chain methods of service and salesmanship is becoming more and more apparent.   It cannot help succeeding because it is economically profitable to all parties concerned.

1. The chain obtains a larger volume of sales.
2. The clerks obtain a larger bonus and more rapid promotion. ·

As a general thing, the better training the clerks receive, the better type of personnel is secured, more profits accrue, and better wages can be paid.

CHAPTER XIV

MAINTAINING MORALE

House magazine.
1. Published in interest of personnel.
2. Maintains contact
    (*a*) Between various links in organization.
    (*b*) By personal bits of information.
    (*c*) By photographs.
3. Makes known the policy of the company.
    (*a*) Articles by executives published.
4. Policy of magazine must be in accord with policy of organization.
Results of morale.
1. Discipline.
    (*a*) Importance of rules.
        1. Each store representative of the whole organization.
    (*b*) Necessity of making clerks see it is for their own good to maintain discipline.
2. Teamwork.
    (*a*) Feeling of goodwill among employees
        1. Towards company.
        2. Towards each other.
3. Increased profits
    (*a*) For company.
    (*b*) For individual members of personnel.

CHAPTER XIV

MAINTAINING MORALE

The morale of an organization may be called its mental state. This mental state is not stationary, but is constantly fluctuating in response to the many influences brought to bear from all sides on the company and its employees. The company which maintains the morale of its organization at a high pitch is usually successful financially, because an upward trend in morale is directly reflected in profits.

"Good morale," says R. S. Woodworth, in his book on Psychology, "means more than willingness for duty; it means 'pep' or positive zest for action. Where the master is able, in the first place, to show the servant the objective need and the value of the goal, and to leave the initiative in respect to ways and means to the servant, looking to him for results, the servant often responds by throwing himself into the enterprise as if it were his own—as, indeed, it properly is in such a case."

The aim of all methods of personnel administration is to maintain this morale, and, where it did not previously exist, to build it up. Maintaining morale for the chain store organization is especially important because of the geographical distances separating the various links and the consequent impossibility of individual supervision of the personnel. Therefore, this feeling of interest in the company and its activities which we call morale must be kept up by other means.

In the case of a factory, morale is a factor in production; in the case of a chain store organization, it is a factor in selling. To obtain maximum results, it is necessary to analyze morale and ascertain by what means it can best be secured.

The Elements of Morale.—There are five points to be considered ordinarily by the chain management in its efforts to improve and maintain its morale.

1. The company must inspire the employee with confidence

in it, in its officers, and in its policies. This is a necessary requisite for morale, since there can be no discipline and teamwork where there is no confidence.

2· The company must give its employees some financial interest in the business as a reward for efficient service.

3. The employee must feel he is working towards a definite goal. Through his own experience and by observing others he must realize that promotion is won mainly by his own efforts. He should be shown how he is progressing from week to week and from month to month.

4. The element of competition should be present. The clerk in the store should be able to compare his achievements with those of clerks in other stores. Furthermore, some degree of responsibility should be thrown upon his shoulders.

5. The company should try to make its employees feel that they are members of one family. That is, it must make them acquainted with each other and with the company. The employee should feel that what touches the company's welfare touches his as well.

No organization can score 100 per cent. on the question of morale, but it is possible to maintain morale at a high level. It is generally accomplished by the use of some or all of the methods discussed in the rest of this chapter. Which particular methods are used depends a great deal on the size of the chain and also on the size of the units in the chain. The question of morale in a five- and ten-cent store organization has two aspects first the morale of the store employees in relation to the store, and second the morale of the store manager in relation to the whole organization. The small chain can do without, and, in fact, from motives of economic operation, must do without such methods of maintaining morale as the house organ. In the very small chain morale is enforced and maintained by daily personal visits of the executive. It is also possible for the various store managers to hold frequent conferences. But, although methods differ, the purpose remains the same, namely, to secure the coöperation of the employee in the activities of the company.

Methods of Creating Morale.—There are five ordinary methods of securing proper morale:

1. Conferences.
2. Daily letters and bulletins.
3. Contests.
4. Rewards and special bonuses.
5. A house organ.

The first two methods will make the employees of the company interested in their work and confident in their own future as well as that of the company. Contests bring in the element of competition. Rewards and bonuses give that financial stimulus which chain organizations have found essential, and the house organ endeavors to create the family spirit, to acquaint the employees with the policies of the company, and to furnish a medium of publicity.

Conferences.—Conferences, of one kind and another, are essential. In all chains they should form part of the routine. There are several types of conferences, strictly business meetings, confined mainly to executives and store managers, and meetings which aim to introduce the element of good fellowship, such as dinners and conventions.

Some chains have an annual convention at which all managers attend who can possibly do so. Policies and plans for the coming year are outlined and explained. The various local men have an opportunity to get away from the somewhat narrowing precincts of their own stores and to obtain a broader view of the organization in its entirety.

Conferences during the year are often held at stated intervals. Where chains are limited in geographical extent, all managers can usually attend. Where chains are more extended, district conferences may be held, and the problems brought up at that time discussed a second time in a conference of district managers. Conferences may take the form of dinners when it is believed the more informal atmosphere will lead to better results.

Where the personnel of a single store is fairly large, as in a department store or five- and ten-cent store, conferences and meetings should be held frequently. As mentioned previously, these conferences may be made the occasion of instructing salesmen and salesgirls in better methods of salesmanship.

Some chains have adopted a policy of giving outings to which all employees are invited. Such a policy increases the feeling of goodwill among the organization.

Special conferences may be held when the percentage of a certain member store shows a marked falling off. The entire staff may be called in to go over the specific problems of the particular store. This avoids any unjust action. Reprimands often do more harm than good, especially as investigation frequently shows that bad conditions are due to external circumstances not apparent at first glance.

Bulletins and Letters.—Keeping up morale is a ceaseless task. Good advice and good intentions are lost sight of unless in some way brought to mind. The store manager appreciates help of this nature. He is constantly reminded of what he already knows but is in danger of forgetting in the stress of the day's work and the monotony of his routine.

Perhaps these bulletins give pointers and tips as to selling goods. Perhaps there is a list of averages in which he can find the position of his own store. A mere list of changes in price of products to be sold usually forms a part of the bulletin, and, although a necessary part, still it is just as necessary to keep in mind the question of the store manager's morale.

In writing these bulletins there is danger, on the one hand, of becoming too prosy and on the other, to use the vernacular, too "peppy." There is a point between the two as is well shown by the following extract on the subject of window trims. See how cleverly instruction, stimulus, and praise are mingled:

"Which One of the Five Senses Produces the Most Dollars?"

"Is it the sense of sight—or the sense of hearing—or the sense of smell—or the sense of taste—or the sense of touch?

"A recent investigation was made to determine through which one of the five senses sales were really made. The results were astounding: 87 per cent. of the people bought the things they saw (in the windows, on the counters, in the showcases, etc.); 7 per cent. bought as a result of hearing; 3½ per cent. through the sense of smell; 1½ per cent. through the sense of touch; 1 per cent. through the sense of taste.

"Think of it!—87 per cent. of the people buy by sight. Doesn't that drive home the importance of attractive window displays? Doesn't that make you stop and wonder whether your displays are as attractive as they can possibly be? Doesn't that make you realize that the time and effort you put forth to trim your windows is worth everything to you?

"Maybe you are smiling as you read this. Perhaps you are saying to yourself that it is old stuff. Yet, we wonder how your windows look at eight in the morning. We wonder whether they are bare or there! We wonder if you are saying that you can't trim your windows early because your stuff isn't out of the oven yet. We wonder if you feel that it isn't worth the effort to trim windows before noon because nobody passes your store before 10 a.m.—and as we wonder, we keep on producing display ideas and showcards just because we known that our progressive managers are everlastingly looking for new stuff—new thoughts —new displays—anything and everything that will help them to make their windows more attractive.

"We know that the live Federal managers have a window trim of some sort at 8 a.m., even if it is just a few cards placed in the window—anything to give the appearance that they are still in business—anything to attract the attention of the average person who passes the store from eight until noon.

"And as you read this message, do you wonder why the stores that always have attractive windows usually do the most business?"

"Has this straight-from-the-shoulder message convinced you that of the five senses, the sense of sight can produce more dollars than all the others? We wonder!"

Note that the above article first proves the value of window displays in making sales, then applies it to the particular problems of the Federal System of Bakeries, and finally brings the matter down to the store manager himself, telling him how to use this bulletin to increase his sales. It is well-written and neither too dignified nor too familiar. Such bulletins as this prove helpful in the maintenance of morale.

Contests.—Nothing is better for the morale of the organization than a good contest with some worth-while prizes for the winner. Everybody is on his or her tiptoes, and sales are bound to pick up. From the chain's point of view it is like the man who advertised he would give $5 for the best bushel of potatoes he received by a certain date, and in a few days had received more than a hundred bushels of prize potatoes. The chain pays a small amount to the winner and received in return the united efforts of the sales personnel. There is a definite goal in view and each member has an opportunity to show what he or she can do.

The most common plan is to give cash prizes to stores making the most sales, to be divided among the employees of that store.

The contest may take the form of the store making the most sales winning, or it may be the store which shows the greatest improvement in sales over the previous month.

The Federal System of Bakeries has evolved a rather novel contest idea. The contest is treated as a horse race, each store serving as a horse and each manager as a jockey. The races are divided into various events. There are national races and in addition there are inter-district races. For example, in July 1921, a purse of $300 was divided with three prizes for each of the six districts in the country.

The results are reproduced from the Federal Sunlight Magazine with details of the contest in the first district.

SUMMARY OF JULY INTER-DISTRICT RACES

A total purse of $300.00, divided six ways to cover the six events which constituted the July Inter-District Races, was awarded as follows:

1st Race—The Knickerbocker Special
First —Little Falls, N. Y	$25.00
Second—Stamford, Conn	15.00
Third —Amsterdam, N. Y	10.00

2d Race—The Keystone Handicap
First —Elizabeth, N. J	$25.00
Second—Meadville, Pa	15.00
Third —Duquesne, Pa	10.00

3d Race—The Southern Sweepstakes
First —Valdosta, Ga	$25.00
Second—Brunswick, Ga	15.00
Third —Jacksonville, Fla., No. 1	10.00

4th Race—Great Lakes Special
First —Rock Island, Ill., No. 3	$25.00
Second—Wabash, Ind	15.00
Third —Belleville, Ill	10.00

5th Race—Mississippi River Suburban
First —Davenport, Ia.; No. 2	$25.00
Second—Knoxville, Tenn., No. 1	15.00
Third —Springfield, Mo., No. 1	10.00

6th Race—Great Western Derby
First —Bartlesville, Okla	$25.00
Second—Long Beach, Cal	15.00
Third —Okmulgee, Okla	10.00

Reports of how races were run. (Note: Names of jockeys have been changed in some instances, but official rewards for July are as given.)

15

First Race

Horses	Jockeys	Position at finish	Percentage of increase in retail sales for July over June
Little Falls, N. Y.............	E. J. Andrews	1	24.0
Stamford, Conn.....	Mrs. Mabel Carrow	2	17.4
Amsterdam, N. Y....	J. A. Schmidt	3	16.7
Norwalk, Conn..............	G. N. Carrow	4	14.6
Albany, N. Y..............	Mary Murphy	5	12.7
Freeport, L. I., N. Y..........	Lela Hatch	6	11.5
Lynn, Mass.................	John Riley	7	11.0
Rome, N. Y.................	Mrs. Lee O'Brien	8	10.3
Hempstead, N. Y.............	Frank H. Baker	9	9.1
Bridgeport, Conn....	Frank Oberg	10	7.8
Boston, Mass., No. 4— Dock Square..............	K. O'Hara	11	7.6
Mt. Vernon, N. Y.......... ...	W. R. Anderson	12	7.4
Binghamton, N. Y..	Mrs. Chris Bleichert	13	7.2
Rochester, N. Y.......... ...	Albert H. Royer	14	6.5
Peekskill, N. Y..............	Mrs. R. Payne	15	5.4
Jamaica, N. Y..............	A. F. Schneider	16	3.9
Yonkers, N. Y.............	H. J. Konecny	17	3.0
Boston, Mass., No. 5— Massachusetts Ave..	A. M. Hobart	18	0.6

Also ran in order named: Boston, Mass., No. 3, Canal St.; Boston, Mass., No. 1, Federal St.; White Plains, N. Y.; Flushing, N. Y.; Boston, Mass., No. 2, Tremont St.; Elmira, N. Y.; Holyoke, Mass.; Brooklyn, N. Y.; Syracuse, N. Y.; Northampton, Mass.; Westfield, Mass.; Buffalo, N. Y.; New York City, No. 4.

Remarks: Little Falls turned in a remarkable performance and led all the way. Stamford, the favorite, could not get up. Amsterdam, who finished third, ran a pretty race. Bridgeport and Albany were raced into submission by Norwalk. The others never had a chance. Winner trained by T. J. Madden.

A contest, to be successful, must stimulate enough interest to bring the winner either money, notoriety, or both. The more publicity given to these contests, the better success they have. If no house organ is published, bulletins should be sent out. If the contest stretches over a long period, bulletins should be sent out giving the status of the contestants.

Rewards.—Rewards are closely allied with contests, the difference being that in the latter case there is open competition, and in the former the result is, as a rule, unsolicited. For example, when an employee of the Whelan organization performs any service which brings him to the attention of the main office, Mr. Whelan would write him a personal letter of commendation and thanks. Inasmuch as contests and rewards must have publicity to be effectual, the letter is mailed in a flaring red envelope so that everyone in the office or store cannot help knowing it has been received and the nature of the contents. To make matters doubly certain, the reward is announced in the monthly bulletin.

Most chains give Christmas presents, at which time special merit may be rewarded. Frequently the basis of the amount of a Christmas present is the length of service, thus placing a premium on steady employment.

All bonuses are in the nature of a reward for work and attention above the average, but reward in the sense of being limited to recognition of acts on the part of the employees beyond the mere duty of routine selling and managing. Recognizing such acts is an excellent method of acquiring the goodwill of the employees.

The House Organ.—House organs published by chain organizations are employee publications, or internal house organs. They are published solely in the interests of the personnel. A house organ is one of the methods of maintaining morale where personal contact is lacking. It reproduces the results of contests, gives personal news about the various employees, and their views on different company matters. It is not only a clearing house for gossip but should also contain certain "inspired" articles from the central office.

Robert E. Ramsay has made an excellent summary of the vital points to be kept under constant consideration in editing a house organ of this nature.

1. Analysis of the policy.
2. Purpose.
    (a) Sales.
    (b) Goodwill.
    (c) Educational.

3. The editor.
4. The name—a freak or unusual name will not wear well and may lead to discontinuance.
5. A sub-title which makes clear the plan and purpose of the publication.
6. Size and analysis of the field to be reached.
7. Frequency of issue—very important and must be lived up to.
8. Cover design.
    (a) Permanent.
    (b) Changed each issue.
9. Style of appeal.
    (a) Language.
    (b) Personality.
    (c) Atmosphere.

In addition to these points it is very necessary to make a budget of expenses of publication. Owing to the constant circulation, this should not be difficult. All material is either "inspired" from headquarters, prepared by the editor, or got from the branches and their personnel. There is no difficulty in obtaining material, due to the universal desire to appear in print.

There is one important point to observe in editing the house organ and that is a careful agreement between the policy of the house and the policy of the publication. The two must be identical. One other point to remember is that the average person objects to "ginger" and "pep" literature. He would much prefer a simple, lucid explanation of the facts and how they apply to him. All sermonizing and moralizing should be done carefully. A busy salesman has no time to read sermons. But he will read articles about his business and about himself and about the other members of the personnel, because he is interested.

House organs are ordinarily illustrated with photographs of various members of the personnel, their stores, their sweethearts, etc. The Federal Sunlight Magazine has the back cover made so that it can be cut out and used for a window paster by the manager.

The editor of the magazine should be in the closest touch with the controlling head of the business, who often looks over the proof before printing. The editor himself, according to Mr. Ramsay, must be author, feature writer, advertising man, investigator, salesman, preacher without seeming to preach, teacher without seeming to teach, reporter, proof reader, and planner.

To conclude, the editor of "The Acme Special," Fred. B. Barton, says: "We try to have this paper hold the Acme family together in a unit, to keep up the family feeling, even though Bill Jones at Acme 6 may only see Tom Smith at Acme 56 once a year. Also we mix in a little educational and inspirational matter now and then. We believe that the paper has some effect in making men satisfied with their jobs and encouraging them to grow into better positions and to look ahead to a real future with our company."

Enforcing Morale and Results.—There are two methods of checking up the morale of a chain organization. The first is to employ a corps of inspectors who will personally see that the policies and plans of the central office are carried out. The second is to allow the personnel to evolve its own morale under the inspiration and educational leadership of the head office. By the second method the responsibility is as far as possible shifted from the chain to the employees.

But, however spontaneous the maintenance of morale may become, the central office of the chain must exercise some supervision. In large organizations this can be done only through a special department which will be in part the personnel department, although it may go under a variety of names. In smaller chains, this supervision must be exercised by some other department, probably the sales department.

Good morale manifests itself in the three following ways:

1. Effective discipline, cheerfully submitted to.
2. Spirit of coöperation.
3. Increased profits to personnel and company.

The first two are necessary to produce the last. Other things being equal, if the first two can be secured, the last will follow as a natural corollary.

Discipline.—What does discipline mean to a chain organization? It does not necessarily mean that the assistant must say "Mister" when addressing the manager, as one chain vainly attempts to enforce. It is something much broader and more important. In a way, every branch store in the chain and every clerk in the store is representative of every other store and clerk in the chain. If one manager allows his store to become dirty and remain so, the trouble is not confined to his store or to him alone, but all the other stores doing business under the same name suffer also. Thus discipline in a chain organization means the uniform observance of policies laid down by the central office as wise and proper.

If it is decided that stores should open at eight o'clock, there should be no exceptions without excellent reason. It is easy to see that a customer who is used to buying from one store in the chain which opens at eight o'clock would not be pleased on going to another store in the same chain to find that it opens at nine. If a clerk in one store of the chain sends away a disgruntled customer, that customer will hesitate to go to another store in the chain, no matter how amiable its clerks may be.

A high morale enforces discipline because the clerks can be brought to see that discipline must be enforced for the good of everyone concerned. Rules and regulations become but printed words without effect unless there is some method of enforcing them. The best method yet found lies in the interest of the employee to obey them without constant inspection. The methods of building up morale, previously described, should have, therefore, as one of their first effects, the maintenance of discipline.

Teamwork.—Teamwork is an essential part of chain store organization, especially since the organization must of necessity be so loosely joined. Therefore, another beneficial result of maintaining a high morale is a spirit of coöperation, not possible to define in so many words, but possible to understand. A chain of stores is a very sensitive mechanism and only the most careful attention to routine makes it possible for it to function well and efficiently. Thus, coöperation between all links of the personnel is a fundamental requisite.

A chain which does not possess the goodwill of its employees may be counted a failure. No matter how methodical and machine-like its methods of supervision, it cannot substitute methods for men. A chain store organization must build up a structure of personalities, not of mere store fronts.

A high morale creates interest in the work because it points out where the employee may better himself and get in line for rapid promotion. The best system of morale is one which points out where the individual himself can benefit. The fundamental idea is to work together for the benefit of each one.

Conclusions.—The question of morale lies between the employer and the worker. Although it is to the ultimate benefit of both parties, the incentive and the control must be furnished by the management. The employee must in a variety of ways be made to feel:

1. That the enterprise is his.
2. That he is fairly treated.
3. That he has a just share in the proceeds.
4. That he has a genuine interest in the purpose of the concern.
5. That he is interested in the work itself.

The composite effect will show itself in an excellent *esprit de corps*. This morale, in turn, will cause greater sales effort, as well as better coördinated sales effort. In fact, for the loosely jointed chain organization, the practical alternatives are between creating and maintaining good morale and suffering under the hardship of the indifference and even hostility of the employees.

CHAPTER XV

THE STORE MANAGER

OUTLINE

Requisites.
1. Personal.
    - (a) Interest in work.
    - (b) Oblivious of long hours.
    - (c) Courtesy.
    - (d) Honesty.
2. Managerial.
    - (a) Sales personality.
    - (b) Ability to handle subordinates.
    - (c) Judgment.

Duties.
1. Clerical.
    - (a) Make daily reports.
        1. Sales report.
        2. Merchandise requirements.
        3. Expenses.
        4. Miscellaneous.
2. Financial.
    - (a) Responsible for receipts.
    - (b) Responsible for stock.
3. Moral.
    - (a) Make store connecting link between corporation and customer.
4. Managerial.
    - (a) Store neat and clean.
    - (b) Stock properly arranged and tagged.
    - (c) Service to customers.

Authority governed by
1. Policy of company.
2. Size of chain and degree of personal supervision.
3. Size of store.
    - (a) Large store manager's considerable authority.
        1. Refund money.
        2. Cut prices.
        3. Make purchases.
        4. Employ help.
        5. Arrange stock.
        6. Etc.
    - (b) Small store's small authority.
        1. Close supervision.

CHAPTER XV

THE STORE MANAGER

No man succeeds in anything he does unless he is interested in it. Few men are satisfied unless they can increase their monetary compensation as a result of their own efforts. The ordinary man prefers to work for himself rather than to work for others. There is much disagreement among chain organizations as to just what the final secret of success in chain management is, but the consensus of opinion on the greatest weakness of the chain is unanimous. The chain is strong in proportion as it holds the undivided and whole-hearted allegiance of its store managers. If a branch store is to compete successfully with independent stores, the man in charge of that branch must feel he is able to earn as large an amount of money as the owner of the independent store next door.

All chains recognize that some inducement must be held out to the store manager. He must be given a bonus, a commission on sales, or encouraged by some other expedient into devoting himself completely to the interests of the chain. In return for his services as evidenced by increased sales, more rapid turnover, etc., the manager receives a larger return, a more profitable store to manage, perhaps advancement into the central organization. In other words, the chain organization must keep the road to promotion wide open. Any stoppage along the route means stagnation. The progress of the store manager is unmistakably evident to the executive at headquarters by the figures as to that store.

Choosing the Manager.—What kind of a man is needed by the chain in order to train him into a capable and efficient store manager? Mr. Woolworth said: "I prefer the boy from the farm to the college man. The college man won't start at the bottom and learn the business." This may be a prejudiced view, but it represents the statement of opinion of one of the great chain store pioneers. And every man in the Woolworth

233

organization must at some time have served behind the counter. For every position there are two understudies, and each place is won by merit. It is a rule never to go outside the organization for a manager or higher position.

When the Penney organization wants men, the following advertisement appears in local papers:

"Men wanted. Well established mercantile concern, operating 313 retail stores, offers:

1. Long and continuous hours of work.
2. The work itself, hard, ceaseless, trying, testing.
3. The work drive unrelenting, day in and day out.
4. And for it, a small living salary, perhaps less than you are getting now."

Mr. Penney says:

"I have generally found the young man coming from the small towns of the Middle West making the best all-round men. They have not been spoiled by big cities and they know how to live within their income.

"The men in our organization must not drink, gamble, or smoke cigarettes. We like to get college men.

"A man is started as a salesman behind the counter. We learn to know him and he learns to know us. If he makes good, time will come when he is put in charge of a store, usually an offshoot of the one where he has been working. The next time he changes, he gets an interest in his first store. If he doesn't have money, we lend it to him. If he is a big success in that store, he can then start other stores."

These statements are enough to show what two authorities think. President Wattley of the National Drug Stores believes in young men, constructively trained, carefully watched, properly placed, and backed by the corporation. He himself had formerly picked the managers for the Liggett stores. His requirements for a manager are that he should have a pleasant personality, ready courtesy, and be strong in discipline—a man who can enforce his discipline with a smile, is, according to him, the one who makes the 100 per cent. success.

Briefly, chains acquire new employees—

1. By offering inducements to men already established in other chains,
2. By taking in men who have already had retail experience in other lines,
3. By training a force of their own.

By such means the chains have, as a general rule, succeeded in acquiring a sales and managerial force far above the ordinary retail average.

The third method is the one usually employed by the large chains and as far as possible by the smaller organizations. If a chain expands faster than the personnel can be adequately trained, then men must be sought outside, but it may prove as dangerous to expand without adequate and capable personnel as it is to expand without sufficient financial reserves.

The first method is sometimes used, but the user runs great risk of incurring the ill-will of the chain from which the men have been taken.

The smaller chain can maintain personal contact with the store managers, while the larger chains must rely on methods. Therefore, the large chain must exercise double care in putting its trust in a man who controls stock amounting to thousands of dollars.

The Duties of a Store Manager.—The duties of a branch manager vary in accordance with the size of the chain, the policy of the organization in regard to delegating authority, and the individual capability of the man in charge of the store. A good manager will always find things to do outside the strict interpretation of his duties as outlined by the central management.

A store manager will, in all cases, have to make daily reports, he will have to see that cash taken in is banked, he will be required to keep the appearance of his store as neat, clean, and attractive as possible. He may have the responsibility of hiring the clerks. He may or may not settle for overhead expenses.

The efficient store manager knows that, in the last analysis, his success in that position which he holds lies in the hands of the purchasing public, and that the way to attract the public is to give them service. A chain store, of course, can give service in many other ways other than by delivering goods and extending credit. A low price is a form of service, a well-arranged and complete stock is another form of service, and courtesy to the customer is still another form. And at this point we might mention the effect of the manager's personality as a form of service.

Authority.—The direct control which the manager has over his store is delegated to him by the central organization as its agent.   Thus the first great point in delimiting the authority of the branch manager is the policy of the company in this respect.

1. *Company policy.*   Some chain systems regard a store manager as merely a clerk over whom supervision must be exercised by other means than direct personal control.   He may not be allowed to hire clerks, to make any purchases, or to withdraw any money from receipts for contingent expenses.   There is no universality or standard practice used in regard to branch managers.

2. *The size of the chain.*   Generally speaking, the smaller the chain, the smaller the responsibility of the store manager. Thus if the chain system were confined to a single town, the manager would probably not be allowed to make any purchases. All goods would come to him direct from the main warehouse.   If a package were broken, he would have to keep the actual package for the inspection of the management or else be charged with the retail price of this package.   He would employ no help, as the central organization would do this.   However, this is not confined to small chains, since the United Cigar Stores train salesmen themselves and then distribute them to member stores.

Where a number of branch stores are close together under the constant supervision of a district manager, their authority will be less than where the units are broadly scattered.   In the latter case, the manager may be almost autonomous.

3. *The type of product.*   The manager of a store containing large floor space and varied stock necessarily must have broader authority.   He has more men and women working under him. His volume of sales is larger, his stock of goods is more valuable. He receives a larger salary.   For example the manager of a branch dry goods store may have to have a large amount of authority.   He may be authorized to refund money, make exchanges, cut prices to meet competition, increase advertising appropriations, employ extra sales help, sell loss leaders, divide departments to suit himself, employ and discharge help, raise and lower wages, purchase goods, veto price recommendations made by the home office, and select the goods he wishes to sell from samples submitted by the purchasing department.   In this case, it is the manager who must meet the competition by adapting his policies to meet local conditions.

In a grocery store, we have the other extreme. There are often many of these stores belonging to one organization in a community. The store manager has no authority as to what he shall sell or the price at which he shall sell. The manager is there to see that instructions from the warehouse or buyer as to prices and goods to be sold are carried out. The goods from the warehouse are invoiced to him at retail prices and he must sell his quota.

The manager of a shoe store carrying a branded, advertised line might be required to conduct his store according to strict rules laid down by the home office as to prices and advertising, but he has latitude in his choice of styles to sell and his method of selling them.

As to the authority of a manager in a five- and ten-cent store, it is said that the manager of each local store is responsible to his district office, which in turn is under the central office, and from that office originate all important orders. The manager has little to say regarding the policies under which the store to which he is sent is to operate. He is transferred by the central office from one store to another, from one city to another, as his supervisor thinks best. As one manager put it: "If it isn't a promotion it's a demotion, and it's not up to you to fuss about it."

From what has been said, it is easy to see that no set rules can be laid down for limiting or extending the authority of the branch manager. In each case, it will be dictated by the policy of the controlling body as modified by circumstances.

Moral Responsibilities.—The majority of chain systems have been able to create an *esprit de corps* which goes a long way towards offsetting the disadvantages experienced in finding and training branch managers. Such a spirit must exist if the chain is to expand and be successful. This feeling is obtained partly, of course, by arranging a scale of remuneration to fit the ambition of the type of man desired, but money alone would never be sufficient. There must be this sense of moral responsibility which the branch manager has for his store.

The manager becomes a part of the system, on the one hand, and a part of the community in which the store is located, on the other. He is the connecting link between the impersonal chain and the customers. He wishes the chain to appear well in the eyes of the public, as judged through his store. Therefore, he keeps it neat and clean, and forgets to note the overtime he spends in making it attractive. He has a feeling of pride in the store and something very much akin to a feeling of ownership. The chains which make the yoke of the necessary accounting routine weigh as lightly as possible, and place the largest premium on the individuality of the store manager, have little difficulty in securing the loyalty of this branch of the personnel. The man who is working for himself pays little heed to hours or wages.

Financial Responsibilities.—The manager is not only morally responsible for his store, but he is financially responsible. He must look out for the stock and for the money taken in from sales. This responsibility differs in actual practice. In some chains no one but the manager is permitted to open the cash drawer or make change. A clerk may take money from a customer, but he has to call the manager to put it in the cash drawer or make change. The rule may seem strict in this case, but it places all responsibility fairly and squarely upon the shoulders of the store manager.

Usually a store manager should be required to put up a cash bond, and any shrinkage in stock which is unaccounted for is likely to be deducted from this bond. Allowance is made, of course, for shrinkages which are unavoidable in any chain. Bonding should be required in chains where the responsibility of the manager financially can be adequately protected in this way. A manager with a great deal of authority naturally cannot measure his honesty by any such method, since his position alone is in the nature of a bond. But for the manager of a small branch store a bond is at once a gauge of his honesty and a guard against temptation.

Ordinarily cash receipts from the daily sales in the branch store are put in the local bank. In some local chains cash is collected daily by an employee of the chain. In the Penney stores receipts are banked, subject to New York draft, three times a week. In some chains, the manager may be allowed to deduct sums necessary to pay current expenses, connected with the operation of the store. In other chains, a "contingent fund" is provided for means of paying such bills and providing change. Every expenditure, however, must be vouchered, and each week the manager must make a report of the condition of the fund and send in his vouchers for verification. This permits depositing the results of each day's business in total and an audit of vouchers plus an examination of cash in the "contingent fund" quickly establishes actual expenditures of the store.

As a general principle, all money taken in by branch stores is concentrated at headquarters. This is done for two reasons:

1. Purchasing functions are centralized in one place and all other major expenses, salaries, bonuses, etc., also are paid direct from the central organization.

2. It is easier to teach the average man how to sell goods than it is to teach him finance. The less he has to do with financial responsibilities, other than those absolutely necessary, the better he performs his other duties.

Knowledge of Stock.—Every properly trained store manager knows his stock thoroughly. This is a fundamental requisite of salesmanship and even although in the majority of cases goods in chain stores sell themselves without the aid or effort of the clerk in expressing their advantages, a knowledge of stock is necessary. Stock must be turned as rapidly as possible. The only way to secure rapid turnover is to specialize on those goods which have shown themselves to be best sellers.

But in all cases there will be some goods that move faster than others. The manager who can keep the slow stock turning over is the most valuable. Thorough knowledge of stock is required before the manager can order properly. He must be able to tell what will sell in his locality. Putting aside all questions of local preferences and seasonal preferences which are treated elsewhere, it is the duty of the manager to serve as the local interpreter between the public and the chain's purchasing agent. In the majority of cases the chain manager is allowed to pick out quantities of any article on the list sent out by the warehouse. The manager is supposed to be able to judge the wants of his customers and about how much they will buy.

The problem of knowing stock varies, of course, immensely with the type of goods sold. The problem of a drug store manager is far more complicated than that of the manager of a grocery chain, or than in the case of a hosiery store or shoe store the sales of which are limited to one product.

Knowledge of stock requires a proper care for details. Price tags should be properly fastened in place and changed promptly. It is bad policy to have a group of articles worth thirty cents marked ten cents because they happen to be occupying space formerly covered by a ten-cent article.

The manager must see that the appearance of the store is maintained at the proper standard. He must not only notify the central office of articles running low, but he must see that these articles are properly arranged when they arrive.

The Manager's Reports.—Daily reports should be made in all chains. The details of the report system, however, vary with the size of the chain and the type of product sold. The larger the chain, the more difficult it is to maintain personal contact with the branch stores. Hence it follows that the management must rely on statistical reports for its knowledge of the actual condition of a store. In small chains of five- and ten-cent stores, centralized within a comparatively small radius, where the owner is in almost daily touch with each store and knows the managers intimately, reports are valuable as checks on his judgment rather than as courts of last resort. It is almost as easy to over-emphasize the value of daily reports as it is to under-emphasize them.

Suppose, in the first instance, we take the daily reports required from branch managers of a large drug chain.

1. There is a daily sales report, showing all sales, cash and charges, and all receipts from sources other than cash sales. The total as shown by the report is deposited in the bank and the main office receives confirmation of this deposit from the bank direct.

2. Managers are required to make copies of all orders for merchandise. One of these is sent to the main office and supplies a constant record of purchases which is used as a check for buying.

3. Statement of condition of "contingent fund" is sent in daily, together with vouchers of bills paid.

4. All invoices for goods purchased are sent to the main office and immediately on receipt are charged against the purchase

account of the store. In order that they may be promptly audited and paid, it is necessary that receipt of the goods be established. For this purpose the quantities are omitted from one of the copies of the original order. When the goods reach the store, they are checked off on this sheet and quantities filled in. If there is breakage or other fault, mention is made on this sheet. It is dated as of the date of receipt of goods signed by and sent in daily by the manager. When this sheet is received in the main office, it is matched up with and attached to the invoice.

Inventory and turnover will be discussed in a separate chapter. Full and complete account of a model system of reports for a grocery chain will be found in the chapter "Controlling Retail Outlets."

Service to the Community.—The store manager, as has been said, is responsible to the organization for the reputation of the member store in the community. His position is much harder than that of the ordinary independent retailer who knows local conditions, and whose hold on the public has been built up through long and intimate service. The manager of a chain store is at once a link in an impersonal organization and a personal representative.

Some chains allow their managers to give special services at their own expense. Other chains make the manager conform to strict rule. The question of deliveries, for example, has come to be regarded in the light of a test of chain store efficiency. Managers in some chains are restricted so that they cannot make deliveries, even if the customer pays a price. The justification of this policy lies in the successful application. But there is and always will be a certain class of customer which wishes and demands service. As competition between chains becomes closer, the question of increased service to promote trade is sure to come up. For example, one grocery chain of fairly large size has resumed delivery service, while still selling goods on a par with competing chains. Deliveries, needless to say, are limited to a very restricted district.

Another disadvantage under which the chain store labors is that much of its trade, owing to the elimination of credits and deliveries, is transient. Yet, on the other hand, certain managers

16

have been able to obtain a regular class of customers, notably in the grocery chains.

This is where the personality of the manager shows its strongest results—in the manner in which service is rendered to the public.

Conclusions.—One most important point has been already treated elsewhere, namely, the method of paying store managers. Although properly belonging here, it was thought better to put the discussion of the principles involved under the chapter on organization, in which the store manager plays a leading part.

This chapter had been confined, as far as possible, to the store manager himself, and his duties towards the organization, and to the qualities which render him valuable to that organization. But considered from any point of view, the store manager is a vital link in the chain store problem. It is necessary to give him the same initiative, incentive, and interest in the business that is possessed by the independent owner of a retail store.

CHAPTER XVI

WAREHOUSING AND PURCHASING RECORDS

    3. Invoices paid but not received.

    4. Invoices pending allowances or disputes.

    5. Invoices pending claims against carriers.

(*c*) Receiving record.

(*d*) Re-checking and figuring unit cost.

(*e*) Entries on books of account and final payment.

(*f*) Permanent invoice files.

CHAPTER XVI

WAREHOUSING AND PURCHASING RECORDS

By John S. Fleek

The warehousing question and the purchasing question are very closely allied. It is a constant process of check and balance. Stock in the warehouse must be kept at normal and the purchasing department must be informed whenever there is a shortage or threatened shortage in supply. As has been shown in the previous discussion of the principles involved in proper warehousing and purchasing, this problem is one of the most important in chain store practice. It remains in this chapter to throw some light on the practical working-out of a typical warehousing and purchasing problem. As grocery chains are by far the most numerous, one of them has been used to illustrate typical accounting method.

Warehousing and purchasing come down, in the final analysis, to careful records of inventories, receipts, and shipments of goods needed to supply the retail outlets. Stock-keeping and stock records should aim to give the buyer the following information:

1. When to buy.
2. How much to buy.
3. From whom to buy.
4. The rate of stock turn.
5. Seasonal variations.
6. Transportation routes and time between order and delivery.

All these questions are likely to come up at any time and the ability to answer them correctly, quickly, and specifically is highly important from a financial point of view. Warehouse accounting is a prerequisite to intelligent buying and the conduct of the business as a whole. It gives the cash value of the goods on hand and indicates clearly whether the business can stand the

245

strain of further purchases.   It also forms a guide to the amount of insurance necessary to carry.

Stock Keeping and Stock Records.—The question which im-

Canned Corn	Size #2					
Curfew Brand	Pkd. 2 doz.					
Mfg. Jno. Jones Co.	Unit					
Page	Maximum 20 cases					
Standing Order	Minimum 5 cases					

Date	On Hand	Ordered		Receipts		Invoiced by
9-1-21	5 cases			9-1-21	15 c.	
9-15-21	19					A. L.
9-29-21	18					
10-14-21	16					
10-28-21	15					J. K.
11-12-21	14					
11-26-21	10					A. L.
12-8-21	5	12-7-21	10 c.			
12-22-21	4					
1-4-22	3			1-8-22	10 c.	A. L.
1-18-22	11					
2-1-22	5	2-2-22	10 c.			

Fig. 30.—Stock record card.

mediately arises here is how to combine, in the most convenient form, both completeness and simplicity.   One form, which may be recommended, employs a 5 × 8 in. vertical card (see Fig. 30) with three main columns "on hand," "ordered," and "received." A separate card is made out for every article carried in stock. At the top, this card bears the name and size of the article and the name of its source, whether manufacturer, grower, or broker. Then it gives the maximum quantity of stock it is desirable to keep on hand of this particular article, and also

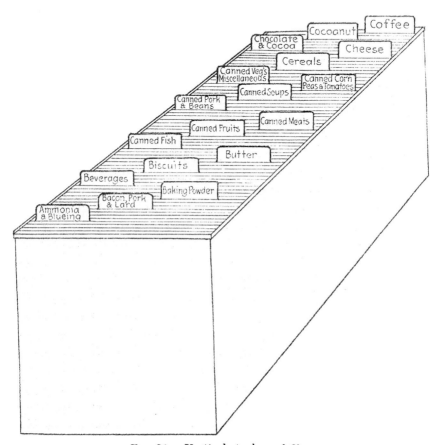

FIG. 31.—Vertical stock card file.

the minimum under which the amount of the article in stock must not be allowed to drop.

All articles leaving the warehouse are entered on these cards which serve to give the buyer information as to when and how much to buy. With some routine buying of steadily moving staple items, a standing weekly or monthly order will serve and, in that event, should be entered on the card. By having the man counting the stock and entering the quantity place his initials in the last column on the card, responsibility for a proper count is fixed.

These cards are to be kept in vertical files and indexed by groups, preferably in the same order as in the price list. All books or files containing data about the merchandise should be arranged in exactly the same order, so that consulting the various files or books will cause the least amount of effort. After a clerk becomes accustomed to the order of arrangement, he turns to the item almost automatically.

Figure 31 shows the arrangement of the cards in the vertical file. The headings on the cards, of course, can be varied at will.

Counting Stock.—Readily moving items should be counted weekly for stock on hand. Those with a lower rate of turnover should be counted bi-weekly, and others only monthly. A schedule can be constructed putting into certain groups for stock taking all articles carried. For example, if business at the warehouse is usually quieter on Tuesday, Wednesday and Saturday, a schedule can be worked out with this in view as follows:

Bi-weekly and monthly schedules taken on Tuesdays.
    Groups, V, VI, VII, VIII, IX, X, XI, XII.
Weekly schedules on Wednesdays and Saturdays.
    Groups I, II, III, IV.
The contents of the groups would be made up as follows:

WEEKLY	BI-WEEKLY	MONTHLY
I. Bacon, pork, lard	V. Baking powder	IX. Ammonia
Biscuits	Canned meats	Beverages
Butter	Canned soup	Canned fish
Cereals	Canned corn, tomatoes,	X. Canned fruits
Cheese	peas	Canned pork and beans
Cocoa and chocolate	Crisco and oils	Canned vegetables,
Coffee	VI. Dried beans and peas	misc.
II. Eggs	Dried fruits	XI. Cocoanut
Flour, meal, etc.	Extracts	Disinfectants and
Milk	Fish, salt	drugs
III. Soaps, laundry	Gelatines	Glassware
Soaps, powder	VII. Honeys, jams, jellies	Paper
Sugar	Macaroni	Polish
Teas	Relishes, pickles, etc.	XII. Soda and lime
IV. Yeast	VIII. Soaps, toilet	Vinegar
Matches	Spices	Woodenware and sup-
Salt	Molasses, syrups	plies
Starch	Tapioca	
Vegetables in season.		

Each chain would find it necessary to make a great many changes in the details of the arrangement outlined above but the fundamental idea can be adopted with little difficulty. On the basis as described here, the following control schedule can be made up for the month.

First week			Second week			Third week			Fourth week		
Tues.	Wed.	Sat.	Tues.	Wed.	Sat.	Tues.	Wed.	Sat.	Tues.	Wed.	Sat.
V	I	III	VII	I	III	V	I	III	VII	I	III
VI	II	IV	VIII	II	IV	VI	II	IV	VIII	II	IV
		IX			X			XI			XII

Under ordinary circumstances, the buyer would be responsible for having this schedule carried out. He takes the cards out of the file on the proper date and gives them to the stock man. The stock man, in turn, makes a physical count of goods on hand as indicated by the card headings and enters the result of his count. Then he returns the cards to the buyer who looks to see whether he needs to make any purchases.

If the buyer purchases anything he records the date and the quantity purchased in the order column, see Fig. 30. When the goods arrive the clerk who is responsible for receiving goods enters the date of receipt and the quantity. He may enter receipts first on a book and then enter the receipts later on the cards.

Methods of Accounting to Arrive at Cost.—In order to give the management the information it needs to carry on the business intelligently, it is necessary not only to build up a stock system that will show the turnover of each item carried, the time to buy, and the amount to pay, but also, by means of a system of cost keeping, to obtain an accurate record in figures from the accounting department of exactly where the business stands and just what is the cash value of inventories. This information should be current and, to be valuable, must be in strict agreement with the financial books. It should be available not only on the dates when the physical inventories at the warehouse are figured, but at all times. These stated physical inventories should then become only a check on the book values by the actual count of stock. If the system is not defective, and if the discrepancy between cash value of book inventory and cash value of physical inventory is slight, it is an indication that the records are working accurately. But if the discrepancy is great, there is a possibility of theft, which should be investigated. A large discrepancy usually is attributable either to theft, a poor system, or the careless handling of a good system.

The method here recommended is a simple one that has proved its value in cost-keeping of wholesale groceries and chain warehouses.

The foundation of all subsequent accounts for merchandise is based on the correct initial figuring and recording of the cost of merchandise purchased; that is, the entries for merchandise

FIRM	QUAN TITY	BRAND	SIZE	UNIT	PRICE	MDSE. DISC.	FRT.	CSH. DISC	FIRST COST	CHANGE COST	RE- TAIL	$

FIG. 32.—Page from cost record book.

on the merchandise account must be at the correct cost figure. For simplicity of illustration, various classifications of merchandise are not separated into separate accounts.

A cost record book is kept by the buyer or buyers. This book is indexed in exactly the same way as the price lists and card file. For a sample of convenient headings see Fig. 32. These include all the necessary information for those who desire it.

When the goods are received, the buyer figures their unit cost (taking net invoice price, not including cash discount, freight, cartage, and the like) and enters such data in the cost record book. At the same time he enters also the selling price in the book. In this way, the cost record book and records hereafter used for figuring cost of merchandise items in detail will give a unit cost that will correspond in proper ratio to the total cost as entered in the merchandise account by the bookkeeper. For example, the following bill is received.

JNO. JONES CO.			
To....................			
2% 10 days		Date.................	
	Price per Doz.	Quantity	Extension
10 Boxes Curfew Corn.........	$1.50	20	$30.00
Less 20% trade discount........			6.00
Net....................			24.00
Less 2%..................			.48
			23.52

The following freight list is for this shipment.

B. & A.—FREIGHT BILL			
To..............		From Jno. Jones Co.	
	Weight	Rate	Amount
10 Boxes Canned Corn..........	500	48	$2.40

The bookkeeper makes the following entries. .

Mdse. purchased	Freight & Cartage	Discount on purchases
$24.00	$2.40	$0.48

The buyer makes the following entries in his cost book.

Firm	Brand	Size	Unit	Price	Mdse. disc.	Frt.	Cash disc.	First cost net	Change cost	Sell price	% Mark up
Jones	Curfew	2		$1.50 per doz.	20%	.01	2%	.11		.15	26%

And the above results he writes on the bulletin, discussed in detail later, as follows:

Item	Cost	Retail
Curfew Corn.............................	.11	.15

From this the clerks concerned in the office enter the information on their cost and selling price lists.

Now assume that store No. 5 orders five cases of this corn. This order comes in on the regular order blank which is described in the section on retail accounting.

When this order has been filled and checked out by the shipping clerk, it comes back into the office to the cost clerks to be figured. From their price lists, which correspond exactly with the cost record book of the buyer, they enter as follows:

ORDER BLANK Store No. 5						
Units			Cost		Retail	
			Price	Amt.	Price	Amt.
5 Cases	120	Curfew Corn	.11	13.20	.15	18.00

Cost figures—WBC Retail—DEF	Posted By GH	Retail................	$18.00
		Cost.................	13.20
		Profit Gross..........	4.80

From this order blank the bookkeeper enters

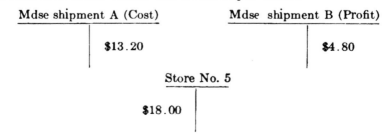

Mdse shipment A (Cost)	Mdse shipment B (Profit)
$13.20	$4.80

Store No. 5

$18.00

Now, let us suppose the fiscal period is at an end. A physical inventory is taken; and Curfew Corn is typical of every item in stock. The stock in the warehouse is counted and found to consist of five cases. This quantity is entered on the inventory sheet by the man counting stock. The inventory sheet is sent in to the buyer (or his assistant) to be priced. He refers to his cost record book (if the market remains unchanged) and enters the price on the inventory. It is next extended as follows:

Description		Unit	Price	Extensions
5 Cases	Curfew Corn.....	120	.11	$13.20
Totals........				$13.20

Since the assumption, for the sake of simplicity, is that Curfew Corn represents the whole stock of merchandise, the bookkeeper takes $13.20 as the total merchandise inventory for closing his books.

It can now be determined how near the book inventory is to the physical inventory. The bookkeeper closes into simple "merchandise trading account" the merchandise purchased and merchandise shipments at cost and freight on purchases.

Merchandise Trading Account			
Purchase................	$24.00	Mdse shipment A at cost..	$13.20
Frt. on purchase.........	2.40	Balance................	13.20
	$26.40		$26.40
Book Val. Inv...........	$13.20		

The book value of the inventory is now seen to be the same as the actual value after a physical count has been priced and extended from the cost record book. In other words, the cost and price lists have been kept in such a way that they tally with the accounts of the bookkeeper. The records used for the daily figuring of merchandise transactions in detail are seen to correspond to the books of accounts, and these figures taken off the books at any time (on short notice) can give a virtually accurate statement of actual condition. This is of great advantage to the management; for it gives at any time the following data:

(a) Cash (book) value of merchandise inventory (warehouse) at cost.
(b) Shipments to the company's retail stores at cost and at retail.
(c) Book profit (Gross) for the whole business and per store.

Price Changes.—The above case assumed is a simple one and an ideal one. As a matter of fact, the market is shifting up or down a great deal; and besides, goods are constantly deteriorating in the warehouse stock. It is necessary, therefore, to set up two more accounts "Warehouse Mark-ups and Mark-downs" and "Salvage."

In the case of the first, suppose that the buyer now purchases ten cases more of Curfew Corn. This time he pays $1.80 per dozen, less 20 per cent. for it. When he comes to figure his invoice, he finds he must raise his cost from .11 to .13, and his selling price from .15 to .18. Then he makes the following entries.

I. In the cost record book he rubs out the old figures, which were in pencil, and puts in the new ones, in pencil also.

Canned Corn

Firm	Brand	Size	Unit	Price	Mdse disc.	Frt.	Cash disc.	First cost net	Change cost	Sell price	%
Jones	Curfew	2		$1.80 doz.	20%	.01	2%	.13		.18	22%

II. On the daily bulletin he makes the following announcement:

Curfew Corn
    Old cost.............. .11   Old retail............ .15
    New cost............. .13   New retail........... .18

The cost clerks get their information and change the price in their books from this daily bulletin. Moreover, the clerk in charge of keeping the retail stores informed of price changes sends them out notice of the retail price change by the methods explained in detail elsewhere.

III. On the warehouse mark-up voucher the buyer enters the item and the old and new unit cost prices and difference. He next signs and dates this and sends it to the stock man. The latter at once goes to the pile or piles of the merchandise listed on the mark-up voucher, gets the physical count, and at once turns it back to the proper person in the office, who figures it and then turns it over to the bookkeeper.

The following entries, for example, are made on the warehouse mark-up voucher:

Warehouse Mark-up Voucher						No. 467 Date 3–1-22
Stock counted	Articles	Old cost	New cost	Mark-up	Am't.	Extension
5 Cases	Curfew Corn	.11	.13	.02	120	2.40
Totals....						2.40

Stock costed on.............by ....
Mark-down figured..........by..........
Entered mdse. cost..........by..........
Entered cost book..........by..........

The bookkeeper now enters:

Warehouse Mark-ups and mark-downs

No. 467 M. U............. $2.40

Now let us suppose the 10 cases ordered the second time come in, and five cases are again sold to store No. 5. And let us suppose that immediately after this comes the periodic physical inventory of the warehouse stock at cost. The books should show the following:

Merchandise Purchases (Billed cost)

Inventory................ $13.20	
Second Lot Purchased..... 28.80	

Freight and Cartage on Mdse. Purchased

Second lot Frt............. $2.40	

Merchandise shipments A (at cost)

	Store No. 5............... $15.60

Merchandise shipments B (profit)

	Store No. 5............... $6.00

Store No. 5

Mdse. Shipments.......... $21.60	

Mark-ups and mark-downs

No. 467 MU............... $2.40	

By transferring these into a single merchandise trading account, we have:

Merchandise Trading Account

Inventory................	$13.20	Shipments A (at cost)......	$15.60
2d lot purchased..........	28.80	Balance (Bk. Inventory)....	31.20
Frt. 2d lot...............	2.40		$46.80
MU 467..................	2.40		
	$46.80		
Inventory................	$31.20		

This gives a book inventory at $31.20. By actual count there should be 10 cases in stock. The counter enters this on an inventory blank and sends it to the office to be costed and extended. The buyer enters the cost from the cost record book at .13 per unit and extends as follows:

10cs. Curfew Corn—240 cans .13—$13.20

Similar entries on the credit side of the ledger should be made in case of a mark-down.

Salvage.—The "salvage" account is set up for the following reasons and in the following way:

Let us suppose that, out of the 10 cases of Curfew Corn, 24 cans or one whole case spoiled while in the warehouse before inventory. How is the merchandise to be credited? If the cans are "dumped" and no count taken, there will be a discrepancy between book and physical inventories. Therefore, a salvage account is set up, and, to take care of this, a system of records known as salvage vouchers is inaugurated.

SALVAGE VOUCHER

No. 40			Folio No	
To			Date	
Condition	Quantity		Cost Price	Extension
Disposition		Entry made on books of account		
By		By . . . . Date		

The stock man has a pad of these vouchers in his desk. As soon as he finds any articles spoiled or damaged, he takes them out of the main stock and segregates them in a separate section

17

called "The Hospital.' At the same time, he fills out a salvage voucher and sends it in to the buyer or merchandise manager. The latter comes out and inspects the goods, determines whether or not they have a saleable value. He then orders disposition of them (whether to be dumped or held in hospital for sale at a price), indicates this on the salvage voucher and brings the voucher into the office with him, where it is figured and turned over to the bookkeeper. Merchandise is credited with the entire amount and salvage is charged. If any goods in the hospital are subsequently sold, salvage is credited with the amount they have brought in.

If we assume the loss to be 24 cans of Curfew Corn, the accounts are as below:

In order to obtain uniformity, economy, and standardization, Warehouse Mark-Down and Mark-Up Vouchers, Warehouse Salvage Vouchers, and Warehouse Credit Memos should all be of the same size and fit the same size post binders. If a physical inventory is now taken, nine cases of Curfew Corn will be found in stock. Extended at .13 per can, they amount to $28.08. Thus the merchandise account closes correctly.

MERCHANDISE ACCOUNT

Inventory	$13.20	Shipments A (at cost)	$15.60
Second lot purchased	28.80	Salvage	3.12
Freight	2.40	Inventory balance	28.80
Mark-up 467	2.40		$46.80
	$46.80		
Inventory	$28.08		

The greatest service the salvage account and salvage system renders is that it informs the buyer of spoilage, in whole or in part, as soon as it comes to the attention of the stock man. By this means, damaged goods can often be sold at once at a price whereas otherwise the goods might not be discovered until all saleable value had departed. When goods are sold from Hospital, salvage is credited and the buyer can reduce his salvage losses. This is particularly true in the case of vegetables, fruits, cheese, meats, butter, dried fruit, etc.

Processes Involved in a Typical Purchase.—It seems appropriate before leaving the warehouse problem to include a few remarks regarding processes involved in the typical purchase and receipt of goods. This will show how the various procedures

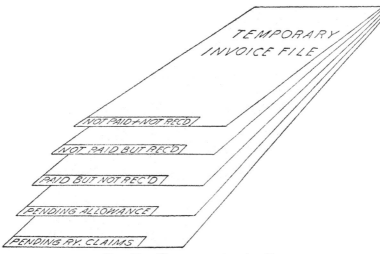

Fig. 33.—Temporary invoice file.

above mentioned dovetail into one another and tend to make the whole central organization function properly.

The buyer learns from inspection of stock cards (or daily shortage list on daily executive report explained later) and subsequent reference to cards, that it is time to make a purchase of a certain article of merchandise. From the information the stock card gives him, showing the average weekly, monthly, or seasonal sales of the past, the buyer determines what quantity to purchase. He then writes the order on his duplicate purchase order, referring to his cost record book for the previous cost, if need be. In the "ordered" column of the stock card, he enters the date and quantity ordered. One copy of the purchase order he keeps in his loose-leaf binder (preferably indexed alphabetically according to firm name of source). The other copy he sends to the source—the manufacturer, grower, or broker.

In the course of a few days, confirmation arrives from the manufacturer, and the buyer notes this on his retained copy of the purchase order and attaches confirmation to it. Later, the invoice arrives. The buyer should now compare the invoice with his purchase order and checks prices, discounts, and terms, marking on the purchase order the date of shipment. It is recommended that the buyer have two loose-leaf binders for his copies of purchase orders; one for current orders not completely shipped; the other for orders completely shipped.

If there are no discrepancies, he puts his O. K. on the invoice, notes in it the discount date, and turns it over to the clerk in charge of the temporary invoice file.

The temporary invoice file should be arranged with the following sections, see Fig. 33:

1. Invoices not paid and not received.
2. Invoices not paid but received.
3. Invoices paid but not received.
4. Invoices pending allowances or disputes.
5. Invoices pending claims against carriers.

In each of these sections the invoices are to be kept loose and arranged alphabetically by commodities, in the same order as the price list and stock record files. This standardizes and facilitates the work of the clerk making entries. This provision gives a regular arrangement for every article carried, and the clerk, as stated previously, turns automatically to the right page. The office clerks have a mental picture of the order of the price book so that when they think of any item they immediately associate it with the standard place in the registered order of the lists and files.

By having five separate sections, provision is made for paying invoices on the discount date, even if goods are not yet received, and for holding invoices pending a settlement before putting in the permanent invoice file and, most important of all, for separating the invoices of goods received from those of goods not received. This last feature greatly aids the clerk who is checking receiving records against the invoices.

To return to a strict discussion of the typical course of a purchase and receipt of goods, when the articles arrive at the warehouse, the stock man enters the quantity and condition on his receiving record, as described heretofore, and the duplicate

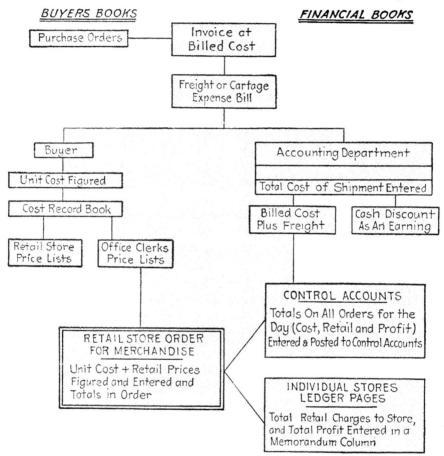

FIG. 34.—Course of purchase order.

copy of this he sends to the clerk in charge of the temporary invoice file. This clerk turns to the section "Invoices not paid and not received," picks out the invoice of this shipment, and stamps it received. He now enters the date and quantity in the "received" column of the proper stock card and then turns the invoice with attached freight or cartage expense bill over to the buyer.

The buyer now refigures the net unit cost per item on the face of the bill and compares this with the figures on his cost record book. If there is any change he takes the necessary steps by means of the mark-up and mark-down vouchers, bulletins, etc., to bring all cost and selling price lists uniformly up to date, and then turns the invoice back to the clerk.

If the goods are in stock for the first time, a new entry is made on the cost record book, and the information is put on the bulletin so that the addition will be made on all lists. The clerk now puts the invoice in its proper section of the temporary invoice file awaiting payment. In this case, it would go into Section Two.

This clerk is responsible for seeing that invoices are paid at the proper time. One of his first duties is to go through the file and turn over to the bookkeeper for payment all the invoices due that day. The bookkeeper, after paying them, stamps them paid, and turns them back to the clerk who puts them either in the temporary invoice file (if goods are not received, or if some question is pending), or files them away in the permanent file.

Conclusions.—This finishes the technical discussion of stock-keeping, stock accounting, and purchasing records. The three are interdependent in the processes of handling the merchandise from its source to the retail store. Figure 34 shows in chart form the various phases through which an order for purchase passes before the receipt of the goods is finally checked off on the individual stores' ledger. This chart might be used for various other types of chain stores, and is not necessarily confined to groceries, although if it were used elsewhere there would have to be modifications.

The forms shown in this chapter are illustrative of a method now in use and should be used suggestively rather than copied exactly. If it merely indicates some ways in which a present system may be made to function more efficiently, the detailed explanation given will have served its purpose.

CHAPTER XVII

SUPERVISION OF RETAIL OUTLETS

OUTLINE

Uniform retail prices throughout chain secured by
1. Price lists.
2. Daily bulletins.
3. Retail mark-ups and mark-downs.
4. Weekly change sheets.

Price lists.
1. Figured by buyer.
2. Sent to store managers.

Daily bulletins.
1. Containing
    (a) Changes in cost.
    (b) Notation of new goods.
2. Duty of clerk to send copy to all store managers.

Mark-ups and mark-downs.
1. Routine practice.

Weekly change sheet.
1. Compilation of all changes on daily bulletins.
2. Store manager held responsible for prices on weekly change sheets.

Policing of retail outlets.
1. Personal visits to store.
    (a) Check up prices.
    (b) Inspect care of store.
    (c) Check cash register.
2. Physical inventory.
    (a) At regular stated intervals.
3. Traveling auditors.

Account methods for retail operations.
1. Regular warehouse shipment order.
2. Credit memorandums for goods returned to warehouse by stores.
3. Daily reports of store managers.
4. Use of special ruled cash receipt book.
5. Use of periodic retail store inventories.
6. Arriving at percentage of retail store profit.

CHAPTER XVII

SUPERVISION OF RETAIL OUTLETS

By John S. Fleek

This chapter contains a model system of controlling retail outlets as used in a moderate sized grocery chain. Other methods are outlined in other chapters, but for a better understanding of the subject, it has been thought wise to follow out one system and one definite example throughout the whole process, in order that anyone really interested in the continuity of the routine followed may find it easier to understand.

The framework of sound accurate accounting methods and of direct merchandise price control must be supplemented by frequent inspection in person by the store's superintendent and the chief executive.

As the organization assumes larger proportions, the executive finds that haphazard supervision of checks and balances and policing can no longer obtain if he is to have efficient control of his business. A regular routine of duties needs to be established so that the individual store account will show actual conditions; the store managers sell articles at the price determined upon; and the superintendent and his assistants follow the stores properly and see that instructions are being obeyed.

Uniform Pricing.—Uniform retail prices, as fixed by the central office throughout all the branch stores, are brought about by the following means:

1. Price lists.
2. Daily bulletins.
3. Retail mark-up and mark-down notices.
4. Weekly change sheets.

Prices are established and proceed from the merchandise department. The buyer figures a unit cost on each article and then, by himself or by the advice of the executive department, the selling price ("retail"). Both these figures are entered in

264

the Cost Record Book—see page 250—which becomes a fountain head of all knowledge to the organization in so far as merchandise prices (cost and retail) are concerned.

The office figuring clerks and superintendent are given complete price lists of all articles carried, for these individuals must have constant records of such information.

Retail store managers are likewise given complete price lists, which are virtually copies of the cost record book, and identical with the office price lists, except that only the retail prices appear therein. The store managers thus know the price at which to sell every item and can put price tags on their shelves accurately.

Were it not for the fact that prices are constantly changing and articles being added to or taken off the selling list, the problem of price control would be solved merely by issuing the lists to the retail managers. But the solution is not so easily achieved and the problem thus becomes one of providing for getting the changes that are known in the office and there recorded in the Cost Record Book to all the books of all the retail store managers. This dissemination of information is brought about by means of (*a*) the daily bulletin, (*b*) the retail mark-up and mark-down notices, and (*c*) the weekly change sheets.

(*a*) The Daily Bulletin is kept in a diary form at a central point in the central offices, so that the office clerks may have ready access to it. In it the buyer enters changes in cost and selling price of the articles carried in stock from the data on his Cost Record Book, and makes notation of new goods just arrived, giving their cost and selling price, and of goods no longer carried. The office figuring clerks make the changes on their price lists from this information and initial the entries on the Daily Bulletin to show their responsibility for having brought the lists up to date.

In order to get this information out to the stores at a given time each day, it is the duty of one clerk to make copies of the Daily Bulletin page, recording only retail prices, and to send them out to all the retail managers.

If speed is desired in transmitting the price changes, the retail managers can be given the latest prices over the telephone, having the messages confirmed later by a copy of the Bulletin.

(*b*) The same clerk makes out mark-ups and mark-downs and prepares notices for all the stores from the information on changes. When the store manager receives a mark-up or a mark-down notice, he counts his stock of the articles enumerated, signs the slip and returns it with his next daily report showing the additional merchandise charge or credit on this report. See Figure 35.

(*c*) Weekly Change Sheets are made out every Saturday and

MARK-UP VOUCHER   N̊ **203**

DATE _____

STOCK COUNTED				ARTICLE	OLD PRICE	NEW PRICE	MARK UP	TOTAL QUANTITY	EXTENSION
MAIN STOCK		WAREHOUSE							

BY ORDER OF _____ DATE _____

STOCK COUNTED ON _____ BY _____
MARK-UP FIGURED ON _____ BY _____
ENTERED MDSE. ACCT. ON _____ BY _____
ENTERED COST-BOOK ON _____ BY _____

Fɪɢ. 35.—Mark-up voucher.

mailed to the retail store managers. Figure 36 shows form in use in a grocery chain. These sheets constitute a compilation of all the changes, additions, corrections, and deductions that have appeared on the daily bulletins, and serve as an additional means of verifying the retail price lists and of bringing them up-to-date. The store manager is held directly responsible for selling his groceries at the prices given on the last change sheet. Consequently, as soon as he receives one, he should at once go over his price list with it, making the necessary changes and corrections.

It is understood that prices on these lists will be entered in

CHANGE SHEET No. G AND WEEKLY BULLETIN

Instructions.

This CHANGE SHEET is issued at the same time that PRICE LIST No. 1 is given to you. Go over your price list at once with this CHANGE SHEET and make the necessary additions and corrections on the price list as per instructions in general order attached.

2. These are the changes of the past week. Owing to the length of time it took to get the PRICE LIST printed, it comes to you a week late. Hence you have all these changes to make at once.

3. BISCUIT LISTS for Loose-Wiles and National will be sent out in a few days.

PRICE CHANGES AND ADDITIONS

Ammonia and Bluing

New   Sawyer's Bluing, large............................ .25

Butter, etc.

New   Diamond Oleomargarine......................... .31
Change Butter tubs...................................... .63

Canned Goods

New   Star Boneless Herring........................... .19
Change Red Salmon..................................... .35
Change Tomatoes No. 2................................ .11
New   Libby Tomato Soup.................... .   .08⅓

Cheese

New   Blue Ribbon, cream...... .... .17
New   Blue Ribbon, pimento........................... .17
Change Mild.............................. .... .37
Change Young America.................................. .39

Cocoa and Chocolate

New   Bensdorps Cocoa, 2 oz......................... .14
Change Beck cocoa, unsweetened....................... .25
Change Beck cocoa, sweetened.......................... .29

Crisco and Oils

Change Mazola, pts...................................... .33

Eggs

New   Monogram eggs.................................. .72

Fish

Change Beardsleys Shredded Cod..................... . .34

Flour, etc.

Change King Arthur, 12½......................... .... 1.15
Change King Arthur, 24½.............................. 2.20
Change Aunt Jemima, pc............................... .20
Change Rice, Flutter, pk............................... .12½
Change Corn meal, pkg................................ .05½
Change Corn meal, bulk............................... .05
         Etc.

FIG. 36.—Form of weekly change sheet.

pencil to facilitate making the many alterations now so frequently necessary.

Thus, by daily bulletins, mark-up and mark-down notices, and weekly change sheets, all price lists in their several degrees of completeness are made to conform with the latest entries on the Cost Record Book, and thus a system of merchandise and price control is established.

Policing of Retail Outlets.—Constant personal supervision and policing of the retail branches is necessary; for in no other way is the central office to know whether instructions are being obeyed and whether the store managers are honest. To provide this, the store superintendent tries to visit each store every day. On such trips he will check up the prices and price list of the manager, will inspect the store for cleanliness, window displays, appearance, and general marketing methods, and will get a check on the cash register.

It is distinctly desirable that the superintendent take a physical inventory of each store at least once a month. This shows up leakage through carelessness and dishonesty in an undeniable manner. If goods are charged against a store at retail from the first of the month, to the amount of $500, and at the time of inventory the cash register shows sales at retail amounting to $400, clearly the store should have an inventory that, when figured at retail amounts, should come to $100.

Many chains have traveling auditors who visit branch stores at specified or unexpected times and take inventory.

Accounting for a Retail Grocery Store.—In the development of a system of accounts to provide the needed information and checks upon retail outlets, it is well to consider what would happen if a new branch were being opened, which we may call, for purposes of illustration, Store No. 35.

The store manager sends to the central office his initial order on the company's order blank. See Figure 37. The order is registered and goes out to the warehouse to be filled. Here the shipping clerk "checks out" the order for store No. 35 as he loads the truck, seeing that the proper quantities and units are entered on the order blank. The driver takes a yellow copy of the order with the goods so that the store manager can check up the items delivered and can use it as a basis for giving a receipt

WAREHOUSE ORDER

Store No.______ Address______________________ Sheet No.______

Manager______________________

DATE ORDERED	DATE RECEIVED	APPROVED	REGISTER NO.	DATE SHIPPED	SHIPPING NO.

Shp'r Check	Quan.	Unit		ARTICLE	SIZE	BRAND	Contained	LOT NO.	Price	COST Extension	Price	RETAIL Extension
			1									
			2									
			3									
			40									
			41									

RETAIL PRICES CHECKED BY		
[1]	[2]	TOTAL COST
		PROFIT
[3] RETAIL PRICES POSTED BY	[4] COST BY	RETAIL
[5] COST FOOTED BY	[6] COST POSTED BY	Store No.______ Receipt Received______

FIG. 37.—Warehouse order blank.

CREDIT VOUCHER No. 702

SALESMAN______________

No. (______________

To______________________________ DATE______________

CONDITION	QUANTITY	ARTICLES	QUAN. TITY	SELLING PRICE PRICE	SELLING PRICE AMOUNT	COST PRICE PRICE	COST PRICE AMOUNT	PROFIT
TOTALS								

	R.R. CLAIM	CREDIT ANALYSIS
Rec'd on______ By______	Claim Entered Against	1. Credit Entered on______ By______
Surv'y'd on______ By______	______R.R.	Against______ Salesman
Disposition______	Date______	2. Credit Notice Card sent
	Amount $______	On______ By______
Error Due to______	Our Claim No.______	3. No Notice Needed______
Approved by______	By______ Traffic Mfg.	4. ______
Date______		Entered on Books Date______ By______

FIG. 38.—Credit voucher.

for the merchandise and comparison with the charge against his store.

The white copy of the order the shipping clerk sends to the office to be extended. The clerks price and extend the order from their price lists, enter the totals for "costs," "retail," and "profit," and the order is then ready for posting.

Orders for the day are bound and numbered in a permanent folio and thus become part of the quasi-sales book, or folio number being used as a check in posting. Totals for the day are posted to the various merchandise accounts.

Store No. 35
Jan. 1, 1922   Folio No. 46

Unit	Article	Size	Brand	Price	Cost	Price	Retail
100	XX	2½	XX	.80	80.00	1.00	100.00

Total cost.. $ 80.00
Total profit..   20.00
Total retail.. 100.00

The bookeeping entries are as follows for January 1:

A. In case of the Journal for Control Accounts (daily total)
Jan. 1, 1921
    Shipments to retail outlets............... $100.00
        To mdse. costs.................... $80.00
        To mdse. profits...................   20.00
B. In the case of Ledger page on Store No. 35

Store 35   Page 142

Date	Folio	Item	Debit at retail	Memo. profit	Date	Folio	Item	Credit retail	Memo. profit
1/1	46	Order	100.00	20.00	1/1	Cm-16	Return	10.00	2.00
/3		Daily	4.40	1.65	/3	c-61	Cash sales	26.75	
		Report			1/4	I-14	Inv.	67.65	
/4		Inv.	104.40 67.65					104.40	

If now No. 35 sends back part of the goods delivered on January 2, the receiving clerk makes out a slip on the credit memorandum, see Fig. 38, entering only quantity and description. An authorized person then inspects the goods and determines whether credit will be allowed. If the credit is O.K'd, it will go to the clerks first to be figured (cost, retail profit) and then to the bookkeeper.

CREDIT MEMO

Cm Folio No. 16

To........................... Date Jan. 2, 1921

| Condition | Quantity | Articles | Quantity | Cost | | Retail | | Profit |
				Price	Am't	Price	Am't	
O.K.	10	XXX		.80	8.00	1.00	10.00	2.00

These credit memos are put in a permanent folio and numbered When the credits are posted, the bookkeeper sends a credit memo post card to the store involved for its use in checking against its other accounts. The entries are as follows:

In the Journal for the entire day, taking totals for the day from the credit memo folio.

January 2, 1922

Mdse. cost.............................. $8.00
Mdse. profit........................... 2.00
To mdse. shipments to retail outlets. $10.00

For Ledger entry, see preceding page.

The Daily Report from each manager, see Fig. 39, brings into the office the complete story of the happenings of the day. The retail business is on a strictly cash basis; hence sales are the direct credit to merchandise at retail charged against the store's Ledger account.

The daily stores report is in six sections. Section 1 shows goods bought and received by the store manager and mark-ups and mark-downs charged against his store through the central office. Section 2 shows the amount paid out for any merchandise

MUST BE WRITTEN IN INK							*Sheet No.*		

Receiving Record   No. 10460   *Register No.*

Store No. _____   *Date*_____

Managers are requested to enter all goods received in the store since previous record was made out, which are not on original Warehouse-Shipment. If nothing is received, write "Nothing" and sign.

Quan.	Unit	FROM	ARTICLE	Price	COST Extension	Price	RETAIL Extension

RETAIL PRICES CHECKED BY			
(1) Cost Figured by	(2) Cost Verified by	TOTAL COST	
		PROFIT	
(3) Retail Figured by	(4) Retail Verified by	RETAIL	
(5) Cost Posted by	(6) Retail Posted by		

*Signature*_____*Manager*

Fig. 39.—Manager's daily report. (Section 1.)

that the manager has bought directly during the day. Section 3 shows the amount paid out directly for expenses by the manager, and Section 4 rebates. A summary of transactions is made in Section 5 and Section 6 is a duplicate summary retained in the store by the manager.

On the assumption that Store No. 35 is opened for business on January 3, 1922, the Daily Stores Report should be sent to the office with the amount of cash equal to the day's sales less deductions. Arrangements can be made with local banks in

MERCHANDISE PAID FOR

No. 10460

Store No_____

Date_____

MANAGER SIGNS EACH TRANSACTION	$	Cts.	SIGNATURE
Write Total in Space Below			
TOTAL TO BE ENTERED ON CASH SHEET			O. K.

EXPENSES PAID FOR

MANAGER SIGNS EACH TRANSACTION	$	Cts.	SIGNATURE
Write Total in Space Below			
TOTAL TO BE ENTERED ON CASH SHEET			O.K.

REBATES

(This covers all money refunded or overcharged, and all over-rings on Cash Register)

MANAGER SIGNS EACH TRANSACTION	$	Cts.	SIGNATURE
Write Total in Space Below			
TOTAL TO BE ENTERED ON CASH SHEET			O.K.

Superintendent signs after having examined and approved all items in spaces above

O. K. for all items-above

_____

Supt

FIG. 39.—Manager's daily report (*Continued*).
(Sections 2, 3, and 4.)

CASH SHEET

Put Bills of the same denomination together and face up
REPORT MUST BE WRITTEN IN INK

No. 10460

Store
No. _____   Date_____

MANAGER'S COPY

REMEMBER

Store No and Date Must be entered in 4 (four) places.

No. 10460

Date _____

	$	Cts.	$	Cts.	
CASH TO_____BANK					Bank
Cash Enclosed Herewith { Bills					Bills
Silver					Silver
Misc.					Misc-
Total					Total
Total Merchandise Paid					Mdse.
Total Expenses Paid					Exps.
Total Receipts for to-day					Total
Salvage Slip Amount					
Total Rebates					Rebates
Previous Statement					Previous Statement
TO-DAY'S STATEMENT					To-day's Statement
To be entered on next Cash Sheet					

To be entered on next Cash Sheet

Signature_____
              Manager

FIGURING OF REGISTER

To be entered by Superintendent

Register Statement_____

Manager's Statement _____

     Difference _____

    Cash on Hand_____

    Over or Short_____

     Sign._____
              Supt.

Store No.

MANAGER

Recd the Sheet
Carefully

FILL IT OUT
CAREFULLY

FIG. 39.—Manager's daily report (*Continued*).
(Sections 5 and 6.)

certain suburbs to collect the money from retail stores and place it on deposit. The total amount of cash sales is credited to the stores merchandise ledger account (see cash receipts). The report is received in the office by the bookkeeper who checks the managers, entries, counts the cash, checks for mark-up and mark-down items on Section 1, which he detaches and turns over to the clerks for figuring, making at the same time entries in the cost column for merchandise items paid for by store manager. This prevents the control merchandise account from

CASH RECEIPTS

DATE	DESCRIPTION	CREDITS				DEBITS				
		✓	CASH-SALES RETAIL STORES	SUNDRIES	MDSE PURCHASES DIRECTION STORE ✓	DIRECT RETAILS EXPENSES ✓	REBATES ✓	SUNDRIES ✓	NET CASH ✓	
JAN. 3	STORE #35	142	26 75		1'	75 485	1 50		1'	25 00
	''									
	''									
	''									
	''									
	''									
	''									
	CONTROL RISK TOTALS FOR JAN. 3	160	26 75		5 00	75 400	1 00		40	25 00

FIG. 40.—Cash receipts book.

being charged twice for items paid for by cash by the store manager.

Section I now becomes a regular store order and goes into the folio binder for the day's business under direct shipment. It is given a folio number and is made ready for posting in the usual way. Later, when invoices arrive from the firms who have delivered direct to the store, they are checked against this section to ascertain their correctness.

Let us suppose that all sections of the daily report sheet have been checked and figured, and duly prepared for the bookkeeping entries to follow:

1. Cash receipts book, see Fig. 40.

2. Postings from this cash receipts book are now made as follows:

1. See ¶ B (Page 270) for Ledger Page on Store No. 35.
2. Expense postings.

Control—Direct Retail Store Expense							P. 400
Date				Date			
Jan. 3	c-61		1.00				

Store No. 35 Direct Expense							P. 435
Date				Date			
Jan. 3	c-61		1.00				

Three other control accounts should be filled in:

Cash Sales of Retail Outlets							P. 100
Date			Date				
			1–3	c-61	Sales	$26.75	

Mdse. Purchases by Cash Direct Stores							P. 300
Date				Date			
1–3	c-61		.75				

Cash							P. 40
Date				Date			
1–3	c-61		$25.00				

The next step in the accounting procedure is the use of the periodic inventory for the retail stores, see Fig. 41. The superintendent and his assistants drop in at a store without warning and take a physical inventory. This is then sent to the central office and figured at retail by the clerks. When figured it is turned over to the bookkeeper for entry on the stores account. If all figuring were perfectly accurate and no dishonesty or mistakes occurred on the part of store managers, the inventory amount should correspond to the balance on this store account.

In practice of course, this never actually occurs. Journal entries must be made to equalize differences between book retail inventories and physical retail inventories.

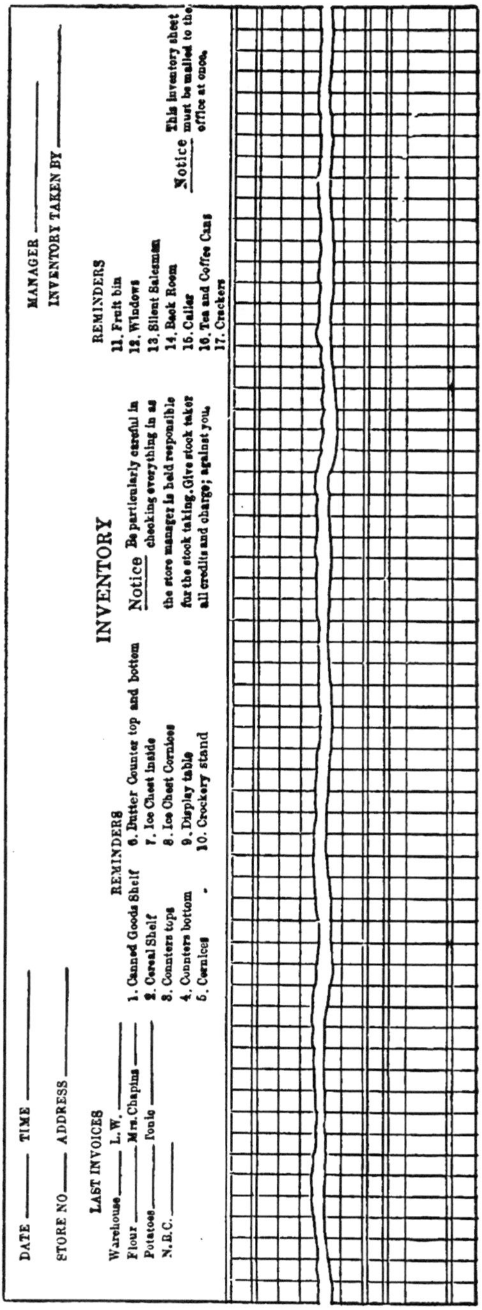

DATE ———— TIME ————

STORE NO.———— ADDRESS ————

MANAGER ————

INVENTORY TAKEN BY ————

LAST INVOICES

Warehouse ———— L. W. ————

Flour ———— Mrs. Clapton ————

Potatoes ———— Poole ————

N.B.C. ————

INVENTORY

REMINDERS

1. Canned Goods Shelf
2. Cereal Shelf
3. Counters tops
4. Counters bottom
5. Cornices
6. Butter Counter top and bottom
7. Ice Chest inside
8. Ice Chest Cornices
9. Display table
10. Crockery stand

11. Fruit bin
12. Windows
13. Silent Salesman
14. Back Room
15. Cellar
16. Tea and Coffee Cans
17. Crackers

Notice Be particularly careful in checking everything in as the store manager is held responsible for the stock taking. Give stock taker all credits and charge; against you.

Notice This inventory sheet must be mailed to the office at once.

Fig. 41a.—Inventory sheet (front).

Book Inventory Charges		INVENTORY	Book Inventory Credits		Statement from Store Receiving Book CHARGES			Statement of Store Credits	
	AM'T			AM'T	AM'T	DATE	State clearly whether Groceries, Produce,Crackers, Allowances	AM'T	DATE	State clearly whether Cash, Mdse., Credit, Reductions, Special, etc.
Inventory Beginning of Month		Store No.	Sales to Date						
Warehouse Shipment		Address	Reductions						
Direct Shipment		Manager	Special Sale Reductions						
Cash Purchases		Taken by	Journal Credits						
Journal Charges		Assisted by	Sundries						
Advances		Date From To							
		Received in office							
		Date Time							
		Figured by							
		Refigured by							
		O'Kd							
		Date Time							
		Physical Inventory							
		Book Inventory							
		Over (black ink)	Total Credits						
		Short (red ink)							
		BOOK INVENTORY							
		Summary Charges							
		Summary Credits							
		balance							
Total Charges		Book Inventory							

FIG. 41b.—Inventory sheet (back).

Let us assume that on the morning of January 4, before any retail sales are made, an inventory of Store 35 is taken. When figured this inventory amounts to $67.65. The bookkeeper would then put the inventory sheet in a permanent file, giving it a number. This, then, becomes the voucher for the subsequent entry on the books on Ledger Page 142 (See ¶B). This being the ideal case, the book balance and the physical inventory agree.

If now the management wants to know the profit on the business of Store No. 35, it can get a very close estimate by taking the difference between the Mem. debit and credit columns for profit on the Stores Ledger page, and getting the percentage of this figure to the net total merchandise charges for the month. This will give the percentage of gross profit on sales for the month.

After the store has been running for some time, it will be found that physical inventories from month to month are approximately the same. For this reason the percentage of gross profit or net shipments per store per month is substantially accurate for the gross profit on net retail sales.

In order to arrive at the net direct retail revenue per store per month, the direct store expense account is deducted from the amount of gross profit (arrived at as above). Similarly, to arrive at the cost value of the retail stores inventory in making up monthly reports of condition a very close approximation can be had by deducting the same percentage of gross profit from the retail value of the inventory as figured.

The profit on shipments of merchandise to the retail stores for the business as a whole can be taken as the gross profit for the entire chain, thus very largely disregarding the retail inventories. But it will be found, as stated above, that after retail outlets are once established, the total retail store inventories for the entire organization are, in the aggregate, about the same, from month to month. From control accounts, therefore, the monthly merchandise statement for the business can be made up with accuracy without considering the retail inventories.

The result would be for a chain, such as we have been describing, as follows:

Retail value, shipments of mdse. to retail outlets..... ————

Cost........................,.......................... ————

      Gross profits on............................... ————

Retail store expense (direct)....................... ————

      Net retail revenue........................... ————

Warehouse... ————

Office and management............................ ————

Fixed charges..................................... ————

Misc. expenses.................................... ————

Total overhead expense carried by retail outlets..... ————

Net profit for the company on shipments to retail

      outlets.................................... ————

Sales direct from warehouse[1]............. ————

Cost on sales from warehouse............. ————

      Net profit on sales direct from warehouse....... ————

Aggregate earnings of the company................ ————

[1] Since wholesaling is not a regular business of the firm, its profits are treated simply as an additional revenue without bearing an allocation of general overhead burden. This is logical because so little expense is involved in making these direct sales.

Conclusions.—This chapter considers the retail store solely from the point of view of the central management. From this point of view, therefore, the branch store is like a private soldier in the army. It must be taken care of, its wants must be administered to, and, like the soldier, it must submit to discipline.

The problem, as it presents itself to the store manager was discussed in a previous chapter. Here, the sole purpose is to make clear the routine of supervision exercised by the central office in two ways: By personal inspection and by daily and other reports. If the process seems long and unduly complicated, it must be remembered that this system of accounting must serve as eyes and ears to the chief executive. A store to him is not a petsodality, it is a link in a chain, and he wants to know whether it is a strong link or a weak one.

It is not claimed that the system for policing and accounting supervision outlined in this chapter is the best or even better than others which have been developed. But to the small chain proprietor, or any retail store owner who desires to branch out with other retail outlets, this chapter should give some very definite ideas.

CHAPTER XVIII

CENTRALIZING EXECUTIVE CONTROL

Outline

Information needed by executive.
  1. Concerning purchasing and warehousing.
      (a) The stock of merchandise.
          1. Adequate supply.
          2. Items short.
      (b) Condition of warehouse inventory and merchandise account.
  2. Concerning central offices.
      (a) Accuracy and up-to-dateness of accounting statistics.
      (b) Billing clerk routine.
  3. Concerning retail outlets.
      (a) Cash sales of each store.
      (b) Warehouse shipments to each store.
      (c) Profit shown by each store.
      (d) Character of orders from each store.
      (e) Condition of retail inventories.
Characteristics of executive reports.
  1. Brief.
      (a) Material concentrated, if possible, on one page.
  2. Up-to-date.
      (a) Preferably for preceding day.
          1. To catch trouble at its inception.
The daily executive report.
  1. Cash sales.
  2. Daily cash balance in banks.
  3. Net operations retail, cost, and profit.
  4. Shortage report.
  5. Routine necessary to follow to get information.
Weekly executive report.
  1. Commonly retail cash sales report.
      (a) Comparison of sales this week with same week last year.
      (b) Total for month this year and last.
  2. Connecting link between daily and monthly reports.
      (a) Indicate course of turnover and sales.
Monthly executive report.
  1. Compiled almost entirely from books of account.
  2. Control account for

      (*a*) Direct retail store expense.

      (*b*) Indirect retail store expense.

  3. Report gives statement of condition for use in

      (*a*) Administration.

      (*b*) Correction.

      (*c*) Planning.

Comparison reports.

  1. Formulated at specific periods.

  2. Compare sales, profits, expenses, etc.

Annual report.

  1. Contains

      (*a*) Balance sheet.

      (*b*) Income account.

      (c) Expense statement.

  2. Serves as final link in executive control.

CHAPTER XVIII

CENTRALIZING EXECUTIVE CONTROL

By John S. Fleek

It is necessary to coördinate and combine all the separate activities and functions of the chain. The executive cannot be bothered with detail. He will not gain the benefits of these methods of better administration unless the information collected

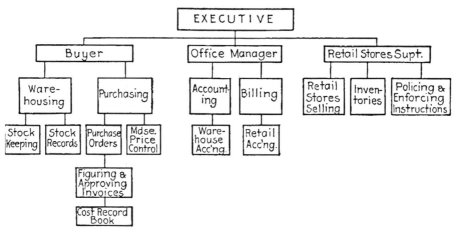

Fig. 42.—Route of statistical information for executive.

at various points is concentrated at one place, in approved reports and at specified times.

It is true that personal foresight at offices, warehouses, and branches cannot be dispensed with by a mere impersonal substitution of routine methods. But, in order that the chief executive may exert his force at the right time and place, such a routine collection of data in the form of reports is almost necessary.

Sources of information for necesary reports for the executive come ordinarily through three channels, the buyer, the office manager, and the superintendent of retail stores. These offices

283

may, in some chains, be divided up or given different terms, but the idea remains the same. The executive must have information obtained from purchases and inventories, finance and accounting, and retail sales by branch stores. Figure 42 shows the progress of information and how definitely the route for each separate item of statistical data can be traced from the bottom of the organization to the top.

What Information to Get.—The information for executive consumption which it is advisable and easy to compile appears under the following heads:

I. Warehousing and purchasing.
    1. Is the stock of merchandise being kept up?
    2. If not, what items are "going short" on orders?
    3. What is the condition of the warehouse merchandise account, warehouse inventory, etc.?
II. Central offices.
    1. Are the bill clerks keeping the work up-to-date?
    2. Is the accounting department keeping work up-to-date?
III. Retail.
    1. What is the standing of each store in cash sales?
    2. What is each store doing in warehouse shipments?
    3. What profit is each store making?
    4. What number of orders are coming back from each store?
    5. Are profits large enough to carry overhead?
    6. What is the condition of retail inventories?

Executive daily reports should, in general, concentrate all essential data on not more than one page. Such reports, when handed to the executive, give him a convenient and portable brief of the condition of his business in all its ramifications. Moreover, a report, to be really effective, must be up to the minute in the information it contains. It should readily reveal any mal-administration. It should pave the way for future plans. For this reason, if a daily report arrives four or five days late, much of its constructive and corrective force is lost; for the evil it presents and brings out or emphasizes for correction has probably by that time ceased to be so obtrusively evident.

Daily and weekly reports, therefore, should come to the executive's desk on the day following that for which the figures are entered. Monthly and other periodic reports should be presented within five or six days of the end of the month. Annual reports naturally take longer to compile, but certainly should be completed during the 30 days following the end of the fiscal year.

The Daily Executive Report.—The daily executive report, appearing on the chief executive's desk by the forenoon of the day following that of the report, gives the brief outline of the course of business during the previous day. The executive not only gets a line on his retail stores, the buying, the accounting department from the daily reports, but he knows also that his office force is keeping its costing and pricing, expending and billing up-to-date. Otherwise the figures under "shipments," and "direct credits" could not be entered.

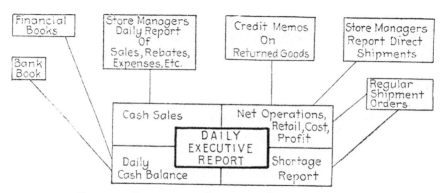

FIG. 43.—Process of making up daily executive report.

Figure 43 shows the procedure required in obtaining the information for the daily executive report as it is made up from the various other detailed reports. It shows how the daily cash balance is found by consulting the bank book and the financial books; how cash sales are taken off the daily report of the store managers, etc. By studying this diagram, the apparently intricate processes of coördinating and concentrating accounts become far simpler.

Figure 44 shows one form of daily executive report. This form is made up as follows: As soon as the warehouse shipments on regular retail store order blanks, the direct shipments from store managers' reports, and the credit memos are figured and extended, the order clerks enter the totals for each store in the appropriate columns and give the algebraic sum (warehouse shipments plus direct minus credits) for the net operations of the day.

One clerk then goes through the warehouse shipment order

STORE	PD.OUT		TOTAL	SHIPMENTS		DIRECT CREDITS				NET OPERATIONS		
	EXP.	MDG	CASH SALES	COST	RETAIL	COST	RETAIL	COST	RETAIL	COST	RETAIL	PROFIT
1												
2												
3												
4												
29												
30												
TOTALS												

EXECUTIVE REPORT   DAY_____ DATE_____

Fig. 44.—Daily executive report form.

DAY_____
DATE_____

EXECUTIVE REPORT

DAILY CASH STATEMENT

FOR BANKS	NAT'L		UNION		CITY		TOTAL BANKS		CASH	
OLD BAL									OLD BAL	
DEPOSIT									STORE RECEIPTS	
TOTAL									OTHER RECEIPTS	
CHECKS									TOTAL	
NEW BAL.									PD. MDSE.	
									PD. EXP.	
									PD. OTHER	
									NEW BAL.	
INITIALS										
SHORTAGE										

Fig. 45.—Daily cash statement.

blanks and lists, under shortage, on the reverse side of the report, the articles (quantity and retail value) which the shipping clerk has marked "short" i.e. he has been unable to fill the order because the articles asked for have run out of stock.

The clerks now turn the report in to the bookkeeper, who enters the amount of cash sales from the figures compiled from the store managers' daily reports. Next he enters the daily cash balance figures on the reverse side of the executive report, Fig. 45. When the bookkeeper has done this, the report is complete and ready for the executive. Entries on the report are initialed by the clerks making them. The report can be conveniently placed on three-ring binder paper and can be kept for permanent record by the executive in such a binder.

Thus the executive has before him daily in a convenient, compact form, a summary of his business and an effective check

	COMPARISIONS		WEEKLY CASH SALES						TOTAL CASH SALES CURRENT MONTH
STORE NO.	THIS MONTH IN ₧ —	QUOTA CURRENT MONTH	— TO —	— TO —	— TO —	— TO —	— TO —	— TO —	
1									
2									
3									
12									
TOTAL									
WAREHOUSE									
AGGREGATE TOTAL									

REPORT OF RETAIL CASH SALES
WEEKLY FOR THE MONTH OF_____ 192_____

FIG. 46.—Weekly cash sales report.

on its functions. By means of the shortage report, the buyer is checked; by means of the daily cash balance, the accounting department is checked, and the retail outlets are checked by the detailed information on the first page of the report.

The Weekly Report.—Chains vary widely in executive accounting control, not so much in the information desired, but rather in the frequency with which it is desired and the completeness of the detail called for on the executive report. Generally it is not considered necessary to include any information on weekly reports except that dealing with cash sales. If the other items are not important enough to be listed daily, they can usually be put off until the monthly report.

Figure 46 illustrates a common form of retail cash sales report to be filled in and submitted weekly. It is found convenient to consolidate this weekly report on one sheet for the current month and with the figures accumulating week by week. Figures for current weeks are compiled direct from the daily executive reports and put on three-ring binder pages for the executive control report book.

As a guide and as a comparison, the first column shows sales for the same month last year, and the second column the quota or mark set for the month this year. The subsequent six columns are for the weekly record of sales and the final column gives the total for the month.

The reason for six columns is to provide for such a month as October, 1921, beginning on a Saturday and ending on a Monday. Weeks are taken as beginning when the month begins and running until the next Saturday or until the end of the month. For example, two of the weeks reported for October, 1921, will contain but one business day.

This cash report gives the chief executive information as to the volume of business his retail outlets are doing, in a desirable form, and in sufficient detail to give him the connecting link between daily and monthly reports, which go more minutely into particulars. These consolidations enable him to ascertain what steps need to be taken immediately to force more sales and a greater turnover, at any one point or throughout his organization.

The Monthly Report.—The monthly report provides a complete analysis and statement of the operations and conditions of business. It gives an operating statement in detail; and moreover combines all this information in a concise form on the two sides of a single sheet of the same standard three-ring binder paper for the executive's control report book. The form, see Figs. 47 and 48, is almost self-explanatory, and is compiled almost entirely from the books of account, although it is possible to check the daily and weekly reports against it.

The cash sales give the needed comparison with profits, years and quotas, as well as with the volume of shipments appearing in the columns to the right. The inventory column serves to show the turnover of each store. Direct expense is seen on the reverse side, Fig. 48, and is that part of the operating expense which can be chargeable directly to the individual store. It is well to keep this separate from the other entries of expense or overhead; for, it might be advisable sometimes to maintain a store that was doing only a little better than making its direct, or as they say in railroading, "out-of-pocket expense" and con-

STORE NO.	CASH SALES				PHYSICAL INVENT. ORIES		MERCHANDISE—SHIPMENT—OPERATIONS						
	SALES FOR MONTH — 192 —	QUOTA THIS MONTH	CURRENT SALES NET	GAIN OR LOSS	DATE	AM'T	AT RETAIL	GROSS BOOK PROFIT AM'T	%	DIRECT EXPENSE	DIRECT RETAIL REVENUE	OVERHEAD ALLOCATED AT — %	NET BOOK OPERATING PROFIT %
1													
2													
11													
12													
TOTAL													
WAREHOUSE													
AGG.TOTAL													

INCOME STATEMENT		BALANCE SHEET				
AGGREGATE BOOK PROFIT NET		OFFICE CASH		COMMON STOCK		
DISCOUNTS EARNED		BANK CASH		PREFERRED STOCK		
SUNDRY REVENUES NET		ACCT'S REC'D		SURPLUS		
WAREHOUSES		NOTES REC'D		UNDIVIDED PROFITS		
MARK-UP		EQUIPMENT		CURRENT PROFIT LOSS		
MARK-DOWN		STORE FIXTURES		ACC'TS PAYABLE		
CURRENT BOOK PROFIT AND LOSS		WAREHOUSE FIXTURES		NOTES PAYABLE		
WAREHOUSE MDSE BOOK RECORDS		OFFICE FIXTURES		OTHER LIABILITIES		
INV. BEGINNING MONTH		WAREHOUSE INV.				
PURCHASES AT BILLED COST		RETAIL STORES INV.				
FREIGHT ON PURCHASES		AT COST				
TOTAL		STOCKS & BONDS				
LESS SHIPMENTS OUT AT COST		OTHER ASSETS				
BOOK INV. END OF MONTH						
SHORTAGE TOTAL						
SALVAGE ACC'T FOR MONTH						
		TOTAL ASSETS		TOTAL LIABILITIES		

Fig. 47.—Monthly executive report.

tributing a small amount towards making the total overhead. Though showing a net loss after deducting its ratio of overhead, such a store assists by increasing purchasing power, or, perhaps, by initiating business for the company in a new and heavily competitive locality.

Thus, there must be a control account for direct retail store

19

DETAILED EXPENSE STATEMENT, MONTH OF					
	MONTH	$		TO DATE	$
DIRECT RETAIL EXPENSE					
SALARIES, STORE MGRS.					
COMMISSIONS					
OTHER CLERK EXPENSE					
RENT					
MISC. DIRECT CHARGES					
TOTAL DIRECT RETAIL EXPENSE					
OVERHEAD BURDEN OR INDIRECT EXPENSE					
WAGES-RECEIVING, HANDLING, AND SHIPPING FORCES					
BOXES AND WRAPPING					
OUTWARD FREIGHT AND CARTAGE					
TOTAL, RECV'G, HANDL'G, SHIP'G EXPENSE					
SALARIES BUYERS					
OTHER BUYING EXPENSES					
TOTAL BUYING EXPENSE					
EXECUTIVES SALARIES					
OFFICE SALARIES					
POSTAGE AND OFFICE SUPPLIES					
TELEPHONE AND TELEGRAPH					
OTHER MANAGEMENT EXPENSES					
TOTAL M'GEM'NT AND OFFICE EXENSES					
INTEREST					
RENT					
HEAT, LIGHT AND POWER					
TAXES					
INSURANCE					
REPAIRS OF EQUIPMENT					
DEPRECIATION OF EQUIPMENT					
TOTAL FIXED CHARGES					
MISCELLANEOUS EXPENSES					
LOSSES BY DEFALCATION					
ADVERTISING					
TOTAL OVERHEAD EXPENSE					
TOTAL AGGREGATE EXPENSE					
NET SHIPMENTS TO RETAIL OUTLETS					
GROSS BOOK PROFIT ON ABOVE					
LESS DIRECT RETAIL EXPENSE					
DIRECT RETAIL REVENUE					
LESS OVERHEAD EXPENSE					
NET BOOK RETAIL OPERATING PROFIT					
BOOK PROFIT ON WHOLESALE SALES					
AGGREGATE BOOK OPERATING PROFIT NET					

FIG. 48.—Monthly executive report (expense statement).

expense and one for indirect retail store expense. The expense sections on the reverse page of the report give in detail the figures for direct and indirect expense.

This report, as made up, gives the executive an accurate statement of the situation each month and is in sufficient detail

	STORE 1		STORE 2			STORE 35		CURRENT TOTAL		LAST YEAR TOTAL	
	AM'T	%	AM'T	%		AM'T	%	AM'T	%	AM'T	%
JAN.											
FEB.											
TO DATE											
DEC.											
TOTAL											
LAST YEAR											
GAIN OR LOSS											

MONTHLY FOR THE YEAR ——
COMPARATIVE NET BOOK PROFITS FROM RETAIL OPERATIONS

FIG. 49.—Monthly comparison form (by stores).

YEAR ——
COMPARATIVE RETAIL CASH SALES STATEMENT

	STORE 1			STORE 35			CURRENT TOTAL RETAIL			LAST YEAR TOTAL RETAIL		
	SALES	INV.	TURN.	SALES	INV.	TURN.	SALES	INV.	TURN.	SALES	INV.	TURN.
JAN.												
FEB.												
TO DATE												
DEC.												
TOTAL												
LAST YEAR												
GAIN OR LOSS												

FIG. 50.—Comparative retail cash sales statement.

to give him adequate data for use in administration.

Figure 49 shows another form of monthly report used in cases where the stock problem is more complicated than in the previous illustration. Here reports are made by departments, as well as by totals. This statement combines comparisons with the actual figures for the month.

Comparative Statements.—In many chain organizations, comparative statements are compiled at specified periods, sometimes weekly as shown previously, and also monthly and yearly. These statements may show sales, profits, expenses or other items of interest regarding the stores and their relative standing from different merchandising aspects. Figure 49 for example, shows a form for comparing the net book profit from retail operations by months. Space, as will be noted, is left for reducing all figures to percentages, the form which makes it easiest for the executives to grasp comparisons.

Figure 50 shows another form for making annual comparison of sales, inventory, and turnover, of the various stores.

It is apparent that figures such as these are of great importance to executives. They enable them to put a finger at once on all weak spots. If one store falls off in sales while other stores maintain a steady average, this fact shows up at once in the percentage column. The same is true of profits. Although the sales of two stores, in gross amounts, may come to the same figure, the net of profits of one may far outbalance the other and, again, these records should show clearly the reason for this deviation.

The Annual Report.—Annual reports are similar to monthly reports. They can well include more detail and, of course, are the final figures for the fiscal period, being compiled after an actual physical inventory of the warehouse stock fixtures and equipment, with depreciation and losses charged off. Practically the same form for the annual report can be used as is used for the monthly report.

The necessary forms are:

1. Balance sheet.
2. Income account.
3. Expense statement.

The annual report comes to the executive as a final link in his system of executive control. It also furnishes the ordinary medium by which the results of the year's operations are made public to stockholders.

Conclusions.—By the means and methods that have been described, the chief executive should be able to put into force an efficient and intelligent administration; for he has first set up the proper methods, and the mechanics for doing the necessary routine; and he has then set up the system of reports which show him they are being carried out as he has prescribed.

Thus warehousing and purchasing and the supervision of retail outlets are coördinated, and the chief executive, with a considerable degree of accurate knowledge, can exert his control and directing force on all parts of his organization effectively.

CHAPTER XIX

FINANCING AND GROWTH

OUTLINE

Methods of financing.
1. New stores financed out of profits from old stores.
2. New stores financed by borrowing money.
3. Absorption of chains by re-organization.

Principles of growth.
1. Steady growth in stores regardless of financial or business conditions.
2. Steady increase in gross sales.
   (a) In organization.
   (b) In individual stores.
3. Constant widening of chain store field.
   (a) In articles sold.
   (b) In services rendered.

Net profits.
1. Do not increase proportionately with gross sales.
   (a) Large turnover allows smaller margin of profit.
2 Dividends more stable than in other classes of industrial stocks.
3. Bonus system allowing adjustment of wages to sales.

Capitalization.
1. Ordinary form.
   (a) Issue of 7 per cent. preferred stock.
   (b) Issue of no-par value common stock.
   (c) Very seldom a bond issue.
      1. Provision for retiring with sinking fund.

Normal growth of chain organization.
1. Single store.
2. Slow growth store by store.
   (a) Gradual evolvement of organization.
   (b) Formation of operating routine.
3. More rapid growth.
   (a) Caused by
      1. Increased economies.
         (a) In purchasing.
         (b) Merchandising.
      2. Increased profits.
         (a) More stores.
         (b) Better operated stores.
      3. Cumulative effect of territorial expansion.

294

4. Combination and stock increase.

Distribution of stock.

    1 Old policy of keeping control in small number of stockholders.

    2. New policy of selling stock to customers.

Methods of selling stock.

    1. Through underwriting house.

        (*a*) Necessitates size and distribution on part of chain.

    2. Through local broker or direct sales or both.

Financial advertising.

    1. Should show present prosperity.

        (*a*) Net sales.

        (*b*) Safety.

        (*c*) Earnings and dividends.

    2. Statement of future prospects.

        (*a*) Reasons for wisdom of purchase.

CHAPTER XIX

CHAIN STORE FINANCING AND GROWTH

One of the remarkable aspects of chain store development is the smoothness with which all financial difficulties have been surmounted. The reason is not far to seek. Most chain systems have done their own financing out of profits. It has rarely been necessary to go to Wall Street for funds.

There are actually three ways in which a chain can finance its natural expansion:

1. Finance new stores out of own profits.
2. Finance by borrowing money.
3. Absorption of other chains by reorganization and exchange of stock, or some other means not requiring new capital.

A chain of retail stores is unlike a manufacturing business, in that the chain rarely has an inventory over its actual and immediate needs. Thus, its expansion in times of depression is in some cases as rapid, and even more rapid, than it is in times of great business activity. Since the chains deal in staple articles, much more so than the department stores and the mail order houses, their earnings do not show such fluctuations. They have financial stability in that they can be counted on to earn a profit regardless of general business conditions throughout the country.

The above statements are subject to some qualification. In 1920, for example, one of the large dry goods chains carried so large an inventory as to wipe out its entire profits on $52,800,000 of business, showing a net loss of $300,000. Its policy of expansion was curtailed, and it was able to regain its position in 1921.

In brief, although it is inadvisable to over-expand in the face of a period of depression, still the chain stores, as a rule, are better equipped to weather such storms than are most businesses.

In passing, it is noteworthy that times of depression are opportune ones for obtaining lease holds.

The question of finance is inextricably connected with the

progress of the various chains. To understand the problems of financing it is necessary to review the progress made by the chains during the last few years and the financial principles along which that progress has been conducted. The larger chains only are considered for the sake of convenience, and also because they are better known to the public.

The Principles of Chain Store Growth.—There are certain phenomena observable about the growth of chain stores:

1. Growth has been steady in spite of financial or business conditions.

2. Gross sales have increased in volume in spite of prosperity or depression.

3. There has been a constant widening of the articles and services marketed through chains of retail stores.

4. Although methods of organization have been different, those chains only have succeeded which have remained true to the fundamental principles of chain store operation, as outlined previously in this book.

The chain store organizations and the two large mail order houses are the only retail agencies which have attained great size and importance in the financial world. The mail order houses depend mainly on rural buying; the chain stores on urban.

No one has been able to estimate, even with approximate exactness, the number of chains in the United States or the number of stores operated by these chains. Only in a few lines has there been any exact census made, such as the drug chains. In the grocery field one concern is spending many thousand dollars in making a census of the grocery field. And, as the number of chains is increasing rapidly every year, the attempt to enumerate them is hardly worth while, lacking definite figures. It suffices to say that the chain store in the last seven years has made enormous strides, not only in the number of new chains, but more remarkably in the increased volume of sales in the old chains. As an example, let us consider the larger chains in the United States and compare their sales over the last seven years:

In each case the gross sales have far more than doubled. In the case of the Penney chain they have increased tenfold. The Kroger Grocery & Baking Company has increased its sales fourfold.

Company	ANNUAL SALES						
	1915	1916	1917	1918	1919	1920	1921
Great Atlantic & Pacific Tea Co.	44,441,199	76,430,565	126,691,919	151,691,919	194,646,99	235,302,877	202,433,531
F. W. Woolworth Co.	75,995,774	87,089,270	98,102,858	107,180,986	119,491,033	140,918,981	147,654,647
American Stores Co.			58,123,807	62,315,465	76,401,889	103,059,303	
... Cigar Stores Co.	31,038,846	35,822,985	42,193,406	52,037,747	61,874,053	80,040,000	78,000,000
May Department Stores Co.	23,309,802	33,404,866	35,631,600	41,179,261	57,962,444	68,254,715	
S. S. Kresge Co.	20,943,300	26,396,000	30,090,700	36,309,514	42,668,152	51,245,311	55,859,011
Kroger Grocery & Baking Co.	12,555,719	23,342,367	25,851,250	34,550,000	34,550,000	50,705,896	
J. C. Penney Co.	4,825,000	8,415,000	14,880,000	21,336,000	28,783,965	42,846,008	46,641,921
S. H. Kress Co.	12,249,590	15,059,683	17,633,100	21,160,111	25,244,131	28,973,847	28,908,985
Jones Bros. Tea	10,905,380	11,077,950	13,252,60	15,832,699	22,231,382	22,743,098	21,889,048

These ten chains, measured by the volume of their sales, are the largest in the United States. The first four in the list operate more than one thousand stores each. Four of the ten are grocery chains, three five and ten cent store chains, and two dry goods chains.

What is happening in the case of the large chains whose sales reports are shown here is happening in the case of thousands of small chains whose member stores are yet too few to mount up to large proportions of gross sales.

Earnings and Dividends.—With few exceptions, chain stores have been able to earn dividends, not only upon their preferred stock but also upon the common. The ordinary form of capitalization seems to be an issue of 7 per cent. preferred stock and a certain number of shares of common, no par value. Some chains have sold their stock at $10 a share to secure wider distribution among the public.

Few chains have any bonded indebtedness and net profits can be applied almost entirely to meeting demands of stockholders, although it must be remembered that a chain company needs a certain amount of capital for new enterprises during the year and this capital is taken out of earnings rather than borrowed, and the amount added to the funded debt.

The following tabulation shows a comparison of net profits earned on the common stock of the two large mail order companies and certain of the chain store companies. The comparison is taken for 1918, 1919, and 1920, that is, during the period of rising prices and falling prices.

EARNINGS ON COMMON STOCK (LAST THREE FIGURES OMITTED)

	1920		1919		1918	
	Net for com.	Net per share	Net for com.	Net per share	Net for com.	Net per share
Sears-Roebuck.............	$11,187	$13.07	$18,331	$26.03	$12,145	$17.63
Montgomery Ward........	†9,468	......	3,652	10.53	3,863	12.97
F. W. Woolworth........ .	8,918	13.87	8,554	17.11	4,982	9.96
S. S. Kresge..............	2,614	26.14	2,140	21.40	1,561	15.61
S. H. Kress..............	601	5.01	1,698	14.15	774	6.45
McCrory Stores.......,....	512	10.24	335	6.69	224	4.48
J. C. Penney..............	†560	......	1,805	114.15	696	44.00
Jones Bros. Tea..........	. 135	1.35	215	2.15	101	1.01

†Deficit.

Profits on common for the Sears-Roebuck Company were practically cut in two in 1920, while Montgomery Ward showed an actual deficit.· Among the five- and ten-cent stores, Kresge and McCrory showed big increases in net each year. Woolworth, because of its adherence to a policy of selling at five and ten cents showed a slight decrease in 1920, but the fall was in no way proportionate to that of the mail order houses. In addition, the company opened thirty new stores during the year. Earnings on the common stock of the Kress Company showed a sharp falling off but still showed enough to cover the four per cent. common dividend requirements.

Figure 51 shows yearly fluctuation in market value of the common stock of the Kresge Company from 1912. Note the great stability during the business depression of 1920 and 1921.

Chain store earnings and dividends show the following trends:

1. Net profits do not increase proportionately with increase in total sales. This is natural since a larger turnover of goods

allows the chain to operate on smaller margin of profit. In other words, the more sales are made, the less money it is necessary to make on each purchase.

2. Dividends paid on chain store stocks do not show that general tendency to fluctuate in times of prosperity and depression which is evidenced by other industrial stocks. That is, the business of retailing on a large scale is more generally profitable than a manufacturing business.

3. The ordinary form of capitalization is an issue of seven

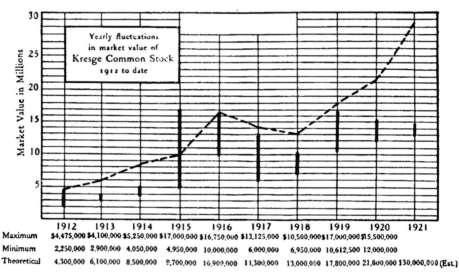

	1912	1913	1914	1915	1916	1917	1918	1919	1920	1921
Maximum	$4,475,000	$4,100,000	$5,250,000	$17,000,000	$16,750,000	$13,125,000	$10,500,000	$17,000,000	$15,500,000	
Minimum	2,250,000	2,900,000	4,050,000	4,950,000	10,000,000	6,000,000	6,950,000	10,612,500	12,000,000	
Theoretical	4,300,000	6,100,000	8,500,000	9,700,000	16,900,000	11,300,000	13,000,000	17,800,000	21,800,000	30,000,000 (Est.)

FIG. 51.—Growth in value of common stock of S. S. Kresge Company. (Merrill Lynch & Co.)

per cent. preferred stock followed by an issue of no par value common stock. Few chains have any bond issues outstanding, and if there are bonds, the general policy is to establish a sinking fund for their redemption as soon as possible.

4. The bonus system of recompensing employees allows a very rapid reduction in labor expenditures whenever sales fall off for any reason whatsoever. In other lines of business this cannot be accomplished either so rapidly, or so easily.

The Kresge Company.—To illustrate better this question of chain store financing the S. S. Kresge Co. has been taken as an example. The company started in business in 1897 with one store. In 1921 it had 198 stores, as far west as Lincoln, Nebraska, and as far south as Norfolk, Virginia. Sales, which were only $5,116,099 in 1909 increased to $55,859,011 in 1921. The margin of net profit has kept between 5.94 per cent. and 8.23 per cent. The company has made a phenomenal showing in net profits per store. In nine years it increased more than 147 per cent., from $7872 in 1912 to $19,463 in 1920, see Fig. 52. Average sales have advanced 123 per cent. or from $121,476 in 1912 to $271,139 in 1920.

The company has followed a policy of financing its expansion almost entirely out of earnings. During the development of the Kresge chain, as with all chain stores following a policy of starting new stores, the old stores have to carry the burden. Thus, the

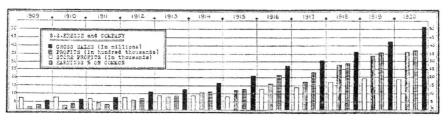

ʻIG. 52.—Gross sales, profits, and earnings on common stock of S. S. Kresge Company
(Financial World.)

reported profits on growing chains rarely show exactly how great an earning capacity the chain is capable of.

The company had one store in 1897, 42 in 1909, 84 in 1912, 157 in 1916, and 189 in 1920. In 1921, this number was raised to 198. More than 80 per cent. of the capital stock has come from reinvestment of surplus earnings. In 1916, when the company was reincorporated, the common stock was doubled and par value changed from $100 to $10. In 1917, the stock had so increased in value that part was changed back from $10 to $100 again. In June, 1920, common stock was increased to $20,000,000 and a note issue of $3,000,000 sold. It is interesting to observe that profits per share of common have not decreased because of increasing the amount of common stock outstanding. They have, on the contrary, kept up at a steady rate of increase (with the exception of 1921).

This account of the financial growth of the Kresge company has been included as a typical example of the method in which chain stores grow financially. The process seems to work out as follows:

1. A single store.

2. Idea of chain of stores. Slow growth over a period of years and ·gradual development of an organization and a system on which to operate.

3. Increased economies in purchasing, merchandising, etc., and increased profits (with the exception of 1921) allow more stores to be opened and territorial extension of operations. At this stage the chain may absorb other chains.

4. Increased capitalization of common stock to keep pace with development. Perhaps increased preferred stock issue to provide extra funds for further expansion.

Kingman Brewster, an authority on the legal aspects of chain store organization, makes the following comment:

"One of the most difficult problems in chain-store or industrial financing is the financing of corporations whose assets are under half or three-quarters of a million dollars. Whoever solves the problem of financing the small business will make a very decided contribution to corporation finance. For the reason of necessity the chains in the early stages have financed their expansion out of earnings. However, I once heard F. W. Woolworth state that such a policy was inconsistent with a desire to obtain a nation-wide distribution within the life time of a single man, and that in his own case he had found it necessary to provide for stock issues (originally $50,000,000 common, $13,000,000 preferred) for the purpose of making his institution a national one.

"J. C. Penney has, I think, used only about $3,000,000 preferred stock, the rest of the financing being done out of earnings. However, his organization, local and administrative, permits of an expansion by what amounts to additional partnerships and is very unusual in chain store operations. Furthermore, it is apparent that the method of financing is very frequently dependent upon the form of corporate organization, and the problem has been to find a method of transition from the business doing five or ten million dollars to a corporate form of organization which would permit of financing a business to do twenty-five millions or more. The obtaining of this change without disrupting the administrative organization is the problem upon which all growing chain organizations are working."

Chain Expansion from the Financial Standpoint.—The first method of expansion, as previously mentioned in the first part of this chapter, is to provide the necessary funds from current earnings of stores already in operation. Such a policy is entirely in line with the inherent conservative idea pursued by chain store organizations in general. By financing a new store out of accumulated cash surplus, there is no heavy overhead charge under which the new store must struggle. All the expenses incident to starting the new branch are already arranged for, and paid before the store opens.

This, of course, does not apply in cases where stores finance themselves. For example, where each store is operated as a separate corporation, it frequently borrows on its improved real estate and obligates itself to pay off the loan out of earnings. This may take a period of five to ten years, but it means of course that the earnings of the local business go into the capital assets.

The method of financing out of earnings, though it is safe, is slow, and men with vision, anxious to succeed, and sure of the soundness of their principles and methods, wish to take short cuts. That is, they wish to borrow the capital from Wall Street or directly from the public. In other words, they wish to float stock, generally preferred, to the public, in order that they may the quicker get a large number of stores into actual operation. This may be accomplished by combining with another chain, not by purchase, but by affiliation, as was the case with the present components of the Woolworth chain. It may be necessary to buy out other chains, and such a sudden drain on the exchequer may make it necessary to seek financial help outside the company.

In the Penney chain, each new store is financed on a partnership basis. In other chains there are special policies pursued in opening new stores, although in each case the central organization furnishes all the capital. It is impossible to lay down any rules for financing other than those which govern the money market in general. The great advantage of the chains has always been that they did not find it necessary to borrow money when money was high. Another point in their favor is that ordinarily there is no large inventory to finance in periods of declining prices. The best insurance for the future is the amount of cash in banks.

Distribution of Stock.—Some chain organizations, in spite of their size, have always kept the control of the company in comparatively few hands. For example, this policy has been traditional with the Great Atlantic & Pacific Tea Co., and with the Singer Sewing Machine Co. Both these companies have pursued a policy of expansion without borrowing, and this explains the small distribution of the stock.

Other companies, and the number of this latter class is growing more numerous, like to have the stock distributed as widely as possible among the public, and especially the public which purchases their goods. For this purpose the par value of the stock is often put at $10 so that distribution among small stockholders may be even wider. The psychology of this, of course, is that owners of stock in a certain chain will purchase goods there rather than somewhere else.

When a chain store wishes to sell stock, it has two alternatives:

1. It may go to a responsible broker and pay him a certain amount for underwriting the stock.
2. It may try to sell the stock directly to its customers.

If a chain store stock issue is to be floated from Wall Street, the issue of stock must be large. The underwriters do not care to handle anything small. It would not pay them to set in motion the machinery for selling stock on a large scale, the newspaper campaigns in various cities, the syndicate members, etc. There are two necessities for floating a chain store stock issue from New York.

1. The chain must be large.
2. The chain must be national or at least sectional.

A chain of stores is known only in the localities where it sells goods. A manufacturing plant is known far and wide over the country because of the wide distribution of its products.

Figure 53 shows the method which Merrill, Lynch & Company used to put before the public the advantages of the S. S. Kresge stock. The graphic method has been employed to show the enormous growth in profits and sales compared with the comparatively smaller growth in number of stores operated.

If a chain, which is local and comparatively small, wishes to distribute its stock, it may call in a local broker or else attempt to float the stock itself. The stock, of course, must be floated

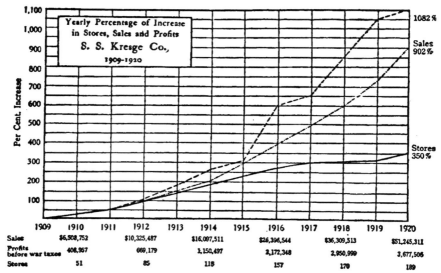
Fig. 53.—Advertisement of chain store securities.

mainly in the district where the stores are operated, because it is difficult to sell stock where the company is not known.

It is of course a function of a broker not only to dispose of stock for the purpose of adding new capital to a chain organization, but also to maintain a liquid market for the securities. In this respect a corporation which has a large number of stockholders is in a much more safe position than where the distribution of stock is localized. There is, as is pointed out in this chapter, the additional interest of the stockholder in the business with which he deals.

If a chain decides to sell its own stock, and this is frequently the case, it can be handled either by a mail order campaign to customers of the chain or by combining this method with advertising.

Financial Advertising.—Many small investors in chain organizations never would have gone to an investment house for their stock. The reason they invest in the chain securities is because they are personally acquainted with its activities and can see for themselves the business done. Therefore, a frequent and sound investment argument is that the dividends from savings invested in chain store stock will help to pay for purchases. It is the same argument which was so successful in selling the stock of American Telephone & Telegraph Company.

There are certain things a chain should show in financial publicity matter:

1. The prosperity of the chain at present. In this category come net sales for the year as compared with past years and the same for net earnings. Next there should be mention of dividend rate at present and in the past, and some statement of the security of the income and the investment.

2. The future prospects of the chain and a concise statement of why this stock is being offered for sale.

Figure 54 shows an advertisement appearing in the local newspapers in districts served by the Waldorf System, Incorporated. An analysis of this advertisement discloses the following facts:

1. Why customers purchase Waldorf stock.
2. The size of the chain and its volume of business.

Why I Want Waldorf Customers to Share in Our Profits

There are hundreds of people eating daily at the Waldorf Lunches who, every three months, are paid back by the Waldorf the money they spent in the meantime for their lunches. They have found one of the most profitable methods of reducing the cost of living.

They are the men and women who have put their savings in the common stock of the Waldorf System, Inc., and own enough shares so that the dividends they have received pay for their lunches the year around.

I am taking this method of talking to our thousands of patrons, as a great many of them are not investors, or are not in touch with investment houses, and are therefore not likely to know what, an unusually safe and profitable investment the common stock of the Waldorf System, Inc., is.

Many of our customers, for instance, do not know that the Waldorf System, Inc., is now one of the largest chains of lunch rooms in the country, spreading over seven States—that it is growing faster than any other chain—that there are now 89 restaurants in 28 different cities—that *every day* about $30,000 is taken in in *cash* sales—that although less than two cents is made on the average meal of 30 cents, the vast volume of 36,000,000 meals a year enabled the Company to pay substantial dividends to owners of Waldorf common stock last year.

Why do I want more of our customers to become owners of our common stock? For much the same reason that every employee in the service of the Waldorf System, Inc., through a profit-sharing plan, participates in the profits of this System, down to the fellows that scrub the floors. Nothing pays so well as taking employees and the public into partnership, so to speak. For one of the reasons you receive more prompt and courteous service in a Waldorf Lunch is because the man serving you feels the pride and responsibility of being something more than a salaried employee.

For instance, you, as a Waldorf customer buy some of its common stock, and thereby become a part owner. You now feel more at home, eating in a restaurant in which you have an owner's interest. You take an interest in everything going on. If you notice some lapse in the courteous service or high standard of cleanliness of the Waldorf Lunches, you report it at once to the management. You will probably be giving us some idea of how a little improvement might be made, as other customer-stockholders have. You become a messenger of good will. For, while, previously, you would tell a friend casually of the good things to eat at a Waldorf Lunch, you now, as an owner, naturally go out of your way to spread the good news of better food. Your interest brings Waldorf more and more business—because it is bringing business to *yourself.* You are not satisfied unless other customers are satisfied—and that spirit helps us in pleasing the 36,000,000 people we serve in a year.

Before we thus publicly invited our customers to become part owners of Waldorf Lunches through purchase of shares of the common stock, we wanted the most positive evidence to show the public how safe and profitable such an investment would be—proof that any man or woman could understand. We now have it.

During the last year Dun's reported 8881 business failures in the United States. Practically everybody knows that many of the largest corporations in the country had to cut off their dividends during the business depression, and that many of them closed down entirely. Yet, since April, 1919, the Waldorf System, Inc., has enjoyed such prosperity that it increased the number of its lunch rooms from 59 to 89—a 50% increase

The net earnings for 1919 were at the rate of $385,467 a year. Although the increased costs of provisions reduced the Company's profits per meal during 1920, the new restaurants acquired and the large increase in the volume of business with careful, efficient management, enabled the company to show net earnings at the rate of $626,703 for 1920.

In 1919 dividends on the common stock were at the rate of 10% per year, cash dividend. In the year just closed, 1920, there were a cash dividend of 10% and two stock dividends of 5% each. Based on the present outlook, I can see no reason why future earnings should not equal or exceed past earnings.

This company—nor any of its officers—has no common stock to sell. It may be purchased like any other stock in the open market through any stock exchange member. The market price is shown daily on the Boston Stock Exchange.

If you have no broker connection, or if you are not familiar with investment matters, I shall be glad to advise you of the name of some responsible investment house through which you can buy Waldorf Common Stock. I shall welcome you as a part owner of this business, no matter how few shares you can buy. And you'll have the satisfaction of having your money invested in a business that has been *proved* safe.

P. E. Woodward. President

WALDORF SYSTEM INCORPORATED

169 High Street
Boston, Mass.

FIG. 54.—Form of financial advertising used by Waldorf System, Inc.

3. The results of customers' owning stock and the value to the chain and the customer.

4. The safety of the investment.

5. Net earnings.

6. Dividends paid.

Conclusions.—As the various chains grow in size, the problem of financing will grow more important than it has been in the past. Even now the capitalization of some of the large chains is tremeudous. For example, the F. W. Woolworth Co. has $100,000,000 of common stock authorized, of which $77,000,000 is outstanding, plus $12,000,000 of preferred stock. The United Retail Stores Corporation was capitalized with $10,000,000 eight per cent. preferred stock, 1,000,000 shares of Class A common stock, and 160,000 shares of founders stock. This means that some of these chains are able to compete in capital with some of the largest manufacturers, and this power behind the chains is rapidly making them a factor to be reckoned with.

Outside financing should be a chain's last resort. The average chain should be able to finance new stores out of earnings. In case of the purchase of other chains or a particularly large expansion program, it may become necessary to seek help outside, and in this event the method will depend on the size and character of the chain. A national chain may be financed from Wall Street; a local chain must be financed locally and perhaps by the chain itself.

CHAPTER XX

INSURANCE

By M. MacIntyre[1]

One has only to consider for a moment the subject of insurance as applied to chain store systems to see its importance. Insurance means protection from liability. It may mean solvency or the opposite. At a comparatively small overhead expense, the chain can guard itself against various losses which it may incur and over which it has no control. These losses fall into three general classifications:

1. Damage to the premises or merchandise, the most frequent cause of which is fire.
2. Liability on account of personal injuries to individuals on or by the property of the chain, through accident.
3. Loss through the dishonesty of employees.

The average chain may look at these problems in two ways: First, it may consider, if the risk is well distributed, that if one store is destroyed by fire, the rest of them will remain unharmed and the loss will be comparatively small, and can easily be borne. Second, it may be argued, if the locations are not distributed, the chances of a severe loss on a single occasion are many times increased. In general, the insurance policies of the various chains are combinations of these two points of view.

The Insurance Broker.—Insurance is a matter of major importance, not to be left entirely to the insurance broker. It does not follow that what the broker has to offer in the way of insurance is the best to fit the individual case. The company, however, particularly if it has been established for some years, knows fairly well where the greatest risks lie. The best policy, therefore, is for it to determine what insurance it needs and then make the broker supply it.

A company gains nothing by distributing its insurance among

[1] Manager of the Insurance Department of one of the largest chain store organizations in the country.

several brokers. It is certainly no cheaper, and it adds complicating factors. If the business is not given totally to one broker, in the event of loss there is complication or confusion in arranging for the adjustment, whereas, if one broker handles the entire insurance business of the chain, it will be found more satisfactory.

Insurance should be awarded on purely business grounds. There is so much competition among rival brokers that the question of patronage is apt to come up. Personal friendships should not be allowed to influence the decision.

The cheaper policy is not necessarily the better policy. In case of a loss, the small difference in premium payments will count not at all. An insurance company can be compared to a savings bank. It is not so much the more favorable rate of interest as the *security* which is desired. It is not wise, therefore, to take the policies of obscure companies, even though they may call for smaller premium payments.

One more caution will not be out of place. Never allow your broker to get a lower rate by some subterfuge. Misrepresentation voids the policy and you never hear about it until the loss occurs.

Insurance Against Fire.—In general, it is unwise to take any part of the fire risk. Over-insurance is better than under-insurance. This statement applies most particularly to local chains whose stores are situated near each other. The statement may be modified in the case of the larger chains. For example, it may be advisable to assume the initial risk, say of a few thousand dollars, for any given store and to insure the excess over and above that amount. This will give a lower insurance cost and may prove cheaper in the end. It should not, however, be resorted to unless the locations are fairly well distributed. There are some chain stores having as many as ten stores in a given conflagration area and risks of this sort are too dangerous for any but an insurance company to carry.

At first thought, it would seem reasonable to suppose that a large chain could carry its own insurance more cheaply than the same security could be had of insurance companies. But, as insurance is based on averages, a series of losses may occur which would cripple the organization, and therefore even the largest chains cannot expect to insure themselves entirely—that is, assume their own risks. The fire insurance company which did not have more locations than the largest chain store organization would be a small one and its losses would soon lead it into bankruptcy.

Chains whose member stores number in the thousands are comparatively few. Chains in the hundreds are still exceptions, so that for the great mass of chains, complete insurance against damage by fire is highly to be recommended.

Real Estate Insurance.—As we saw in the chapter on "Locating the Store," chain store systems may have to enter the real estate business themselves in order to get the most desirable locations for their own stores, and by that we mean that it may sometimes become necessary to purchase or to take the lease of an entire building, or at least of more space than is actually needed, in which to conduct a link in the chain store system. This brings up questions of real estate insurance. Among the forms of real estate insurance commonly carried are fire insurance on buildings, rents, leasehold interest, and improvements.

1. *Building Insurance.*—If a lease of an entire building, and almost invariably, if what is known as a ground lease is taken, the lessee (the chain store system) is required to keep the building insured for the benefit of the landlord. If, when making the lease, the fire clause does not provide that the repair or rebuilding of the premises shall be performed by the lessor (the landlord) insistence should be made upon providing that the building insurance should be in the names of both landlord and lessee as interest may appear. Building insurance frequently contains "loss payable" clause in favor of a mortgagee. It is important to note that it is not necessary for the mortgagee interest to appear in all policies, but only in such number of them as may be required to make up the amount of the mortgagee's interest. In other words, to have a mortgagee clause or designation in some policies and not in others does not render the insurance non-concurrent.

The question of amount of insurance is important. If the lessee is responsible for deficiency of insurance in case of loss, it is advisable to insure for full insurable value regardless of any co-insurance clause. One hundred per cent. co-insurance should never be used in building policies. Insurable value is not replacement value, but replacement value less depreciation. Recently it has become possible to carry insurance against loss in connection with a fire due to depreciation, but prior to that time a loss due to depreciation had to be borne by the lessee or the landlord according to the terms of the lease.

2. *Rent Insurance.*—There are several forms of rent insurance—rental value (occupied or vacant), rent (occupied only) and leasehold interest (rent paid in advance). It is sometimes difficult to know which form should be used. Generally speaking *Rental Value* form should be used in the following two cases:

A. When an owner leases a building to a number of tenants whose leases contain provision for abatement of rent in case of untenantability due to fire and or termination of lease with or without refund of rent paid in advance.

B. When the lessee of an entire building, under a fire clause providing for no abatement of rent, leases various portions to different tenants with provision in lease for abatement of rent in case of untenantability due to fire.

The *Rent* (Occupied Only) form should be used where an owner leases to a single tenant under the conditions above described, or where a lessee of an entire building under fire clause providing for no abatement of rent, sublets the entire premises to a third party under terms providing for an abatement of rent. In many insurance jurisdictions there is a difference of 25 per cent. in the rate between the two forms in favor of the Occupied Only form, which should be taken advantage of whenever possible.

Rent Paid in Advance.—Where a lessee is holding under a lease providing for an abatement of rent in case of untenantability due to fire, but not providing for refund of rent paid in advance, he should insure under the leasehold interest form.

3. *Leasehold Interest.*—There are several forms of leasehold insurance, including rent paid in advance, anticipated profits and bonus. The first form differs from the others in that it refers to rents paid or to be paid. The other forms are designed to guard against the loss due to fire through the termination of the lessee's lease, of the benefits of moneys invested, or of profits which, during the term of the lease, would have accrued. The amount collectible under these forms is automatically reduced according to the unexpired term of the lease on any given date.

4. *Improvements.*—Improvements are betterments made to

existing buildings, and a lessee may insure its interest in such improvements against damage to or the loss of them by fire in its own name. A landlord is not generally under the obligation to restore improvements made by a tenant, although an owner usually does so unless the improvements are of an unusual character or expensive. It should be kept clearly in mind that, if a lessee erects a new building on vacant land, it does not constitute an improvement within the meaning of the improvement form of insurance. The same would have to be insured as a building in the name of the lessee *as owner* with a special clause providing that it is standing on leased ground if, by the terms of the lease of the ground, title to the property did not immediately pass to the landlord. If title passed, then the building must be insured as such in name of the ground landlord, and the lessee as interest may appear, *with the consent of the landlord*.

Fire Insurance Policies.—There are two types of general fire policies, first, floater policies, and, second, blanket policies. These are in contra-distinction to ordinary policies applying to a specific location. A blanket policy covers, let us say, any given number of locations in the chain. A floater policy, on the other hand, covers all present locations and any others which may be acquired of the same class. It is necessary, of course, to carry specific policies on warehouses or office buildings where the value of the unit is especially large.

In the larger cities, and these are where the greatest number of chain stores are located, the 80 per cent. co-insurance clause is in current use. It is important to make a study of this clause. It does not mean that it is necessary for the chain store organization to carry any part of its risk. As an example of what the clause is, let us assume that the insurable value of the property is ten thousand dollars and that eight thousand dollars of insurance is carried. If a fire loss of anything up to eight thousand dollars is sustained, it may be collected from the insurance company in full. On the other hand, if only seven thousand dollars worth of insurance were carried, then only seven-eighths of the actual loss could be recovered, and so on in the same proportions. In other words, you must insure 80 per cent. of the value of the property if you wish to collect the full amount of the partial loss. Otherwise, it is only possible to collect proportionately.

Plate Glass Insurance.—Since window display forms such an important part in chain store merchandising, there are many plate glass windows to be considered in the insurance problem. Chain stores having several hundred stores may perhaps safely assume their risks on plate glass insurance. If you have been carrying insurance, and wish to see how it would work out in your own case, get figures for the last two years as to breakages, and get a glass concern to give you a figure as to the cost of making replacements. Allow a 25 per cent. salvage for glass recovery. Compare the cost of replacement minus salvage with the premiums you paid including the reinstatement premiums (wherever a breakage occurs, it is necessary to get a new policy, and to pay a so-called reinstatement premium).

If the cost in two years is less than the premiums which it would have been necessary to pay, then it may be well to experiment for a year in assuming your own risk, setting up on the books a fund to take care of breakages, this fund to be equal to the premiums you would have paid.

The reason the company can assume such a risk as this is that, even though a heavy series of losses should occur, they are limited in any single case.

Public and Employers' Liability Insurance.—Insurance against accident on the premises costs little and the possibilities of incurring damage suits are great. It is likewise necessary to insure employees under the compensation law. These are cases of protection against events which are not very likely to happen, but, in the event of their occurrence, the claim for damages may be large.

In choosing the company in which to take out this class of insurance, the best is none too good. Liability cases give rise to claims which may not be settled for years, and you want to be sure the insurance company will be doing business at that time. If the insurance company fails, it is well to remember that the liability of the chain organization is not in any way lessened thereby.

Chains in certain lines may find it necessary to carry special liability insurance. For example, chain drug stores should carry druggists' liability insurance against wrong filling of prescriptions and also against incorrect delivery.

Since most chain stores use automobiles for transportation of goods between stores and warehouses, if not also for retail delivery, automobile liability insurance should be carried. It is well to have this in the same company which covers the public liability in stores, since there are frequently border-line cases. If there are two insurance companies involved, it would permit a dispute, whereas if there is only one company, there can be no excuse for its not shouldering the entire responsibility.

Every accident of any kind should be reported to the insurance company, even though there are no personal injuries. The latter may develop, and failure to give notice may prejudice the insurance.

Other Forms of Insurance.—Burglary and hold-up insurance is almost a necessity, especially since it is known that the member stores operating on a cash and carry basis take in a great deal of money.

Protection against messenger and paymaster robberies should also be carried. This may be included on the same policy with the burglary and hold-up insurance.

Life insurance on executives drawn in favor of the corporation or firm may be desirable as a means of offsetting temporary loss of business or the lessened ability of the new incumbent. This is a matter for individual decision.

Group insurance may, or may not, be an important stabilizing factor in labor turnover. Where the wages in a trade are practically fixed, as in cases where employees are unionized, the additional attraction of group insurance may prove alluring. But where there is no fixed rate, the employees seem to prefer an increase in wages rather than to have insurance protection, regardless of how small this increase may be. That is, the employee of the retail store class prefers the small immediate advantage to the greater advantages which would accrue to his dependents after his death.

Employees will not stick to one chain merely on account of group insurance, if they can go to another chain which also offers them group insurance. This defect, of course, may be obviated to some extent by making the insurance inoperative during the first six months.

Group insurance is a question which affects the liability of the company in no way.   Its purpose is rather towards making the employee more satisfied and contented, and in reducing the labor turnover.   Each chain must decide whether it answers this purpose from the circumstances and factors which bear on its own case.

Bonding Employees.—Chain store employees should, without exception, be bonded.   This does not mean that there is a large percentage of dishonesty among chain store employees, but there undoubtedly is great opportunity for dishonesty in various ways, and this should be discouraged by the company in every possible way.

The purpose of bonding employees is not so much on account of the expectation of recovering losses, as for the elimination by the bonding company of dishonest employees.   To recover losses on a bonded employee it is necessary to prove dishonesty. Most thefts from chain stores are made in small quantities and detection of any individual delinquency is difficult.   Furthermore, all losses not proved against dishonest employees must be borne by the employer.

The bonding company's real function is to serve as an investigator of the character of the chain's employees.   No bonding proposition which does not contemplate a thorough and immediate investigation of the prospective employee's record is any good.   The bonding business is founded on the average honesty of the human being, and its success is determined by narrowing the risk, in so far as possible, through elimination of dishonest individuals.

The way to prevent losses is not to have employees who steal. Bonding is one way of selecting honest individuals, as well as a means of protection against defalcation.

Conclusions.—A chain store system makes use of every economy possible in its effort to make the purchasing and merchandising mechanism 100 per cent. efficient.   Therefore, it is important to make sure that a lack of protection where protection is necessary and possible should not nullify the merchandising economies.   That is, insurance should be adequate.

The problem, of course, differs for the chain with three stores and the chain with three hundred, not in principle, but in the variety of risks to be assumed.   The larger the company and the larger the number of branch stores operated, the larger the opportunity for self-insurance. In the largest chains, there should be a special department to take care of insurance problems, to decide on the necessity of protection and the amount of insurance which should be carried, premium necessary to pay. But do not neglect your insurance problems. It is worth while to pay for the protection insurance gives.

CHAPTER XXI

THE MANUFACTURER'S CHAIN

It is necessary at once to sound a caution against confusing chains which manufacture with the manufacturer's chain. The former is primarily a retailing organization and in no case limits its sales to the articles it manufactures. It sells what the public wants and if it can make the public want goods of its own manufacture so much the better. The true manufacturer's chain, on the other hand, is limited to a manufacturer who aims to dispose of a part or all of his output through his own retail outlets.

The immediate causes of a manufacturer starting a chain of retail stores may be many, but the majority of them come down, in the end, to dissatisfaction with the methods of distribution. Many companies find the jobber and the retailer extremely unsatisfactory. In times of depression, these outlets become choked, and the manufacturer is compelled impotently to wait until the road is clear. In times of prosperity, jobbers and dealers send in order after order, but when the turn comes they are just as quick with their cancellations.

Manufacturers who start retail stores, therefore, do so usually with the clear purpose of distributing their products more directly. That they have had no retailing experience is too often lost sight of at the beginning. Manufacturing and retailing functions are almost diametrically opposed. It takes a different type of mind in the executive and an entirely different type of organization for these two functions. In addition, there are the ever-present questions of whether manufacturing or retailing is more important to the company, and the question of which one should prevail. The fact that there are many successful retail chains operated by manufacturers does not alter the fact that the manufacturer has to face an exceedingly difficult problem.

Advantages Possessed by the Manufacturers' Chain.—A manufacturer should take careful stock of what is to be gained before definitely deciding to enter the retail field. In other

318

words, he must budget his prospects. On one side of the page he must put the advantages he expects to gain and on the other the obstacles which he must be prepared to surmount. He must carefully weigh the results.

The following discussion is based on an excellent article on the subject which appeared recently. In the first place, what can the manufacturer hope to gain by starting a chain of retail stores?

1. If they are properly managed, he should receive almost 100 per cent. coöperation in backing up his consumer advertising. This brings out immediately one of the causes of dissension between the manufacturer and the dealer. The manufacturer wants his product given first preference by the jobber and dealer and the same feeling is shared by his rival manufacturers. This may be obviated by granting exclusive agencies, but whether exclusive agencies are the best form of retail merchandising for manufacturers is open to question.

2. Retail prices can sometimes be lowered. This is a very real advantage in any retailing proposition. The chain, however, immediately experiences the condition of affairs encountered by the Regal Shoe Co. where the company was selling shoes in its own stores at less than the Regal agency around the corner. What is the answer? Price is such an important element in chain store competition that the manufacturer might profit by it. Indeed, the ability to sell at a lower price would almost be necessary to make the manufacturers' chain successful in a short time.

3. Any service work demanded by the retailer can be rendered more satisfactorily. Naturally the management can install the most modern merchandising policies and see that they are uniformly carried out in the stores. In other words, the manufacturer will initiate his own service rather than wait for a dealer who may not see the need for it or, if he does, may not have sufficient interest to bring it to the attention of the management.

4. Substitution can be more surely avoided. The importance of this point will depend largely upon the company's present relations with its retailers.

5. The consumer and his tastes can be studied at first hand. This is a real advantage and one which many manufacturers have taken advantage of. In this case the retail stores are not created primarily for profit and the stores are usually few in number to be used as a laboratory.

6. The product itself can frequently be improved as a result of direct contact with the user.

7. It is possible to develop new sales arguments.

8. The results obtained through the retail stores can be applied in dealing with other retailers outside the organization.

9. Advertising and display material can be made uniform and used to much greater advantage than if merely distributed to agencies or retailers.

10. Road salesmen can be trained in retail stores.

11. By the publicity attained, new dealers may be secured to handle the product.

So much for the tabulation of advantages. The following are some practical advantages, as found by representative manufacturers:

One of the main reasons for manufacturers opening retail stores was the larger volume of sales. In many cases it was a last resource. In some cases, stores in particular communities have been opened only because of the peculiar character of the competition there. They might be called strategy stores. Some stores have been started when a market had to be created for a new product; sometimes when there were no dealers in the field, such as was the case with automobiles. Sometimes stores were started when goods were so novel that dealers hesitated to take them up. This was true of Dennison's retail stores in the early days. Dealers would not carry a large enough stock. The present Dennison stores are more like warehouses than stores.

As far as reducing the retail price is concerned, one company was found which had succeeded in selling its goods at from 15 per cent. to 20 per cent. less.

There are technical products which demand service. The Waterman Fountain Pen Co. has several retail stores. Yawman & Erbe and the Library Bureau are further examples.

Manufacturers' stores may serve as experimental laboratories and training schools for salesmen. The manufacturer can study the buying public through his retail stores. S. E. Summerfield, president of the Gotham Hosiery Co., says that through his New York stores he can get information regarding public taste he could not secure in five or six months through other dealers.

Chain Shirt Shops were created to try out the selling of Olus combination shirtwaist and drawers for men, which had not worked well in the regular trade. They did not work here either, but the retail stores are excellent outlets for other men's wear. The Dennison stores, according to Advertising Manager Schuyler Van Ness, are used as laboratories to get first hand criticism of goods from home consumers. Defects can be discovered immediately.

Some manufacturers have found that one of their stores conducted profitably is of more value in convincing retailers of the value of the product than anything else. The Gotham stores are frequently visited by buyers. The retail store often gives the product backing in the eyes of the public.

The Redfern Corset Company's stores are maintained almost entirely to train dealers' department heads and saleswomen in the art of corset fitting, alteration, merchandising, and stock-keeping.

When Dennison moved the location of his Philadelphia store, a nearby retailer threw out his entire department, and a year later put it back with double the size because of increased calls for Dennison goods.

These experiments have been cited at length because they illustrate the variety of uses to which the manufacturer may put his retail outlets. The manufacturer who is thinking of starting a chain of retail stores should carefully take all these points into consideration.

Disadvantages.—The disadvantages which the manufacturer must overcome when starting retail stores are so serious, that it becomes a desperate remedy for a situation which can be solved in no other way. The disadvantages may be listed as follows:

1. It has taken years in nearly every case to get stores on a paying basis. Many times they have been operated at actual financial loss.

2. There is always the danger of trying to compete with the company's own retailers unless, like Browning, King & Co., the retail stores absorb the company's entire production.

3. Frequently the retailers object strongly to a retail store operated by the company and while the stores of the company may be successful, sales may fall off sharply in agencies.

4. Since the manufacturer must maintain the highest standards in his stores, he has a high overhead.

5. The chain must obtain the services of an experienced retail manager. This is essential. The manufacturer himself is not competent to look after the retailing end of the business. The whole question of the personnel becomes more difficult owing to the lack of personal relations between the management and the retail end of the business.

6. The manufacturer is limited to his own line of goods. In this way he may be at a disadvantage in comparison with independent dealers or chains. It is also claimed that the manufacturer's chain does not respond quickly to change in public taste because the initiative generally comes from the manufacturing instead of the retail end.

21

The manufacturer can now see just what points he must consider before starting a retailing venture. In nearly every way he is at a disadvantage when compared with the retail chain selling the products of others as well as its own, but the fact that there are successful chains run by manufacturers is sufficient evidence that the enterprise is by no means hopeless. The manufacturer must weigh the following points:

1. What is my purpose in entering the retail field?
2. Is there no cheaper and more easy way out of the difficulty experienced in distributing or selling the product?

Organization.—When the manufacturing end is in control, chain organization may differ in various ways. The essential point is the degree of control exercised by the directors of the manufacturing company and, in some measure, the degree with which they exercise the power actually in their hands.

Following are some of the ways in which the retail outlets and the manufacturing enterprise can be and are coördinated:

1. Where the whole output of the factory is sold through retail outlets of the company. This is the simplest form of manufacturers' chain because it eliminates the intricate dealer and agency question. In this class come such chains as Browning, King & Co. who started in 1868 to retail their own products and now own seventeen stores. The Library Bureau for forty years has followed the policy of selling all its goods through its own stores. The Singer Sewing Machine Co., with 6,000 stores in all parts of the world, and 1,800 in this country alone, is one of the most imposing examples of a successful manufacturer's chain.

2. Chains which sell through their own retail stores and also through independent retailers or agencies. Most manufacturers' chains fall under this classification. The W. L. Douglas Shoe Co., the Regal Shoe Co., A. G. Spalding & Bros., etc., are examples of this type. Naturally such a system involves much more accounting than the first type. It is in cases like this that goods are billed to member stores at wholesale, rather than retail prices, to avoid a double system of accounting at headquarters.

3. There is the further type of manufacturers' chain, small in size, which is not designed primarily for retail outlets. The

Gotham Hosiery Co. is an example of this type. Sales for 1921 through its three retail stores in New York amounted to over a million and a half dollars. In the tiny shop on West Thirty-fourth Street there are eighteen sales girls placed as close to each other as they can stand. Nothing is sold but Gotham Hosiery and, as there is little looking around or pricing, the turnover is exceedingly rapid. Warner Brothers Co., makers of Redfern corsets, have stores in New York City, Chicago, and San Francisco. The Sherwin Williams Co., paint manufacturers, have retail stores in many cities.

Many manufacturing companies are run under the committee plan where the heads of the organization, in conference, map out procedure and development. Naturally they attempted to extend this plan to the retail stores, but found it did not work. Chain stores need centralized control, chiefly because they themselves are so scattered that there must be some well-defined bond holding them to the central organization. A committee is too impersonal. It is too cumbersome. It takes too long to function. It cannot keep pace with local conditions. Every chain should have some sort of executive in charge who knows his business and who is in direct control of an able staff of subordinates.

Some manufacturers' chains have solved the problem of organization by forming a separate holding and operating company to manage their retail outlets. Whatever form of control is chosen, it should always be borne in mind that the selling and the manufacturing must be divorced and, that if either is to furnish initiative for change in policy, this should preferably come from the retail end as being closer in touch with public demand.

The Product.—R. A. Bruce says that, for chain store purposes, products must be divided into two classes:

1. Convenience goods which can be sold without disturbing existing distribution to any great extent.

2. Articles demanding personal service which will interfere with existing trade relationships.

In the first case it is perfectly possible for Page & Shaw to have a retail store of its own in the middle of a block and to have agencies in two drug stores, one at each end of the block. The reason is that candy is a convenience article and people generally buy it wherever they are.

In the second case people will go out of their way to get a particular article. The manufacturers of shoes operating retail stores and also giving agencies are up against this problem.

The product can be considered in a different light, however. If the manufacturer makes a product which is extremely limited in its use, such as a door-hinge, it is quite evident that a chain of retail stores would not be worthy of serious consideration. His logical outlet is the dealer and his logical appeal to the public through advertising.

But in the case where the product itself is the entire output of an industry such as shoes, hats, shirts, clothing, etc., it is equally evident that the product is fitted for sale through a manufacturers' chain. That is, as far as the product itself is concerned, there is sufficient demand from the public to support a store dealing exclusively in this product.

The Agency Problem.—To what extent can the manufacturer compete with himself? When the field is already supposedly occupied by retailers handling his products, is it possible for him to start his own stores in such a way as to keep the loyal coöperation and help of existing agencies? This is a problem the individual manufacturer must solve in his own way. It is difficult to see how a certain amount of friction can be avoided. A retailer will naturally resent the entrance of the company into his district with a retail store of its own. He feels that it is going to affect his business adversely. Whether it does or not depends largely upon the company and the assistance it gives the agency when compared with the assistance rendered its own stores.

The Regal Co. for a long time maintained two separate policies in regard to its own stores and its agencies. Then it was discovered that customers had very often to pay more for their shoes at the agencies than at the company's stores. There was a very thorough investigation of the whole problem and it was found that the agencies were getting little or no coöperation. As a result the policy of the company was reversed. The agencies were, to a certain extent, taken into the company. Their own store managers were ordered to give the fullest assistance to the local agency. The district managers were told to give the problems of the agency the same attention they would give the problems of the store managers. An attempt was made to make the agencies feel the company was working with them rather than in competition with them. The most important concession was a leveling of price charges so that agencies obtained shoes at exactly the same price at which they were delivered to the company's own stores. Furthermore, the company's stores were made warehouses from which agencies could draw in emergency for supplies of shoes, thus avoiding the necessity of waiting until the company's nearest warehouse could ship the goods, and perhaps saving many sales. A policy such as this is bound to work out to the benefit of both parties, since it is based upon team-work and coöperation rather than competition.

The Personnel.—As in the case of the normal retailers' chain, the personnel is the weak link. The company must pay high to secure a good man. He should be given a share in the company if possible. It is difficult to get good men because, in the upper ranks, very few chain executives shift from one company to another. Their interest in profits keeps them attached to one concern. When a manufacturer starts a chain of stores, he is naturally prompted to look outside for his men. Whereas a retail chain can start with one link and train up men, he must secure men trained elsewhere, especially since he has not the requisite retail knowledge to train them himself.

When the company has secured a man whom it believes capable of taking full charge, he should be allowed to have considerable latitude. He knows, supposedly, a great deal more about the problems the manufacturer will have to encounter in his new undertaking than anyone in the company. If the company has chosen its man wrongly, it can dismiss him and choose another man, and this is far less harmful than hampering him at every step with commands and suggestions. One good plan would be to appropriate a certain amount of money and then tell the retail manager to go ahead on that basis, rendering strict account of expenditures at frequent intervals.

What has been said in other chapters in regard to the personnel will apply equally well here. To all intents and purposes, the member store is run exactly as the member store of a retail chain. There is a manager with a share in the profits and clerks who probably receive some sort of a bonus for sales.

The manufacturer may regard it as necessary to maintain one

or more stores at a loss, because of competition or because it is desired to open up new territory, etc.   In this case some arrangement should be made by which the manager of the local store which is not earning money should be recompensed proportionately to his effort.   This is especially important as it would pay to have a good man located at this point.

The Operation of Manufacturers' Chains.—It may be of value to present some of the aspects of chain store operation as applying specifically to the manufacturer's problem.   These may be grouped under the following headings:

1. Territory.
2. Purchasing.
3. Accounting control.
4. Sales policies.
5. Advertising.

1. *Territory.*—Every manufacturers' chain is a potential national chain, although, in actual fact, the retail stores may be grouped within a small radius and the rest of the country covered by agencies.   Yet by means of these agencies the company has paved the way for the installation of a retail store of its own whenever it considers conditions warrant.

The best results are often secured through retailing the entire production through the manufacturer's own stores.   The Singer Sewing Machine Company, for instance, the most conspicuous example, has divided the United States into territories, which are in turn sub-divided into one hundred or more divisions. The company maintains outside salesmen as well, who turn all the business they secure into the store covering the territory in which the sale is made.

The Regal Shoe Co. has six selling districts, determined by volume of sales rather than extent of territory.   It is divided into the Southern, the Northern, the Pacific, the Middle West, and the two Metropolitan divisions of New York.

This question of territory is much more important in the case of the manufacturers' chain because of the previously discussed agency question and the nature of the product.   On the one hand it is necessary to secure the loyal coöperation of the agencies and on the other the efficient operation of the retail stores.

2. *Purchasing.*—Purchasing, as such, does not exist for the retail branch of the manufacturers' chain. All goods are invoiced to the retail stores at cost of manufacture by the company. Thus, one great source of chain economy is at one stroke removed. The purchasing function is a mere choice of lines to be stocked by local managers. As hitherto explained, this slows up the entire process of transferring the purchasing desires of the public to the source of supply. Consequently, a manufacturing chain is far more likely to be caught with large inventories by sudden shifts in buying habits and style or perhaps of periods of prosperity or depression.

3. *Accounting Control.*—Accounting is just as necessary in the manufacturers' chain field as in the retail chain field. It is, however, more difficult to obtain the same accurate results if agencies are used for partial distribution. But all manufacturers with retail chain stores recognize the necessity of scientific statistical control both for purposes of sales analysis and for individual store efficiency.

4. *Sales Policies.*—When a manufacturer sells through agencies, his desire is to sell the product. The dealer is important only through the volume of sales of the company's product. When the manufacturer runs a retail store or chain of stores, the individuality of the store takes on prime importance. What an agent does reflects on the agent more than on the company. What one of the company's own stores does reflects directly on the company itself. Thus the sales policy must be modified to take into consideration the retail links.

The great sales problem is the question of price. Must the company's own stores sell at the same price as the agencies? Suppose there is an overstock of goods. Should agencies and stores combine in sales effort to clear out these stocks? Unquestionably it is very difficult for the manufacturers' chain to reduce prices. Various expedients are tried. Merchandise is shifted from stores where it will not sell to stores where it will. More general still is the practice of giving a premium to the salesman on sales of slow-moving goods.

Price in a manufacturer's chain is a local question far more than in the case of the retail chain. For example, competition in one city may be especially strong, due to local manufacturing and local retailing. The problem here is quite different from that of another city where competition may be weak and sales easy to make. A price-cut is generally a last resort, after all other methods have failed. However, it may be essential in case of an over-supply of seasonal goods.

A manufacturer does not sell a number of brands; he sells one brand and that his own. All sales effort, therefore, is concentrated on establishing the preëminence of this particular brand over others in the field. In a retail chain, if one manufacturer's brand fails to sell, it can immediately be discarded, but the manufacturer who runs his own retail store must make his brand successful.

5. *Advertising.*—The general advertising policy of the manufacturer's chain must be made up with reference to the following considerations:

(a) The interests of the retail stores.
(b) The interests of the agencies.

Many of the manufacturers' shoe chains do national advertising in the interests of both. When it comes to local advertising, there has been some reluctance on the part of the local managers to run advertising matter which would help the agencies as well as themselves. This view, an essentially narrow one, has been generally discarded in favor of the policy that whatever helps the sales of the product will eventually help everybody concerned.

Conclusions.—The retailer who starts a chain of stores is beginning at the bottom, and whatever manufacturing operations he may eventually take up, they are always in response to a direct demand from the retail outlets, and an advance indication that the products manufactured will be disposed of immediately at a profit.

The manufacturer who starts a chain of retail stores in the endeavor to make his distribution more direct, or more uniform, or for any other reason, is commencing at the top and working down. He has to create a market for his product which is already being manufactured, and he must do this against strong competition. He should choose an executive capable of handling the retail end of his business who will see to the choice of sites, the building up of a personnel, sales policies, etc. And the manufacturer is always hampered more or less by the inelasticity of the product he manufactures to shifting demand, a factor which the retail chain capitalizes immediately.

Whether a manufacturer should start a chain of retail stores is an individual question, depending on capital available, and a careful study of all the problems brought forward in this chapter.

CHAPTER XXII

THE GROCERY CHAIN

The chain store idea in this country originated in the grocery field and it is but natural that it should there have its strongest hold even if we do not take into consideration that the selling of food products is our most important retail activity. The business of the average independent grocer is not large enough and in many cases never can be large enough to develop maximum efficiency in purchasing, merchandising, and accounting. Thus at the start the chain grocery store occupies a favored position in the way of competition. Some chain grocers do not even consider the independent competition but only that of other chains.

Although there are no exact figures, it is estimated that there are about 4,000 wholesale and 350,000 retail grocers in the United States. Alfred H. Beckmann, Secretary-Treasurer of the National Chain Grocers' Association, is authority for the statement that there are less than seventy-five responsible chain grocery store organizations, operating not over 50,000 stores. Taking into consideration the fact that only one seventh of the total retail grocers are made up of chain links, there seems to be a broad field still undeveloped. Naturally, with the spread of the chain stores and the elimination of the weaker independent stores, the number of wholesale grocers will also decline, since the chain organization takes upon itself the functions of the jobber, that is, the purchasing from the manufacturer, the warehousing, and, incidentally, the profit.

The metropolitan districts have served best up to this point for grocery chain development. Within a few years they have advanced from supplying 12 per cent. of the retail grocery trade to supplying one half of it. In Philadelphia, which is the stronghold of the chain grocery store, the percentage is even higher.

The Chain Grocery Field.—There are several types of so-called grocery chains. We have the regular chain grocer handling all brands asked for by customers and selling a private brand in competition, we have the self-service type handling nationally advertised goods only, and we have the restricted-products type, handling tea, coffee, butter, eggs, and a few dry staples. Last, we have a few quality grocery chains, giving delivery, allowing credits etc., which are frowned upon by the cash-and-carry type.

1. *The regular grocery chain.*—In most respects this type of grocery store is no different from its independent competitor. It carries approximately the same products, but not so many lines, there are no "shelf warmers," and the tendency is always towards packaged goods where possible. In methods, of course, the chain grocery is infinitely superior to the independent; the same is generally true of location. This type of chain store normally does some manufacturing or distributing on its own account. The larger chains do a great deal of their manufacturing; the smaller chains concentrate on some particular line, such as breadstuffs.

2. *The self-service type.*—This is a new comer to the chain field, and long enough time has not yet elapsed to demonstrate the exact possibilities inherent in such a scheme. It seems better fitted for the grocery field than any other, and, as pointed out elsewhere, it is more adapted for downtown sites than for suburban. These stores sell only nationally advertised goods, following out their policy of handling only the best known articles and products.

3. *The restricted-products type.*—A great many of these stores started out as retailers in teas and coffees and found it convenient to take on additional lines, butter, eggs, beans, etc. In general, the stock of the chain grocery store is more restricted in number of items than the independent store, but the tendency seems to be to enlarge the line of goods carried once it is proved conclusively that there is a public demand for the new products.

4. *Quality chains.*—This type of chain started from a single store always and then acquired branches. In many cases the management still dislikes the word chain as applied to this organization because it is felt that a chain denotes cash-and-carry, which is precisely what they seek to avoid. As is natural, these chains are comparatively small, first, because their class of trade is limited to those with money, and second, because it is

so much more difficult to standardize the individual service on which the trade of this type of chain is founded.

Rarely, as in the case of Chas. M. Decker & Bros., both cash-and-carry and service stores are operated by the same management.

The Grocery Chains.—In the last ten years or, in fact, from 1910 onward, there has been tremendous growth in the chain store organizations. There was a long-felt want in the community to be filled. The prejudice against the chain store had almost vanished. When the war broke out, and prices rose to unprecedented heights, and even staple commodities were scarce, the chain store progress was rapid. In the short space of three years, from 1914 to 1917, the Great Atlantic & Pacific Tea Co. opened over twenty-two hundred new stores.

Contrary to the drug field, where the Liggett Co. is far in the lead, in the grocery field the different chains are strung out with the Great Atlantic & Pacific Tea Co. in the lead, the American Stores Co. second, and the Kroger Grocery & Baking Co. third.

The following list gives an idea of the more important grocery chains operating at this time, although this list may be incomplete or inaccurate as far as some chains may be concerned, owing to the rapid growth and the difficulty of obtaining information. The majority of this list was compiled by the National Chain Grocers' Association.

LIST OF CHAIN GROCERY CONCERNS

NAME	HEADQUARTERS	APPROXIMATE NUMBER OF STORES
Alabama		
Hill Grocery Co	Birmingham	71
Arizona		
Arizona Grocery Co	Phoenix	4
Arkansas		
Cox's Cash Stores	Little Rock	38
California		
H. G. Chaffee Co	Los Angeles	66
Federal Grocery Co	Los Angeles	90
Sam Seelig Co	Los Angeles	106
Von's Grocery Stores	Los Angeles	24
Heller's, Inc	San Diego	20
Colorado		
Snodgrass Food Co	Trinidad	25
Connecticut		
Davey Bros	Bridgeport	
Logan Bros	Bridgeport	41
District of Columbia		
Sanitary Grocery Co	Washington	170

NAME	HEADQUARTERS	APPROXIMATE NUMBER OF STORES
Florida		
Whiddon Cash Stores	Jacksonville	29
Georgia		
L. W. Rogers Co	Atlanta	145
Indiana		
Standard Tea & Grocery Co	Indianapolis	85
Illinois		
Consumers Sanitary Coffee & Butter Co.	Chicago	70
Logan Tea Co	Chicago	30
National Tea Co	Chicago	369
Iowa		
Benner Tea Co	Burlington	17
Kentucky		
The Quaker Maid, Inc	Louisville	78
Maryland		
Knoblock Bros	Baltimore	25
C. D. Kenny Co	Baltimore	70
J. W. Crook	Baltimore	110
Massachusetts		
John T. Connor Co	Boston	307
E. E. Gray Co	Boston	150
M. O'Keeffe, Inc	Boston	330
The Ginter Co	Boston	150
Country Club Stores	Boston	62
Economy Grocery Stores	Cambridgport	53
H. P. Hood & Sons Co	Charlestown	46
A. H. Phillips, Inc	Springfield	96
Michigan		
C. F. Smith Co	Detroit	240
Wright & Parker	Detroit	187
Missouri		
Union Pacific Tea Co. of Missouri	Kansas City	50
Montana		
J. M. Sawyer Co	Billings	
New Jersey		
National Grocery Co	Jersey City	375
Great Atlantic & Pacific Tea Co	Jersey City	7,000
Eagle Grocery Co	Jersey City	184
Mutual Grocery Co	Newark	62
American Food Co	Newark	56
Aaron Ward & Sons	Newark	26
Lehman & Co	Newark	56
Chas. M. Decker & Bros. Thrift Stores, Inc	Orange	161
Great Eastern Stores Co	Paterson	60
New York		
National Economy Stores Co	Auburn	50
H. C. Bohack Co	Brooklyn	210
Thomas Roulston, Inc	Brooklyn	400
Globe Grocery Stores, Inc	Brooklyn	222
Grand Union Tea Co	Brooklyn	197
S. M. Flickinger Co	Buffalo	205
Thrift Grocery Stores, Inc	Buffalo	87
E. T. Donahay Co	Buffalo	25
John H. Kamman Co	Buffalo	30
A. F. Beckmann & Co. Inc	New York City	63
James Butler, Inc	New York City	629

NAME	HEADQUARTERS	NUMBER OF STORES

New York (*Continued*)

NAME	HEADQUARTERS	NUMBER OF STORES
Gristede Bros. Inc.	New York City	64
Progressive Grocery Stores, Inc.	New York City	60
Daniel Reeves, Inc.	New York City	297
Atlas Stores, Inc.	New York City	49
Andrew Davey, Inc.	New York City	179
L. Oppenheimer, Inc.	New York City	37
Park & Tilford	New York City	11
Schaffer Stores Co.	Schenectady	31
Community Stores Co.	Syracuse	21

Ohio

F. W. Albrecht Grocery Co.	Akron	63
A. B. Flory	Canton	40
Kroger Grocery & Baking Co.	Cincinnati	997
Foltz. Grocery & Baking Co.	Cincinnati	68
Fisher Bros. Co.	Cleveland	132
Matt. Smith Grocery Co.	Cleveland	101
Thrift Grocery Co.	Toledo	53

Oregon

Skaggs United Stores	Portland	33
Twentieth Century Stores	Portland	24

Pennsylvania

Shaffer Stores Co.	Altoona	30
Almar Tea Co.	Philadelphia	78
American Stores Co.	Philadelphia	1,276
Huey & Matthews	Pittsburgh	72
P. H. Butler Co.	Pittsburgh	194
S. B. Charters Grocery Co.	Pittsburgh	68
Donahoe's	Pittsburgh	33
Union Supply Co.	Pittsburgh	58

Rhode Island

Mayflower Stores Co.	Providence	121
Nicholson-Thackeray Co.	Pawtucket	60

Tennessee

Parham-Lindsay Grocery Co.	Chattanooga	52
Mr. Bower's Stores, Inc.	Memphis	50
H. G. Hill Co.	Nashville	92

Texas

Star Cash Stores Co.	Dallas	48

Virginia

D. Pender Grocery Co.	Norfolk	100
Jamison's Chain Grocery Stores	Roanoke	

Washington

The Marr Stores	Spokane	24
Groceteria Stores Co.	Seattle	29

Wisconsin

Union Food Stores Co.	Milwaukee	51

A glance at the above list shows that in the grocery line, far more than in the drug line, the chain idea has gained great impetus. As soon as a chain grocery obtains over 25 member stores, it is placed in a position of advantage, both as to purchasing economies and the inevitable publicity attached to the activities of the larger chains.

The Great Atlantic & Pacific Tea Co.—There was but one Great Atlantic & Pacific Tea Co. store in 1859. To George H.

Hartford, who died in 1917, is due the credit for initiating the first successful retail grocery chain. The idea, as conceived by him, was carried out and is still being carried out. Stores are added only as they seem warranted. Yet owing to the great size of the chain, the new links come with surprising frequency. A glance at the table below shows increase in number of stores operated since 1910.

1910	372	1916	2,866
1911	404	1917	3,232
1912	447	1918	3,799
1913	628	1919	4,246
1914	1,001	1920	4,508
1915	1,726	1921	4,744

From 372 stores to 4,744 stores in 11 years is a notable achievement, even considering that it is a chain of retail stores. Furthermore, the company does a great amount of business in foodstuffs. In 1919, it sold 50,000,000 pounds of coffee; 35,000,000 pounds of butter; 20,000,000 dozen eggs; 150,000,000 pounds of flour; 200,000,000 pounds of sugar; 300,000,000 pounds of potatoes; 68,400,000 cans of milk; 200,000,000 cakes of soap. The company employs approximately 17,000 men.

The Great Atlantic & Pacific Tea Co. is the only great national grocery chain. It has succeeded in solving sectional difficulties and in establishing its stores in all corners of the United States. After experimenting with various policies, it abandoned credits and deliveries in 1912 and later on adopted the policy of selling products asked for by the customers but of manufacturing as much as possible of its own products to compete either in price or in unit volume of the product.

Other Chains.—The American Stores Co., as explained elsewhere, is a combination of several smaller chains to form the second largest grocery chain in the country. But the Kroger Grocery & Baking Co. is, like the Great Atlantic & Pacific Tea Co., the creation of one man. B. H. Kroger in 1884 owned one store in Cincinnati, Ohio, called the Great Western Tea Co. In 1885, he had three stores, each located on what he considered a profitable site. At an early stage in the development of his chain, he adopted two policies.

. o y irect in so ar as possi e.

2. To sell his products at as low a price as was consistent with the cost to him, regardless of competitors' prices.

Needless to say, he incurred immediately the enmity of the independent grocers, the jobbers, and the wholesalers, and of many manufacturers who disliked seeing their prices cut. In 1891 he had seven stores, and in 1902 thirty-six.

As soon as he had laid up some money he spent it in advertising in newspapers. The appeal, of course, was based on low prices, and this policy, also, was bitterly resented by his opponents. But it allowed many of his stores to turn their stock twenty times a year, and he continued. As he came into contact with middle-men who refused to sell as he required, he turned them down and started manufacturing on his own account. He made cake, candy, and canned goods, and put up his own brand of coffee. Then he bought fifteen grocery stores at Dayton, Ohio, and changed the name to the Kroger Grocery & Baking Co. In 1904, he bought a packing house and made the retailing of meat one of his major activities, although meat is not sold in all stores. In 1908, sixty stores were added at one stroke. Mr. Kroger has founded a bank in Cincinnati, built an interurban railroad, and owns a great deal of real estate. And his chain of stores keeps on growing. Not content with cutting out wholesalers, he has cut out commission brokers, and is buying his produce direct from the farmers on a commission or cash basis.

The story of the Kroger Grocery & Baking Co. is typical of many other chains. But there are peculiar features in individual chains. The Ginter Co., operating a medium-sized chain of grocery stores in and around Boston, also operates a chain of restaurants serving food at moderate prices. This venture has proved very successful, both from the point of view of the restaurant business and from the publicity obtained.

The Piggly Wiggly Co.—In five years, the business of the Piggly Wiggly Co. grew from nothing to $5,000,000 a year. In 1916 the first Piggly Wiggly store opened in Memphis and three years later Piggly Wiggly Stores Inc., was formed. This corporation acquired immediately about 125 stores out of about three hundred privately-owned stores which were operating the Piggly Wiggly patent. On October 1, 1920, 515 stores were operating in 150 cities in 28 states, of which the company owned 340.

The idea was invented and patented by Clarence Saunders of Memphis, Tenn. It was to standardize everything down to the last degree. First the store was standardized, then the stock, then the personnel, and finally the customer. That is, the customer has to do the work of picking out what articles he wishes, thus saving the time and labor of the clerk.

Mr. Saunders, as the Dry Goods Economist says, had experts study handling and serving, with the idea of eliminating all lost motion, decreasing handling costs to a minimum, and cutting out all waste. Thus the modern up-to-date labor-saving devices for the handling of goods are found in the Piggly Wiggly stores. Devices are arranged so that employees handle merchandise only once, and porters and others employed in the store each have a definite task to do. Though they may be in the aisles while the customers are passing through them, they are forbidden to touch any merchandise or aid the customer in selecting merchandise. Their job is standardized. They have so much to do, no more, no less, and are forbidden to go beyond the work assigned to them.

The management has attempted to reduce the operation of the individual store, as far as possible, to a science and, with this view in mind, it has formulated a complete set of rules governing all probable contingencies. For example, if the customer by accident causes any damage the rule reads as follows:

"Should the customer inadvertently or through any other cause knock from a shelf a bottle or package of anything that breaks and is thereby ruined for sale, and should the customer or any visitor do any damage about the store which is not done with malicious or wilful intent, it will be considered the duty of the employee who sees damage result through action of such customer or person to tell that person that such a one is not in any wise to blame; even should such a person offer to make payment, the money must be refused and customer made to feel that such accidents will happen sometimes."

Even the number of keys to the store is mapped out in a little booklet setting forth the conduct of the stores and the store personnel.

The Piggly Wiggly stores, as Mr. Saunders says, are an experiment in practical store psychology. People laugh when they

22

see the name for the first time, but they are interested and they remember it. The next time they go by, they stop and make a purchase and immediately cease laughing. On the shelves they not only see what they are intending to buy but also many other things they had not intended to purchase but the sight of which makes them realize they would like to have that particular item. Thus sales per customer are increased. The basic principle of the standardized store layout and equipment is that each customer must pass all products for sale.

The Degrees of Standardization.—All grocery chains are fairly well standardized. But there is a difference of degree. It becomes such a science in the larger grocery chains to get every possible penny that they keep a check on how much paper and string each store uses so as to eliminate waste. Also they charge each store with the wood boxes that hold the canned goods and allow credit of five or ten cents a box when boxes are returned to the warehouse.

The larger the chain, the more the tendency towards standardization, due of course to lack of contact of management and personnel. In the case of inventory, for example, many chain stores keep an almost exact-to-the-penny inventory of the stock each store contains. These records are so exact that, if there is a ½ cent a pound drop in the price of navy beans, they weigh up the beans in each store and credit that store for the reduction on the books. Similarly, if beans go up ½ cent, each store is charged with that extra ½ cent for every pound of beans in stock. Working this way, it is possible to tell almost to a penny whether the management is getting every bit of profit which that store makes, or whether the store manager is making something for himself. Such a microscopic treatment of price changes is best suited for a large chain, but in the smaller chains it is simpler to check up on price changes no oftener than once a week. Some chains require weekly changes on staple goods and intermittent changes on dairy goods which may vary considerably during a period of seven days.

The larger chains can afford to demand a closer standardization of method because they can afford to operate the machinery. Every refinement in accounting necessitates the weighing of the result to see whether it justifies the expenditure in clerk hire.

The small or medium-sized chain must adapt its standard practice to its resources, just as the independent store keeper cannot compete with the chain store on the ground of individual store efficiency of operation, but must resort to service to retain a hold on his customers.

The Location.—Generally the grocery store seeks the cheaper locations, but as its chief hold is in the residence districts, rents are not so high, and it can usually obtain locations near the center of business. Location, however, is one of the essential features of chain grocery operation, as great reliance is placed upon the efficiency of the window display.

It was discovered by experience that one chain could locate near another and not cause any perceptible diminution in the trade of either store. In fact, some stores have claimed that their business was positively increased. Relying on this fact, some curious results have happened. In some communities a single chain store has become well established. A rival chain wishes to establish a branch there, and judging that the original chain has already done the missionary work of prospecting for a site, it establishes itself as closely as possible to the original chain store, sometimes next door. Sometimes a third chain follows and fixes itself near the first two.

In one town the original chain store was located at some distance from the center and the other two chain stores settled in close proximity. The result was that the trade was not sufficient to go round and a fourth chain store, locating afterwards at the center, obtained the bulk of the trade. In other words, there is naturally a saturation point for chain stores at a certain location.

Grocery chain stores do well in suburban localities, and in recent years have invaded quality locations with surprising success. Automobile trade has had much to do with this as in this case the fact that the chain does not deliver makes little difference. The discovery that chain stores could prosper in rich localities marked a new phase of chain store development.

One point to notice in regard to the location of the grocery chain store is that it is situated in many cases in small communities supporting no other type of chain enterprise. In this respect it has been the pioneer. In no other field has the chain idea been extended so far as to cover small communities.

The Manufacturer and the Chain Grocery.—Strangely enough, it was a long time before the manufacturer could be brought to see that his best interests lay in coöperating with the chain store instead of working against it. He labored under the mistaken impression that the chain idea was only a fad and that if he openly incurred the hostility of the wholesale grocers, he would find himself in the long run left out. Although wholesalers originally fostered the chain stores, they became their bitterest enemies as soon as the chains began to try to buy direct, and to pocket the jobbers' discount.

A. H. Beckmann, for many years secretary of the National Wholesale Grocers' Association, and now, Secretary of the National Chain Store Grocers' Association, has the point of view of one who is well acquainted with both sides of the question. He says that in selling responsible chain grocery store organizations, the manufacturer eliminates a considerable overhead expense in the cost of travelling salesmen. The chain is able to buy carloads where the individually-owned grocery can buy only in small quantities.

Most manufacturers recognize the economy of the chain store's distribution both in buying and selling. The so-called retail grocer must necessarily buy from the wholesaler or jobber on account of his small volume in buying, and his credit risk, which the wholesaler or jobber must assume. The wholesaler or jobber is compelled to maintain a large sales force to take care of the retail trade, in addition to which the manufacturer employs specialty salesmen who call on the retailer also, and turn over the orders taken to some jobber for execution, all of which adds to the cost and for which the consumer must pay.

A manufacturer desiring to place his product on the market through a chain of stores—whether it operates 50 or 5,000 stores—need send only one representative to the headquarters of the chain grocery store, where the sale is consummated, if the article has merit, and immediately distribution follows in all stores operated by that chain. This is a decided advertising advantage.

In large cities distribution by manufacturers could be handled economically and it is only a question of time when the larger ones will have distributing organizations similar to the National Biscuit Co., Procter & Gamble Distributing Co., Kirkman & Son, the Heinz Co., and other manufacturers. The jobber or wholesaler will develop into a manufacturer even more than he is now, or handle specialties, for, as the chain store increases, so does the wholesaler or jobber decrease.

The average retailer, or rather the majority of small retailers— and they are in the majority—have as a rule little capital when they enter business, and the wholesale grocer extends a line of credit in addition to furnishing the opening stock. Immediately the retailer is established, he is called upon by the salesmen of other wholesale grocers—a duplication of overhead expense—and the wholesaler, who is really entitled to all that retailer's business, finds his sales diminishing and is obligated to wait the pleasure of the retailer for payments on goods purchased, ranging from 30 to 60 days, or even longer, further emphasizing the credit evil. Not less than 75 per cent. of retail grocers require credit accommodation of the wholesale grocer, while the chain grocer both buys and sells for cash.

Conclusions.—Nothing said in the course of this chapter should lead the man ambitious to start a chain of retail grocery stores to think the task is easy and that all that is necessary is to open a series of stores and wait for profits. The reverse of the case is more often true. The owner of a chain of grocery stores is confronted with the keenest kind of competition, not only for trade but also for sites, and in merchandising policies. The fact that the competition is ordinarily conducted on a fair and square basis does not render it any less formidable.

There are six fundamentals for success in this line, irrespective of other factors;

1. Sufficient capital.
2. The right location.
3. Purchases direct.
4. Economies in operation. Cash-and-carry.
5. Well-known, high-grade merchandise.
6. High turnover and low margin of profit.

CHAPTER XXIII

THE DRUG STORE CHAIN

Next to the grocery field, there are more chains in the drug field than anywhere else. The chains are not particularly remarkable for their size but rather for their numbers. In 1921, there were 303 drug chains operating over three stores, in all 1763 stores. In 1920 there were 315 chains but only 1563 member stores. This illustrates an evident tendency towards combination among the chains, a symptom which is common to nearly all types.

The chain store movement in the drug field has come comparatively late. The difficulties in the way of standardizing drug store operation were far greater than in the case of the grocery or the cigar field. They were even greater than in the case of the five and ten cent store field. Most of the present drug store chains have been operating but a few years, notably the National Drug Stores and the United Retail Chemists Corporation both newcomers, yet both among the first ten in size. The Liggett Co. is by far the largest and bids fair to keep this position for some time.

Figure 55 shows the relative position of the drug stores operating 10 links and over. Twenty-one chains operate 618 stores or over a third of the total of stores operated by the entire 303 chains. This clearly illustrates that the drug field is yet essentially a small chain field. But the fact that large capital and modern methods in the National Drug Stores and the United Retail Chemists Corporation have made such rapid growth points to a probable exploitation of the drug field by chains to a much greater extent than at present.

Within a year of its organization, the National Drug Stores Corporation had 21 stores in operation and in 1921 it had 27. Although most of its stores are located in New York City, it purchased the Guilford chain in Rochester, New York, and has stores in Massachusetts, New Jersey, Connecticut, and Pennsylvania.

The Mykrantz Co. was organized in 1912 and at one time had thirty stores in operation in Columbus, Ohio, and its vicinity, but six stores were closed during 1921. The Dow Drug Co. was organized in 1915 and now operates 22 stores. The Miller-Strong Co., organized in 1908, now has 26 stores in Buffalo and surrounding cities. The history of the other chains is similar.

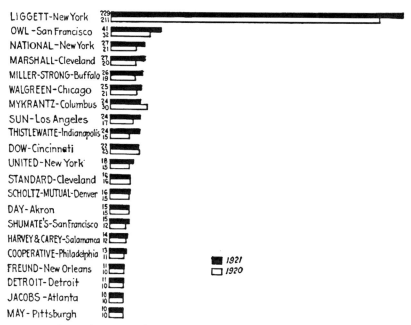

Fig. 55.—Chart showing relative positions of leading drug chains during 1920 and 1921.

Expansion has come only in recent years, even when founding dated back twenty years or more.

The Louis K. Liggett Co.—The Louis K. Liggett Co., operating 229 stores, and in a fair way to become a national drug chain, is the largest factor in the drug field. No discussion or description of this company is possible without a preliminary account of its connection with the United Drug Co. This company was formed in 1902, at a meeting in Boston of 35 retail druggists. Mr. Liggett, the guiding spirit of the organization, who had been a traveling salesman for Chester Kent & Co., manufacturers of Vinol and other proprietary medicines, had been impressed with three evils in the drug trade.

1. There was a tendency of manufacturers to force retailers to overstock.

2. There was substitution by the dealers of their own preparations in place of those of proprietary companies.

3. There was a failure to maintain the manufacturer's indicated resale price.

The original 35 members drew up resolutions to the following effect:

1. The company was to manufacture only for stockholders.

2. There was to be only one stockholder in each town.

3. The company was to make and market at the outset at least 100 remedies, all of which were to be sold under a single blanket trade-mark.

4. Six of the 100 remedies were to be advertised extensively in season.

5. The first lines to be advertised were to be a dyspepsia cure and a catarrh cure.

6. All of the products, except the advertised remedies, were to be sold to the stockholders at such a price as would not net the corporation more than 25 per cent. on its gross selling price.

7. Each preferred stockholder had to purchase as much stock in the company as the cost of the first year's advertising in his city.

8. Control of the corporation was to be in the hands of the druggists themselves.

9. As long as a stockholder owned common stock, he was to be a perpetual agent.

The company, in addition to manufacturing drugs, has been interested in the manufacture of perfumery, of candy, and of stationery. Liggett also organized the Drug Merchants of America, a company formed to purchase other goods than were manufactured by the company for use in agencies.

The Louis K. Liggett Co. was organized in Boston in 1907, five years after the foundation of the United Drug Co., to relieve the United Drug Co. of risk of loss from a controversy as to the Boston agency. This dispute had originally started between the United Drug Co. and the Riker-Jaynes Co. This was the beginning. In 1910 the Liggett Co. had 26 stores while the Riker-Hegeman-Jaynes people controlled 58. In 1900 the

Hegeman Co. had four stores in New York and the Wm. B.
Riker Co. had two stores, also in New York.

By a process of combination the Riker-Hegeman-Jaynes
people in 1916 had operating 107 stores. In this year the
Liggett Co., operating 45 stores at the time, bought them out.
Since that time the Liggett Co. has expanded steadily and to its
policies and practices are due in great measure the present idea
of the chain drug store as a retail outlet which can sell almost
anything.

Analysis of Drug Chains.—In 1900, the 14 leading drug store

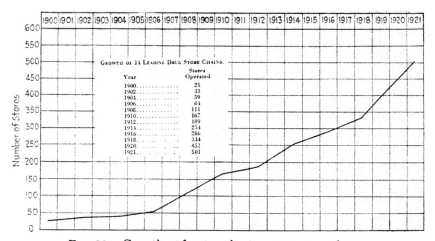

FIG. 56.—Growth of fourteen leading drug store chains.

chains of the country operated only 25 stores, that is, such of
them as were in existence at that time. In 1921, these 14 chains
operated 501 stores, or 20 times as many as in 1900. This is a
fair rate of growth but not when it is considered what a field
there still remains to develop. Of over 50,000 retail druggists in
the country 1,763 of them are members of chains.

Chain drug stores have, as yet, confined themselves mainly
to the urban sections, with few attempts to cultivate the smaller
towns and outlying sections. This, of course, is a phase in all
chain development. Pick the easiest sites first. But in the
next few years the growth of the chain drug stores should show
a tendency towards the smaller towns and a tendency also to

drop some of the strictly non-drug lines which would not prove profitable in small communities, owing to the smaller turnover.

Figure 56 shows in graphic form the growth of the 14 chains at two-year intervals The growth in member stores went on uninterruptedly during the period of depression of 1920 and 1921. The figures, compiled by the Druggists Circular, include the following companies: The Louis K. Liggett Co., the Owl Drug Co., the National Drug Stores Corp., the United Chemists Corp., the Mykrantz Co., the Dow Drug Co., the Marshall Drug Co., the Miller-Strong Drug Co., the Sun Drug Co., the Standard Drug Co., the Scholtz-Mutual Drug Co., the Day Drug Co., the Jacobs Pharmacy Co., and the Peoples Drug Stores.

Figures furnished by the Druggists Circular and Drug Store Merchandising form the basis for an analysis which has been prepared of the extent of the chain movement in the retailing of drugs. Drug chains with only two stores have been included in this survey because otherwise a great many towns would have been left out, and these two store chains are all larger chains in embryo form.

If the number of firms operating only two stores are added, the total number of chains is more than doubled. While the number of chains operating three stores or more is only 303, the number of chains operating two stores and more is 691, with a total of 2,627 stores.

The names of those chains operating ten or more stores are the only ones mentioned. In every other case the name of the state and the town where the store operates is given, with the number of chains in that town and the number of stores in each chain. The great number of chains with but two stores gives food for thought. It shows that a great many of the smaller retailers are beginning to take advantage of the chain idea.

A much fuller analysis of the situation would be necessary than is given here, for any person seriously contemplating establishing a chain of drug stores throughout the country, but the following figures will give a fairly general idea of the situation in the country as a whole and afterwards in the various cities and towns.

When # appears before any name it means that the chain operates stores in other places than where it is credited.

SUMMARY OF DRUG STORE CHAINS

State	No. of chains	Total stores
Alabama	4	12
Arkansas	4	12
California	34	175
Colorado	9	37
Connecticut	8	28
Florida	3	12
Georgia	16	61
Idaho	2	9
Illinois	65	219
Indiana	21	97
Iowa	8	32
Kansas	5	13
Kentucky	18	50
Louisiana	18	59
Maine	1	2
Maryland	13	33
Massachusetts	28	84
Michigan	48	154
Minnesota	22	63
Mississippi	3	8
Missouri	34	97
Montana	2	6
Nebraska	5	17
Nevada	1	3
New Jersey	12	28
New York	75	417
North Carolina	6	17
North Dakota	1	6
Ohio	51	264
Oklahoma	14	51
Oregon	3	7
Pennsylvania	57	211
Rhode Island	9	34
South Carolina	4	13
Tennessee	11	32
Texas	19	73
Utah	5	33
Vermont	1	3
Virginia	6	20
Washington	15	52
Washington, D. C.	12	36
West Virginia	7	16
Wisconsin	11	31

DETAILS OF DRUG STORE CHAINS BY STATES
Alabama—12

Town	Chains	Stores	Total
Birmingham........	2	3	6
Mobile.............	2	3	6

Arkansas—12

Argenta...........	1	3	3
Fort Smith........	1	3	3
Little Rock........	2	3	6

California—175

San Francisco......	#The Owl Drug Co.	..	41
	Shumate's Pharmacies	..	15
	1	..	6
	#1	..	5
	2	4	8
	5	3	15
	3	2	6
Los Angeles........	#Sun Drug Co.	..	24
	1	5	5
	2	4	8
	1	3	3
	7	2	14
Napa.............	#1	5	5
San Bernadino.....	1	3	3
Riverside..........	1	3	3
Oakland...........	1	4	4
	1	2	2
San Diego.........	1	2	2
	1	3	3
San Luis Obispo.....	1	3	3

Colorado—37

Denver.............	#Scholtz-Mutual Drug Co.	..	16
	2	3	6
	3	2	6
Grand Junction.....	1	3	3
Pueblo............	1	2	2
Trinidad..........	1	4	4

DETAILS OF DRUG STORE CHAINS BY STATES (*Continued*)
Connecticut—28

Town	Chains	Stores	Total
Bridgeport..........	J. A. Leverty & Bro.	. .	10
	1	2	2
Hartford..........	4	2	8
New Haven........	1	2	2
Waterbury........	#1	6	6

Washington, D. C.—36

	People's Drug	11	11
	3	3	9
	8	2	16

Florida—12

Jacksonville.........	1	5	5
	1	2	2
West Palm Beach ...	#1	5	5

Georgia—61

Atlanta............	Jacob's Pharmacy Co.	10	10
	1	5	5
	1	4	4
	2	3	6
	1	2	2
Athens............	1	4	4
Augusta...........	1	2	2
Dover.............	1	2	2
Eublin............	1	2	2
Columbus.........	1	2	2
	1	3	3
Macon............	1	5	5
	1	4	4
Savannah..........	1	8	8
	1	2	2

Idaho—9

American Falls......	1	3	3
Boise.............	1	6	6

DETAILS OF DRUG STORE CHAINS BY STATES (*Continued*)
Illinois—219

Town	Chains	Stores	Total
Chicago	Walgreen Co.	25	25
	Central Drug Stores	10	10
	3	7	21
	1	..	6
	4	4	16
	20	3	60
	20	2	40
Danville	4	2	8
Elgin	1	3	3
	1	2	2
Jacksonville	2	3	6
	1	2	2
Peoria	1	4	4
	1	3	3
	1	2	2
Quincy	1	6	6
Rock Island	1	3	3
Springfield	1	2	2

Indiana—97

Indianapolis	1	7	7
	1	6	6
	1	4	4
	6	3	18
	4	2	8
	Clem Thistlewaite	24	24
Clinton	1	3	3
Gary	1	3	3
Fort Wayne	#1	9	9
Muncie	1	3	3
	1	2	2
South Bend	#1	5	5
Terre Haute	1	5	5

Iowa—32

Burlington	1	4	4
Davenport	2	4	8
	1	3	3
Des Moines	1	8	8
	1	3	3
Sioux City	1	3	3

DETAILS OF DRUG STORE CHAINS BY STATES (*Continued*)
Kansas—13

Town	Chains	Stores	Total
Crowsburg	1	2	2
Hutchinson	1	3	3
Kansas City	1	2	2
Ottawa	1	3	3
Wichita	1	3	3

Kentucky—50

Town	Chains	Stores	Total
Covington	1	3	3
Louisville	1	6	6
	5	3	15
	8	2	16
Bowling Green	#1	5	5
Frankfort	1	3	3
Paducah	1	2	2

Louisiana—59

Town	Chains	Stores	Total
New Orleans	Paul Freund, Inc.	11	11
	1	6	6
	7	3	21
	8	2	16
Bogalusa	1	5	5

Maine—2

Town	Chains	Stores	Total
Bangor	1	2	2

Maryland—33

Town	Chains	Stores	Total
Baltimore	1	8	8
	1	4	4
	9	2	18
	1	3	3

DETAILS OF DRUG STORE CHAINS BY STATES *(Continued)*
Massachusetts—84

Town	Chains	Stores	Total
Boston............	2	4	8
	6	2	12
Allston............	1	3	3
Bridgewater.......	1	3	3
Brookline..........	1	3	3
Cambridge.........	1	5	5
East Boston.......	1	3	3
Lowell............	1	2	2
Lynn..............	1	3	3
New Bedford.	1	3	3
	1	2	2
Marlboro..........	1	2	2
Onstable..........	1	4	4
Plymouth.........	1	4	4
Quincy............	1	3	3
Roxbury..........	1	4	4
Salem........ ...	1	6	6
	1	3	3
Springfield..	2	3	6
	2	2	4

Michigan—154

Town	Chains	Stores	Total
Detroit............	Detroit Drug Co.	11	11
	2	5	10
	2	4	8
	6	3	18
	15	2	30
Adrian............	1	3	3
Ann Arbor.........	1	3	3
Battle Creek.......	1	3	3
Bay City..........	1	3	3
	1	2	2
Flint..............	1	8	8
Grand Rapids..	5	3	15
	2	2	4
Ishpeming........ ..	1	3	3
Lansing............	1	3	3
	2	2	4
Muskegon	1	4	4
Menominee....... .	1	3	3
Port Huron.........	1	3	3
Pontiac............	1	3	3

Details of Drug Store Chains by States (*Continued*)

Minnesota—63

Town	Chains	Stores	Total
Minneapolis.........	2	5	10
	2	4	8
	1	3	3
	5	2	10
St. Paul...........	1	4	4
	1	3	3
	5	2	10
Duluth.............	3	2	6
Rochester.........	1	3	3
Virginia...........	1	6	6

Mississippi—8

Glendora.........	2	3	6
Meridian..........	1	2	2

Missouri—97

St. Louis..........	1	..	5
	4	4	16
	4	3	12
	9	2	18
Kansas City.......	1	4	4
	7	3	21
	6	2	12
Joplin.............	#1	6	6
	1	3	3

Montana—6

Butte.............	2	3	6

Nebraska—17

	1	3	3
Omaha............	1	5	5
Fairfield..........	2	2	6
	1	3	3

Nevada—3

Ely..............	1	3	3

DETAILS OF DRUG STORE CHAINS BY STATES (*Continued*)
New Jersey—28

Town	Chain	Stores	Total
Harrison..........	1	3	3
Jersey City........	1	3	3 —
	1	2	2
Newark...........	2	3	6
	6	2	12
West *H*oboken......	1	2	2

New York—417

Town	Chain	Stores	Total
New York City.....	#Louis K. Liggett Co.	229	229
	#National Drug Stores Corpora-tion	27	27
	#United Retail Chemists' Cor-poration	18	18
	1	4	4
	11	3	33
	7	2	14
Albany............	1	4	4
	2	3	6
Amsterdam........	1	3	3
Auburn...........	1	4	4
Brooklyn...	1	8	8
	1	6	6
	2	4	8
	6	3	18
	7	2	14
Buffalo............	#Miller-Strong Drug Co.	26	26
	4	3	12
	7	2	14
Corning...........	1	3	3
Dunkirk...........	1	3	3
Elmhurst..........	1	7	7
Elmira............	1	3	3
	2	2	4
Interlaken........	1	2	2
Lockport..........	1	3	3
Middletown....... ..	#1	7	7
Oswego...........	1	2	2
Plymouth..........	1	3	3
Rochester..... ...	5	3	15
Salamanca..	#*H*arvey & Carey	14	14
Yonkers...........	1	3	3

To avoid confusion, the Liggett stores have been grouped in the New York chains, because the majority of the stores were located there, but actually the distribution is as follows. Italics indicate change in 1921.

(Liggett's International, Ltd., now controls the chain of 630 Boot's Chemists' Shops in England, so the Liggett interests actually operate nearly 1,000 retail drug stores.)

The Liggett stores are located in the following cities:

Albany, N. Y	1
Allston, Mass	1
Atlanta, Ga	2
Augusta, Ga	1
Bangor, Me	1
Binghamton, N. Y	1
Birmingham, Ala	1
Boston, Mass	15, *19*
Baltimore, Md	1
Bridgeport, Conn	1
Brockton, Mass	1
Brookline, Mass	2
Brooklyn, N. Y	12
Buffalo, N. Y	3
Cambridge, Mass	1
Charlotte, N. C	1
Chattanooga, Tenn	1
Chester, Pa	*1*
Cincinnati, Ohio	3
Columbus, Ohio	2
Detroit, Mich	4
Des Moines, Iowa	1
Dallas, Tex	1, *2*
Elizabeth, N. J	*1*
Far Rockaway, N. Y	1
Fitchburg, Mass	2, *1*
Fort Worth, Tex	1
Germantown, Pa	1
Haverhill, Mass	1, *2*
Hartford, Conn	1
Holyoke, Mass	1
Jacksonville, Fla	*2*
Jersey City, N. J	1
Johnstown, Pa	*1*
Kansas City, Mo	2
Lancaster, Pa	1
Lawrence, Mass	1, *2*
Lewiston, Me	1
Long Island City, N. Y	1
Lowell, Mass	2
Lynn, Mass	3
Malden, Mass	1
Macon, Ga	1

Manchester, N. H	1
Meriden, Conn	1
Minneapolis, Minn	4, *5*
Mt. Vernon, N. Y	1
Montclair, N. J	1
Nashville, Tenn	*1*
Newark, N. J	2
New Bedford, Mass	1
New Britain, Conn	1
New Haven, Conn	1
New Orleans, La	2
Newport, R. I	1
New Rochelle, N. Y	1
New York City, N. Y	61, *55*
Oklahoma City, Okla	1
Passaic, N. J	*1*
Paterson, N. J	2
Pawtucket, R. I	1
Philadelphia, Pa	9, *8*
Pittsburgh, Pa	1
Pittsfield, Mass	1
Portland, Me	1
Poughkeepsie, N. Y	1
Providence, R. I	4
Reading, Pa	1
Richmond, Va	1
Rochester, N. Y	3
Salem, Mass	1
St. Paul, Minn	1, *2*
Saratoga Springs, N. Y	1
Schenectady, N. Y	1
South Boston, Mass	1
South Norwalk, Conn	1
Springfield, Mass	1
Springfield, Ill	1
Stamford, Conn	1
Syracuse, N. Y	2
Tampa, Fla	*1*
Taunton, Mass	1
Toledo, Ohio	*6*
Trenton, N. J	1
Troy, N. Y	1
Utica, N. Y	1
Washington, D. C	7, *8*
Waterbury, Conn	1
White Plains, N. Y	1
Wilkes-Barre, Pa	1
Wilmington, Del	1
Worcester, Mass	2
Yonkers, N. Y	1

Town	Chains	Stores	Total
Durham..........	1	2	2
East Durham.. ...	1	3	3
Charlotte..........	1	4	4
Raleigh............	1	3	3
Wilmington...... ..	1	2	2
Winston-Salem... .	1	3	3

North Dakota—6

Fargo.............	#1	6	6

Ohio—264

Akron...........	Day Drug Co.	15	15
	1	8	8
	3	3	9
Canton...........	#1	8	8
	1	6	6
	1	3	3
Bellaire...........	1	4	4
Cincinnati.........	#Dow Drug Co.	22	22
	2	4	8
	3	3	9
Cleveland.........	Marshall Drug Co.	23	23
	Standard Drug Co.	16	16
	1	9	9
	1	5	5
	1	4	4
	9	3	18
Columbus.........	#Mykrantz Drug Co.	24	24
	1	3	3
Dayton............	2	4	8
Elyria.............	1	3	3
Kenton...........	#1	4	4
Lima.	1	3	3
Lorain............	1	3	3
Marietta......... ..	1	3	3
Martins Ferry... ...	1	3	3
Salem.............	1	3	3
Springfield...... .	1	3	3
Toledo........... ...	2	5	10
	5	3	15
Warren.....	1	3	3

DETAILS OF DRUG STORE CHAINS BY STATES (*Continued*)
Oklahoma—51

Town	Chains	Stores	Total
Oklahoma City	1	5	5
	1	3	3
	1	2	2
Fairview	1	3	3
Guthrie	1	2	2
Lawton	1	2	2
Muskogee	1	5	5
Enid	1	3	3
Okema	1	3	3
Savannah	1	6	6
Shawnee	#1	5	5
	1	3	3
Tulsa	#1	4	4
Vernon	1	5	5

Oregon—7

Portland	1	3	3
	2	2	4

Pennsylvania—211

Philadelphia	#Co-Operative Drug Co.	13	13
	#1	8	8
		5	10
		4	8
	2**3**	3	78
	1	2	2
Altoona	1	5	5
Ben Avon	1	3	3
Erie	• 1	2	2
Harrisburg	#1	8	8
	1	3	3
Johnstown	1	4	4
Midland	1	3	3
Pittsburgh	May Drug Co.	10	10
	#Gilchrist-Simpson Drug Co.	10	10
	1	6	6
	1	4	4
	6	3	18
	4	2	8

DETAILS OF DRUG STORE CHAINS BY STATES (*Continued*)
Rhode Island—34

Town	Chains	Stores	Total
Providence........	1	7	7
	2	5	10
	5	3	15
	1	2	2

South Carolina—13

Town	Chains	Stores	Total
Anderson.........	1	2	2
Columbia..........	1	3	3
Greenville..........	1	5	5
	1	3	3

Tennessee—32

Town	Chains	Stores	Total
Chattanooga.....	2	3	6
	2	2	4
Knoxville..........	1	4	4
Memphis..........	3	3	9
Nashville..........	2	3	6
Union City........	1	3	3

Texas—73

Town	Chains	Stores	Total
Abilene............	1	3	3
Brownwood.......	1	4	4
Coleman...........	1	4	4
Dallas.............	1	5	5
	1	4	4
	2	3	6
Fort Worth........	1	9	9
	1	6	6
Hillsboro...	#1	4	4
Houston...........	#1	4	4
	3	3	9
Kingsville..........	#1	3	3
San Antonio.......	1	4	4
	1	3	3
	1	2	2
San Benito........	#1	3	3

DETAILS OF DRUG STORE CHAINS BY STATES (*Continued*)
Utah—33

Town	Chains	Store	Total
Salt Lake City......	#Schramm-Johnson	11	11
	#1	9	9
	1	3	3
Logan..............	#1	6	6
Provo.............	#1	4	4

Vermont—3

Springfield.........	1	3	3

Virginia—20

Norfolk...........	2	5	10
	1	3	3
Portsmouth........	1	3	3
Richmond.........	2	2	4

Washington—52

Centralia..........	1	3	3
Olympia...........	#1	4	4
Seattle...........	1	8	8
	1	5	5
	7	3	21
Spokane...........	2	3	6
Tacoma...........	1	3	3
	1	2	2

West Virginia—16

Charleston.........	1	3	3
Huntington........	1	2	2
Parkersburg.......	2	2	4
Wheeling..........	#1	5	5
	1	2	2

Wisconsin—31

Madison...........	1	4	4
	2	2	4
Milwaukee.........	1	3	3
	4	2	8
Racine............	1	6	6

The preceding analysis should give any druggist a fairly complete idea of the chain competition he will have to face in any particular locality.

Amount of Business Done.—It is difficult to arrive at any accurate figures which might indicate the total amount of business done by retail druggists in the United States and what percentage of it is done by chain organizations, but the following attempt at such a compilation has been made by the Druggist's Circular:

There are approximately 50,000 retail druggists in the country and, according to typical figures published by the Bureau of Business Research at Harvard University, and to reports of investigations conducted by pharmaceutical journals, credit bureaus, and others interested in the subject, each of these retailers sells about $25,000 worth of merchandise every year, making a total of $1,250,000.000 annually for the group.

Figures furnished by 15 of the 21 larger chain organizations show that these 21 corporations sell $76,000,000 worth of goods each year—practically six per cent. of the total amount sold by all the retail druggists in the country. In other words, these 21 corporations receive $6 of every $100 spent each year in the drug stores of the country.

The annual receipts of the Louis K. Liggett Co., operating about 200 stores during 1919, were $30,000,000. The Owl Drug Co., with 30 stores, sold $8,124,000; the Mykrantz Co. with 30 stores $1,250,000; the Jacobs Pharmacy Co. with nine stores $1,200,000; the Scholtz-Mutual Co. with 14 stores and the Miller-Strong Co. with 19 stores each, $1,250,000, etc.

The fact that the chain drug stores as yet do so little of the drug business proves that there is a large field still waiting for chain development.

Location.—The drug store is one of the lines of business where it seems that the proper site is necessary. Even the retailer recognized this fact, as the term "corner drug store" indicates. As stated before, up to this time the chain drug stores have sought out the busy down-town corners where the largest amount of traffic passes. There is a limit, however, to this phase of development and the time should shortly come when the suburban districts will be invaded by chain drug stores.

The key of business success is percentage, and when $500 a month rent is paid for a store it is considered not in terms of dollars, but in percentage. If the location can bring four per cent. business all well and good. If not, the location must be changed.

The first point of differentiation between the chain drug store and the independent store is in location. The chain store relies on the transient trade secured by its down-town location while the independent drug store relies on regular customers. The result of this location leads to the second point of differentiation, the type of product sold.

The Product.—The great danger that the chain drug store has had to face is to avoid becoming a department store. Owing to its advantageous location, it found itself able to sell almost anything from fresh eggs to phonographs. There was also a tendency towards the soda fountain and away from the prescription counter. This, however, was found to be a mistake, as the prescription counter turned out to be a very vital part of the drug store's pulling power. Without the prescription counter, the drug store lost its individuality. Some drug chains introduced lunch counters which served sandwiches and salads, following out the soda fountain idea. The success of this feature depends largely of course, upon the location of the store.

At present, the products carried in drug stores are not standardized. The purchasing department of each chain decides what the stores can sell and stocks up accordingly. Customers have got in the habit of going to the drug store for almost anything they desire. One way for an up-to-date druggist to forecast the products he should carry is to observe the success of his competitors with their lines. Writing paper is universally stocked. Hair nets at one time were not carried by the department stores, and were taken up by a large drug chain with success. Other drug stores followed this example and stocked hair nets successfully. The chain stores as a rule set the fashion for products which can be carried by drug stores. If the experiment works with them, others follow their example.

Advertising.—The third point of differentiation is the advertising. The chain store advertises; few independent stores can. The chain, owing to its metropolitan location, can take full pages in the big dailies and be sure that the results of this advertising will be spread around among its stores. It does happen occasionally that an independent store, desirous of obtaining a reputation as a price cutter, will run cut-price advertisements, but these attempts are rare and not always successful.

The problem of the small suburban druggist is a difficult one. How is he going to let people know what he carries? This same question is going to confront the chain drug store when it invades suburban locations. The answer seems to be that the metropolitan advertising of the chain will have to serve for the suburban districts, most of the inhabitants of which read the city daily papers. Many of these suburbanites already buy at chain drug stores in the city and the extension of the chain to the suburb will only make the purchasing easier for them.

Sales Policies.—The largest chain drug store organizations do their own manufacturing in large part. And they obtain jobbers' discounts on proprietary medicines. Thus they have at once the facilities for making themselves cordially disliked by their independent competitors and by manufacturers. They can cut prices and they can sell their own goods.

The one-cent sale has already been discussed. The chain drug store, like the chain grocery store, relies on loss leaders frequently, of which the one-cent sale idea is only a novel form. As for substitution, the practice is slowly dying out and the customer may be fairly certain of getting what is asked for.

Conclusions.—The situation in the drug field seems to be briefly as follows:

1. There is but one large chain in the field; there are about twenty chains operating between 30 and 10 stores, and a great many small chains.

2. The drug chains have as yet availed themselves of a very small part of the total possibilities.

3. There is already a tendency to enlarge the number of stores per chain and decrease the number of chains.

4. The chain drug store has an advantage over its independent competitor in location, sales turnover, advertising, management, and a knowledge of the principles of retail store operation.

CHAPTER XXIV

THE FIVE-TEN-TWENTY-FIVE-CENT STORE CHAINS

The five and ten cent store chain differs from the drug and grocery chains not so much in principles of operation as in physical characteristics. There is the same necessity for careful accounting and for routine practice but there are certain factors which complicate the situation, such as the following:

1. The five and ten cent store chain has a labor problem. Each five and ten cent store has in its employ a certain number of clerks, usually a less highly trained selling type, working for lower wages.

2. The size of each unit in a five- and ten-cent store is inevitably large, and because of the wide variety of goods carried it is necessary to secure requisite turnover.

3. Goods are sold at a fixed price, five, ten, twenty-five cents, or in some cases the stress is laid on the odd cents, three, nine, and nineteen cent stores. The price problem is at once made simpler and more difficult. The labor of registering and following up constant price changes is removed, but, on the other hand a sufficient variety of goods must be found to retail at these fixed prices.

4. A five and ten cent store satisfies a much larger area than either the grocery or the drug chain store. But because all classes of small articles used in every day life are sold, that is, convenience goods, the five and ten cent stores have been able to operate profitably in communities with eight thousand inhabitants. Contrary to other types of chains, the five and ten cent store originated in a small town in Pennsylvania and it was some time before it was operated in large cities. But the necessary distance of the various units of these chains from other units of the same chain causes a more decentralized organization. Each manager has more responsibility.

The Field.—The size, the territory covered, and the publicity connected with the operations of a few of the largest chains in the field have almost made it appear as though this class of chains was limited to a few strikingly successful examples, and that the field was entirely closed to the "little fellow." As a matter of fact, however, there are many small chains. The following table will give some idea of various chains in the field. It has been difficult to obtain the statistics for this tabulation, which is at best an approximation.

Company	Head office	No. of stores
F. W. Woolworth Co	New York, N. Y.	1,189
S. S. Kresge Co	Detroit, Mich.	199
McCrory Stores Corp	New York, N. Y.	152
S. H. Kress	New York, N. Y.	150
Metropolitan Stores		150
McLellan Stores Co	New York, N. Y.	50
W. T. Grant 25¢ Stores	New York, N. Y.	45
P. C. Murphy,	Pittsburgh, Pa.	43
Duke & Ayers, Inc	Dallas, Texas	29
Graham Latimer	Ottumwa, Iowa	20
F. & W. Grand 5, 10, 25¢ Stores	New York, N. Y.	19
Morris 5 & 10¢ Stores	Bluffton, Ind.	19
J. J. Newberry & Co.,	Stroudsberg, Pa.	18
Spurgeon Mercantile Co	Chicago, Ill.	15
A. L. Duckwall Stores Co	Abilene, Tex.	12
H. L. McElroy Co	Bowling Green, Ky.	11
National 5, 10 & 25¢ Stores	Omaha, Neb.	11
Read Stores Co	Kansas	11
Trick Bros. Co	Benton Harbor, Mich.	9
Charles Tremayn's Stores	Ashley, Pa.	8
Kuhn's 5, 10 & 25¢ Stores	Nashville, Tenn.	8
Wm. H. Cobb	Sharon Hill, Pa.	7
Greene Bros	Lowell, Mass.	7
Taylor, Knobel Co., Inc	Tacoma, Wash.	7
Trimmers Stores	Carlisle, Pa.	6
Hested Stores Co	Fairbury, Neb.	6
John W. Tottle, Ba	Baltimore, Md.	6
A. A. Grimes 10 cent Stores Co	Kansas City, Mo.	
F. E. Nelson Co	Manchester, N. H.	6
L. J. Everett Corp	Jamestown, N. Y.	6
W. W. Joseph 5 & 10	Pittsburgh, Pa.	5
Schulz Bros. & Co	Chicago, Ill.	5
J. Da Silva	Freeport, N. Y.	5
Neel Cunningham,	Chicago, Ill.	5
Acme 5 & 10 cent Stores	Philadelphia, Pa.	5

There are many additional chains operating four, three, and two stores, but the above list is sufficient to give an idea of the competition. The five and ten cent store field seems to be essentially the small town of which there are so many in Pennsylvania and the Middle West.

Most of these stores never advertise and thus local chains are not known beyond the precincts of the territory they serve. The store is usually well located, painted in brilliant colors, usually red, and its window display well taken care of.

The F. W. Woolworth Co.—F. W. Woolworth made himself one of the best known men in America out of nickels and dimes. He lived to see the completion of the Woolworth Building, the highest edifice in the world, and the opening of the chain's thousandth store on Fifth Avenue, New York. The story of his rise to success has often been told, but a book dealing generally with the subject of the chain stores would be incomplete without it.

Mr. Woolworth was born in Rodman, Jefferson County, New York, in 1852. He was the son of a farmer and was brought up on a farm. But his ambitions lay along business lines. He took a course in a commercial college at Watertown, New York, and then went to work with the drygoods firm of Augsbury & Moore at Watertown. The first three months he received no salary. Then he was paid $3.50 a week. After two and one-half years he was receiving $6 a week. W. H. Moore, when he was earning $10 a week in 1877, gave him an opportunity to rearrange the stock in the store. He did this, making up a five cent table with a price card inviting customers to take their choice. Mr. Moore was induced to back a five cent store in Utica, New York, but sales were not large enough to carry the store. It was closed. Woolworth immediately started another store in Lancaster, Pa., which sold out over 30 per cent. of the stock on the first day. Sales for the first year were $6,750. This was the first five and ten cent store in successful operation.

Mr. Woolworth was wise enough to see the vast possibilities ahead of him, but he had no organization and no financial backing. He first took his brother, C. S. Woolworth, into partnership with him in a store in Harrisburg, Pa. This store was unsuccessful. It was closed and another opened in Scranton, Pa., which quickly established itself. In July, 1886, a small office was opened in New York.

The early growth of the present Woolworth chain was due to the training of men in the organization who later established chains of their own, culminating in the final merger of 1912. S. H. Knox, Mr. Woolworth's cousin, went in with Mr. Woolworth, and was associated with him for five years until 1889, when he started for himself.

Carson H. Peck was next taken from the Utica store and was brought to New York to help manage the stores and buy merchandise. F. M. Kirby started in with C. S. Woolworth in Scranton, Pa., where his entire office furniture was an old drygoods box. Earle P. Charlton started with Mr. Knox and chose the New England field for exploitation, beginning business for himself in 1896. After the division of the stores, Mr. Charlton extended his activities to California and the Pacific Coast. Thus from the Woolworth organization has developed five successful chains. The national aspect of the Woolworth chain has already been discussed in connection with the merger of 1912.

Hubert T. Parson, now president of the F. W. Woolworth Company, started with Mr. Woolworth in 1892 as an accountant. He became secretary of F. W. Woolworth & Co., and at the time of the merger naturally became secretary of the enlarged company.

The Woolworth chain, like the Liggett chain, is far ahead of all competitors in the field, and like the Liggett chain, is a combination of stores. While the Liggett stores have invaded England, the Woolworth stores have gone into Canada.

Five and Ten Cent Store Policies.—More than any other type of chain retailing organization, with the exception of the self-service store, the five and ten cent store relies on the goods to sell themselves. The constant object of the chain management should be to secure articles which sell easily. And practically the whole secret of the five and ten cent stores' selling program is display. Beginning with the windows, which are changed weekly, the whole store is arranged with the one idea of displaying goods to the best advantage. Each counter is a miniature store in itself with articles arranged according to their display value. Traffic routes should be and ordinarily are studied with a view to arranging the location of the merchandise.   Mention has already been made of the necessity of having jewelry in the front, and the policy of putting household goods in the basement.

The fundamental rule, therefore, for a five and ten cent store is to choose merchandise which will sell and display it where the

FIG. 57.—Selling peanut brittle through Woolworth store.

public can see it to the best advantage.

The second fundamental is the facilitating of sales by having the customer pick out the article desired and handing it to the salesgirl with the money.

All five and ten cent stores are cash-and-carry.

The window display of the five and ten cent store chains is always attractive, because of the number of articles displayed, the brilliant coloring, or the idea behind the display.   Figure 57 shows a window display in the Woolworth store at Los Angeles,

California. The large card carries the words "We sold ninety million pounds of candy last year." The safe in the center of the display was made entirely out of peanut brittle and was an exact duplicate of a real office safe. The combination and handle were made of white candy, as was also the lettering on the top of the safe. Coins were tumbling out of the safe into the large plate, made also of peanut brittle. The idea behind the whole display was that the public could bank on Woolworth candy as evidenced by popular approval in the shape of the ninety million pounds of candy sold the year before.

The Labor Problem.—The five and ten cent store normally has t o contend with lack of interest and ignorance on the part of the sales girls. The lack of interest is due to the small· wages paid and the ignorance is, in great part, due to the large labor turnover. The low wages have been caused by a general feeling that since the goods were of such a nature that no sales effort was necessary, the class of girl hired could be of an inferior type. The natural result is an inefficient clerk.

The New York State Department of Labor investigators found that thieving was included by almost every manager as one of his greatest problems. The universal display of goods and indiscriminate use of cash registers make thieving comparatively easy. Both salesgirls and the public take things. One manager resorted to weekly inventories and shrinkage reports to check up losses apparently due to thieving. One store manager placed an empty box, done up carefully in paper and string, on a front counter. It promptly vanished and in the course of a half hour 22 of these empty boxes had disappeared.

A great deal of the ignorance, dishonesty, and lack of interest among the salesgirls can undoubtedly be removed if the turnover is stabilized, and by the introduction of carefully planned methods of employment, as suggested in the chapters dealing with personnel problems.

Wages paid are ordinarily as low as possible. The high turnover tends to create plasticity in wages. The five and ten cent store will pay just enough to give it a sufficient supply of girls, with rarely any attempt at making them permanent workers.

The following tabulation shows the wages of women employees in a representative five and ten cent store in a small city in

New York State, as tabulated by the New York State Department of Labor, division of Women in Industry.

WOMEN'S WAGES IN A REPRESENTATIVE 5 AND 10 CENT STORE IN A TOWN
OF THE SECOND SCHEDULE
1915–1921

Wage rate	1915, number of women	1916, number of women	1917, number of women	1918, number of women	1919, number of women	1920, number of women	1921, number of women
$ 4– 4.99	10	8					
5– 5.99	8	4	2	2			
6– 6.99	8	7	19	11			
7– 7.99	1	2	3	6	11		
8– 8.99	..	1	1	2	4	5	
9– 9.99	1	..	..	1	3	4	
10– 10.99	..	1	1	..	2	1	9
11– 12.00	1	..	..	1	2	4	7
12– 12.99	..	..	..	..	2	2	
13– 13.99	..	..	..	1	..	1	
14– 14.99	..	..	..	..	..	..	4
15– 15.99	..	..	..	..	1		
16– 16.99	..	..	..	..	..	..	1
17– 17.99	..	..	..	..	..	1	
18– 18.99	..	..	..	..	1		
19– 19.99	..	..	..	..	..	..	1
20– 20.99	..	..	..	..	..	1	
Total	29	23	26	24	26	19	22
Median wage	$5.56	$5.88	$6.76	$6.86	$8.38	$10.00	$11.22

With the advance in wages from 1915 on, the number of employees fell off. While there were 29 in 1915, there were but 19 in 1920. That is, the decrease in number of employees nearly kept pace with the wage increase. It would be interesting to have figures on sales in this store to see whether higher wages were conducive to sales efficiency or the opposite.

There is a tendency in the five and ten cent store chains, as in department store and other retailing agencies, to better the condition of the salesperson. It is recognized, at least in theory, that they have a right to a living wage and the policy of store managers to make a good showing by reducing salaries of his salesgirls to the minimum is frowned upon, and justly so.

24

Hours.—There is no set time for opening or closing five and ten cent stores, In general, they conform to the custom of the community. As a rule, stores in large cities open at nine o'clock and close at five or six, but in small cities and towns the hours are apt to be longer. In the majority of small towns the stores must remain open Saturday afternoon while in cities they usually close during the summer. Stores of the same chain, one in a

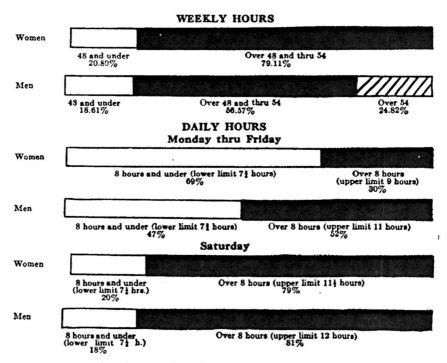

Fig. 58.—Schedule of working hours in five and ten cent store chains.

residential district and one in a business district, may keep different hours although in the same city. Independent stores are likely to keep longer hours than the chain stores.

The amount of actual sales in five and ten cent stores is small before 10 a. m. but clerks must be on hand at 8:30 or 9 a. m. to prepare for the day's business, restock counters, etc. Customers begin to come in large numbers from 11 a. m. on.

Figure 60 is taken from the New York Department of Labor investigation and shows the various working hours of men and women for the entire week, for Monday through Friday, and for Saturday alone.

Approximately 80 per cent. of the women worked over 48 hours a week. From Monday through Friday 30 per cent. worked more than 8 hours a day but with an upper limit of 9 hours. Sixty-nine per cent. worked under 8 hours but at least as much as 7¾. The men worked longer, 52 per cent. of them working over 8 hours with upper limit of 11 hours. On Saturdays it was apparent that everybody was worked to the limit. Sixteen per cent. worked 11 hours a day and 51 per cent. worked 10 hours.

The best wages were found to be in stores with the shortest hours, and workers were paid less where hours were longest.

Price and Manufacturing.—Before the war, some chains had gone up to a 25-cent limit but a great many of them remained at the 10-cent limit. Now the F. W. Woolworth Co. is practically alone in pursuing the ten cent policy. All its competitors, although still calling themselves five, ten, and twenty five cent chains, in reality have boosted the price as high as one dollar or over. It was discovered that the average sale of the department store is under one dollar and the chains immediately capitalized this point and branched out more in the line of dry goods and less in that of crockery and glass.

That this price widening has been successful is proved by the record of the stores that have followed this policy, particularly the Kresge organization. But that goods can still be made and sold at retail for ten cents is also conclusively proved by the Woolworth organization, the profits of which have steadily gone on. There is evidently a field for both types of chains. The Kresge stores and others following the higher price policy are able to offer goods for sale which naturally the Woolworth stores cannot do. But there are many staple articles which can be made to retail at ten cents and these will always prove a definite drawing card, even for the chains with higher-priced policies.

While the war forced many chains to raise their price limit, the Woolworth Co. adopted the policy of manufacturing those things which it could not induce others to manufacture. When the war made it impossible to get any more D.M.C. crochet cotton, it induced a manufacturer to devote his whole spinning output to making crochet cotton which the Woolworth chain put out under the private brand name of "Woolco." By following out this policy of having articles manufactured under contract exclusively to meet their own demands, the Woolworth organization is taking a long step forward.

The small variety chain cannot hope to practice such economies, but it has the advantages and the disadvantages of the fixed price. Unquestionably the low price appeal of the five and ten cent store has proved its greatest sales asset.

The Manufacturer and the "Five-and-Ten."—It was a long time before manufacturers could be brought to see the advantage of producing articles that could be retailed for ten cents. It is true that all manufacturers cannot modify their products to meet this need, but there are a great many that can, and many of these are doing so at the present moment.

It is a rule of selling that the best known article, and the one with the best reputation, will sell better than the unknown, unheralded product, no matter how good the latter may be. Therefore, manufacturers must come up to the standard of excellence set by the five and ten cent stores. Their product must sell itself, and they must pave the way for this sale by publicity, and they must keep the way paved so that this article will sell. The weak point so far has proved to be when the manufacturer desired to sample his article where its hold was weakest. This is in direct opposition to the policy of the chain to sell it where it is strongest. The natural result is that, as all the stores in the chain do not necessarily sell the same articles, the samples are sold only where the demand proves satisfactory, and the manufacturer is brought up sharply where he was in the beginning. His product will sell only where his publicity has been successful.

Publicity must precede distribution through ten cent store chains. Otherwise the samples cannot compete with already established lines.

Mention has been made elsewhere of the value to the manufacturer of this sampling and the publicity it gives the product. The customer in the ten cent store sees an article on display with a familiar name. It costs only ten cents. She buys it, likes it, and the next time it is more than likely she will purchase a full-sized package through the regular channels.

Sampling pays both the ten cent stores as well as the manufacturer. It gives him the prestige incident to carrying a well known brand. It relieves him of the imputation of retailing only cheap articles.

Stock.—The five and ten cent store is and should be an exact reflection of the community's likes and dislikes. This is easier in the case of individual five and ten cent stores because of the wider scope allowed the manager in selecting his goods. Allowance also is made for small communities, where naturally stock must be more closely watched with regard to its turnover, than it is in cities where slower moving articles can be merchandised profitably.

Five and ten cent chains frequently grant temporary concessions to manufacturers. They are considered excellent publicity and in many cases serve as a drawing card for the store rather than as an attempt to sell the goods. The arrangement ordinarily is that after the concessionaire moves on, the chain is given the agency and a certain percentage of profits made during the concession.

Permanent concessions very often form miniature chains within chains. This may be in the case of the music counter which is run by a special company having a branch in each of the stores. Such a department is considered an added attraction and an inducement for customers to come to the store. A singer will often draw a crowd to the store. One chain grants a grocery concession in its stores as a drawing card.

Conclusions.—The newcomer in the variety field has much to contend with—strong competition, efficient methods, operating economy, large stock, etc. But there are also some points in his favor. By carefully choosing his location he may be sure of a certain percentage of trade. The five and ten cent store as a non-advertiser must rely on location. A customer will not normally walk out of his way to trade at one five and ten cent store rather than at another. He goes to buy a certain staple article and he expects to find it at any five and ten store rather than at a particular one.

The customer should also be able to procure a standard stock to sell within the prescribed price limits. But such a venture necessarily demands a certain minimum of capital without which it would be folly to begin.

CHAPTER XXV

DRYGOODS AND CLOTHING CHAINS

The selling of drygoods and clothing, shoes, hats, etc., has, from the earliest times, always been an important retailing activity and it is to be expected that the chain should have made considerable inroads in these fields. Whenever the question of public taste enters the selling equation, however, there are new difficulties to surmount. The ordinary forms of clothing are not convenience goods, but rather are shopping lines. Therefore, the turnover is likely to be slowed down. A customer does not come in and say "I shall take this or that." He says "Let me look at this or that," and, if it does not suit, the customer goes away. Therefore, the problem of the chain retailer of drygoods and clothing is to pick out only those lines which the majority of people will choose. That is, there must be no ultra styles, there must be no odd sizes, and the stock must be limited in supply of seasonal goods to what surely can be sold. Chain drygoods and clothing chains cannot afford to purchase far ahead. The Penney chain, which has been the most successful in the drygoods field, makes it one of its cardinal policies to buy no more than is immediately needed.

Another point which may cause difficulties to the drygoods chain is a difference of demand in different sections. This can be overcome only by allowing the local manager considerable latitude in his choice of stock. Although there may be a central purchasing organization, still that body acts in the closest coöperation with the local stores, and buys only what is certain to be approved by local managers. Even shoe manufacturers running their own local retail stores are careful to consult the local manager in advance of manufacture about styles for the coming season.

In the case of shoe chains, the type of demand may be different in one section of the town from what it is in the other. Hat chains, haberdashery chains, and clothing chains all have many seasonal problems to meet.

This type of chain retailing shopping lines has to do a great deal of advertising, and consequently, it is possible that in some cases location may not play so important a part. In the Penney chain, for example, the appeal is through price and quality.

Shoe stores, however, retailing cheap shoes, which come practically under the class of convenience goods, must find suitable locations. All stores, of course, must locate in the section devoted to the trade they wish to capture. A shoe store retailing quality ladies' shoes would be out of place in the financial district.

In the case of the dry goods store, the control is far more decentralized than in the case of the haberdashery, the hat, or the shoe store. The dry goods store usually has but one link in a town, while the other types of store have several. In general, the manager of the dry goods store hires his own clerks, chooses, if not purchases, his own merchandise, pays his incidental expenses, attends to local advertising, etc.

Even where chains have gained strong hold in drygoods and clothing lines, the general policy has always been to sell only the standard styles and sizes and at low or moderate prices.

The Drygoods Chains.—There are but two dry goods chains with a large number of unit stores, the Penney and the Perkins chains. But there are several organizations, such as the Associated Drygoods Co., and the May Department Stores, whose gross sales mount up into many millions. Thus two types of chain drygoods stores may be distinguished.

1. *The small-unit type.* This class carries lower-priced merchandise, standard styles and sizes, employs few clerks, is located in small towns, generally in the South and Middle West, Pennsylvania, and New York. Purchasing is ordinarily done at headquarters in this type of chain, and close watch is kept of individual stores by careful accounting methods. This type of drygoods store comes in direct competition with the small independent drygoods stores in medium-sized towns.

2. *The large unit type.* These are found in the large cities, and carry a much more diversified and better line of goods. The control however, of the central organization over the

member stores is much less. In some cases, it is merely financial, limited to stock ownership in a holding company, and there is much question whether this control is sufficient to entitle the organization to be called a chain.

The largest field in the drygoods line seems to be that offered by the small towns. The chain store can usually offer a much better stock than its local competitor, and by careful watching of sales can shift merchandise around in order to avoid loss, yet at the same time secure adequate turnover.

Following is a list of the most prominent chain drygoods stores as compiled by the Fairchild Company:

	No. of Stores
Affiliated Retail Stores—Pittsburgh, Cleveland, St. Louis, Milwaukee, etc.	12
Associated Dry Goods Co., New York	9
Belk Bros. Organization—North Carolina	17
Buchanan Co., Hillsdale, Mich.—Illinois	8
Broadwell's, California	4
Clarke Brothers, Pennsylvania	19
Consolidated Drygoods Co., Western Massachusetts and up-state New York	5
W. P. Chamberlain Co., New Hampshire and Vermont	8
Cole Bros., Missouri and Kansas	6
Cherry's, California, Oregon and Washington	6
Chaffee, central New York State	4
Dives, Pomeroy & Stewart, Pennsylvania	5
Efirds Department Stores, Inc., North and South Carolina	19
Emrich chain, Illinois	6
D. G. Fowler Co., Pennsylvania and Indiana	7
Graham, Sykes Co., Texas and Oklahoma	16
J. M. Gidding Co., New York, Duluth, Philadelphia, and Cincinnati	4
Goodnow-Pearson Co., Fitchburg, Mass.	13
Gilmer's Inc., North and South Carolina (controlled by United Retail Stores Corp.)	18
Kline's, Middle West	4
Irwin Cloak Co., Ohio and Missouri	3
M. Luria & Co., up-state New York	9
Lynch-Fuller Corp., western New York	5
May Department Stores Co., Middle West	4
Mercantile Stores Corp., New York National	25
W. H. McAllister, Sycamore, Ill.	18
Parke, Snow, Inc., Boston, Mass	8
J. C. Penney Co., Middle West and West	313

No. of Stores

D. Price & Co., New York	3
Perkins Bros. Co., Texas	350
Rorabaugh Co., Kansas, Illinois and Oklahoma	6
Ross Stores, Inc., New Jersey and New York	5
D. G. Ramsey Bros., Kansas and Missouri	5
Smith Bros. Co., Pennsylvania	6
John Stillman, Michigan and Indiana	4
Albert Steiger Co., Springfield, Mass	7
Seitner & Co., Canton, Ohio	3
Weiler Syndicate, Indiana, Illinois, and Ohio	7

This list, like other lists of chain stores, is not complete because of the constant changes which are taking place in the chain store field. Old chains are constantly adding new links, absorbing other stores or chains, or new chains are rising up.

Gilmer's, Inc., as noted in the list, has been acquired by the United Retail Stores Corp. It is too soon as yet to tell whether the methods which made the United Cigar Stores Co. so successful can be applied with equal profit to a drygoods chain such as Gilmer's, which sells in the medium-sized southern cities, such as Winston-Salem and Durham, North Carolina, and Roanoke and Lynchburg, Virginia.

The drygoods field is still the field of the small chain, and the question has not been settled how far the chain idea can be applied to the drygoods store, properly so-called.

Men's Wear and Haberdashery.—There have been small chains dealing in men's wear, mostly local, for years. It is only in the past few years that a number of chains have sprung up and spread with great rapidity. Their growth has been almost too large for safety; but war conditions helped them along and enabled them to get on their feet before the period of deflation came. The chain haberdashery stores get as close as possible to the convenience class. A man will buy a shirt, a collar, or a necktie at almost any store while he will go out of his way to buy a suit of clothes.

The following four chains deserve mention:

Chain Shirt Shops, Inc., New York City	52
Weber & Heilbroner, New York City	20
United Shirt Shops, New York City	31
Paramount Shirt Shops, New York City	10

There are, in addition, a large number of small chains, with two, three, four, or five member stores, all apparently prosperous, but showing little signs of further expansion.

The Chain Shirt Shops, Inc. is controlled by the Phillips-Jones Corporation, manufacturers of shirts, etc. In a sense, therefore, it is a manufacturer's chain, although the control is only through stock ownership. The company has 25 stores in New York City alone, and has spread as far as Boston, Philadelphia, and Rochester.

The United Shirt Shops started out in Johnstown, Pa., as the United Dollar Shirt Shops. This was in 1916. The rapidly advancing prices caused by the war made it advisable to change the name to the United Shirt Shops. The growth was rapid, and at present the chain is the third largest in the country dealing in haberdashery.

The rapid growth in this field was due to an unquestioned need for better methods, better stuffs, fairer values, and new merchandising ideas. Furthermore, haberdashery seemed to be particularly fitted to the economies possible to effect by applying chain methods of purchasing and accounting.

Jacob Kagan and A. Fred Podren have described the method they followed in installing an accounting system for a chain of retail men's wear shops. Where the chain is too small to maintain a warehouse, as most of them still are, goods are sent to the stores with memorandum of goods shipped, but with no prices. The manufacturer sends the office a duplicate of the memorandum containing, however, the cost prices. The store manager signs a receipt and forwards it to headquarters. To avoid delay, the central office, as soon as it receives notification of shipment from the manufacturer, sends invoices to the stores of the goods at retail prices, and these invoices arrive in advance of the goods.

Cash received for goods sold is rung up on the cash register, and cumulative record of sales is thus kept. Every evening, the cash register readings are put on the daily cash report, the difference between the previous reading and the one for the day in question forming gross sales for the day. The store manager deposits all cash at the bank and the bank teller stamps report in space provided. See Fig. 59.

On the reverse side of the form is place for all cash expenditures. If paid at the store, an amount must be deducted from deposits at the bank, but the better way is to have them paid by check from the central office.

Figure 60 shows a simple form of inventory for use in small

FORM A

CHAIN
HABERDASHERY
SHOPS

DAILY CASH REPORT

Store No.______ ____________ Manager
Day of Week Month Day Year

Register Reading After Last Sale Today
Register Reading After Last Sale Yesterday
SALES FOR TODAY
Expenditures (see reverse side)
BALANCE—DEPOSITED IN BANK

O. K.'d by Approved by

Name of Bank
City or Town

(BANK STAMP)

DEPOSITED BY

CHAIN HABERDASHERY SHOPS
BOSTON, MASS.

Date Deposited 192

Bills
Specie
Checks on
"
"
"
"
"
"
TOTAL

Manager:—Please itemize your expenditures on the reverse—NOW.

Reverse Side, Form A

CASH EXPENDITURES

Store No........ Day.................. 192

Paid the following expense items:
Help (give full details)

Ice Water
Express
Postage
Removing Rubbish
Other Items (list each individually)

Total (carried on Reverse Side)

Manager.

Remarks, Suggestions, etc.

Fig. 59.—Form of daily cash report used in haberdashery chain.

haberdashery chains. Columns are provided for different-priced articles in the store. The quantity only is placed in the price column. Total inventory can quickly be found by multiplying and adding totals.

This way of taking stock, according to "The Haberdasher," is quick, and supplies all information in which the accounting

Form B

Store No......... Address ....
Date ...... Time...... Register Reading.......
Manager ....
Inventory taken by ....

CHAIN HABERDASHERY SHOPS

INVENTORY

DO NOT SIGN this Stock Sheet unless you are Sure it is **ACCURATE**

69	75	96
105	8	97
31	9	2
71	16	19
89	105	77
209	73	87

455	211	282
63	95	98
318	156	276

TOTAL—OVER

Reverse Side, Form B

BOOK INVENTORY CHARGES			INVENTORY	BOOK INVENTORY CREDITS		
Inventory Beginning			Store No.	Sales to Date		
Shipments			Address	Reductions		
Journal Charges (*Transfers, etc.*)			Manager	Special Sale Reductions		
Advances			Taken By	Journal Credits (*Transfers, etc.*)		
Sundries			Date—From to	Sundries		
			Figured By			
			Physical Inventory			
			Book Inventory			
			Over (black ink)			
			Short (red ink)			
			BOOK INVENTORY			
			Summary Charges			
			Summary Credits			
			Balance			
			Book Inventory			

FIG. 60.—Form of inventory in haberdashery chain.

department is interested. This department (accounting) is interested only in the amount of merchandise represented in dollars and cents. Its lookout is not as to the kind of merchandise in the stores.

The reverse side of the inventory form contains space for general and special information, and for book inventory charges.

Each store manager is supposed to keep a store ledger, in which he charges himself for goods received and credits himself for cash turned in. All his entries are made at retail prices. In times of rapid price changes, there will be entries for mark-ups and mark-downs. Where goods are frequently changed from store to store, there should be space for transfers.

The above system is exceedingly simple, and is not recommended for any but small chains which cannot afford the overhead expense necessary to install a more complex accounting system. This method lays the responsibility for watching the particular items in stock on the store manager himself as checked up by the district superintendent. In more complete systems, inventories contain detailed account of all items in stock.

In the men's furnishing shop, as well as in the hat store and the shoe store, the element of salesmanship enters. Service is far more important than it is in the drug store, the grocery store, or the five- and ten-cent store. But the sale is complicated whenever a choice is to be made by the customer, and where the attitude of the clerk may mean a large or a small sale. A good haberdashery salesman will build up a collar sale into a shirt sale. The higher type of salesmanship required, the more difficult it is to secure adequate control in a chain. Thus the problem of the personnel is even more important in stores dealing in shopping lines than it is in those handling convenience goods only.

Hats.—Chain stores in the hat industry have existed for fifteen years, and in that course of time have expanded slowly, and not with the remarkable activity characteristic cf the chain haberdasheries. The following list shows the leading retail chain hatters, dealing in headgear alone.

	STORES		STORES
Sarnoff-Irving	52	Long's Hat Stores	23
B. H. Kaufman	50	Truly Warner	21
Wormser Hat Stores	36	Kenton Hats	14
Snyder's Inc.	25	Young's Hat Stores	11

In addition to the above list, there are several local chains. There are also many general chain store organizations which carry hats, such as Browning, King & Co., the Menter stores, etc.

The chain hat stores started by holding closely to the cheaper grades. Truly Warner and Kaufman have kept to a fixed price limit, but Sarnoff-Irving, which formerly had a $2 limit, now handle hats as high as $7.

A chain hat store has to contend with the desire of the average customer to have a distinctive hat, while it must be the policy of the chain to furnish a standard hat. This explains the tendency of the chain hat stores to hold to the cheaper grades. The large hat manufacturers ordinarily give their agencies to independent hatters.

Clothing.—This field may be divided broadly into men's and women's clothing. In the men's clothing field, there is Browning, King & Co., with 28 stores, which manufacture only for themselves, the Rogers Peet Co., which operate stores of their own and give agencies, and such chains as the Monroe Clothes Shops, with 11 stores in New York. The field is an exceptionally difficult one for a chain organization to handle successfully, owing to the rapid changes in style, price, etc.

The problem of retailing women's clothing through chain stores is even more difficult. Nevertheless, the Bedell Company, of New York, operates a chain of seventeen retail stores for the sale of women's suits and cloaks.

The New York Waist Co. operates a cnain of stores in New York and Brooklyn, selling women's waists. The National Hosiery Stores, with nine shops, the Gotham Hosiery Co., with four and some others with but two links, sell women's hosiery.

Shoes.—The retailing of shoes has offered real opportunities for chain organization, and especially to the manufacturers of shoes, to start retail chains under their supervision. The number of small chains is legion, and there is a comparatively large number of moderate-sized chains.

The chain shoe field is remarkable for the number of firms manufacturing and at the same time managing retail stores. As a matter of fact, shoes are sold in six different ways:

1. Independent shoe store,
2. Manufacturer-owned store,
3. Department stores,
4. Privately-owned chain stores,
5. Independent stores having exclusive agency for some manufacturer,
6. Mail-order houses.

We are concerned here only with classes 2 and 4. Class 2 is the commonest form, and seems to find it possible to make a success. The privately-owned chain is at a disadvantage, and must content itself with retailing a cheap grade of shoes. The following is a partial list of chain shoe stores, both manufacturer and strictly retail:

	STORES
Newark Shoe Co., Baltimore, Md.	300
W. L. Douglas Shoe Co., Brockton, Mass.	107
G. R. Kinney Co., Inc., New York City	102
Regal Shoe Co.	56
Hanan & Sons.	
George E. Keith (Walkover).	
Beck-*H*azard Stores, Inc., New York City	28

The following chains operate more than three but less than ten, and the list does not pretend to be complete, as there are many more throughout the country:

Adler Shoe Co.	Thomas G. Plant Co.
I. Blyn & Sons	Dr. Read Cushion Shoe Co.
Bouve-Sterling	Rice & Hutchins
Edwin Clapp & Son	Rival Shoe Co.
Emerson Shoe Co.	Star Shoe Co.
Ground Gripper Co.	Stetson Shops, Inc.
London Shoe Co.	United Shoe Stores, Milwaukee, Wis.
D. Loventhal's Sons	Wildfeuer Bros.
I. Miller & Sons	

In addition to shoe stores proper, there are several chains of shoe repairing shops, such as Klein's Rapid Shoe Repair Co., in New York. There are also some shoe-shining chains.

The great problem in merchandising shoes has always been securing turnover in all lines. There is a choice of two evils, either to prune stock to bare necessities and lose customers, or to accept a reduced turnover. One small shoe chain has found its solution in reducing the time of selling a shoe to eight minutes per customer. If the customer cannot make up his mind in that length of time, he is politely advised to look somewhere else. This shoe chain has adopted a form of self-service, allowing the customer to put on the shoes and fit himself. In this way, one clerk can handle several customers at the same time. In spite of this innovation, the stores are making money and securing a turnover of ten times annually, more than twice what the average chain shoe store expects to obtain.

CHAPTER XXVI

OTHER CHAIN FIELDS

The development of chain stores has followed the lines of least resistance. First those fields were taken up and exploited which were devoted to the retailing of necessities and of products which every individual uses constantly. The grocery chain, the drug chain, the five and ten cent store chain, and the clothing and apparel chains are all in this class.

But with the development of chain stores, with the better functioning of method and the cumulative force of a successful enterprise, the chain store idea has grown in two directions.

1. It has been extended to the retailing of articles which cannot strictly be called necessities, but which many people find necessary to their comfort. In this class come the tobacco and confectionery chains, which are founded on habit, and the optical chain, which is based on defective vision. In many cases there have been long established chains in these fields, but with the exception of the United Cigar Stores Co., their growth has been slow compared with that of the grocery and five- and ten-cent store chains.

2. It has been extended to the retailing of products which necessitate special service. In this class comes the restaurant chains where food has to be prepared and served. It also includes chains of hotels, theatres, and places of amusement which have successfully applied the principles of chain operation to their special problems.

The Retail Tobacco Chains.—Some of the most efficient and profitable methods of chain operation have been developed in the tobacco field. The United Cigar Stores represents a case where a man saw opportunity and seized it. When George J. Whelan decided that his eight stores in Syracuse, New York, were not large enough to satisfy his ambition, and came to New York City, a new era was opened in chain store development as well as in retail tobacco merchandising.

The independent cigar stores had been losing ground steadily to the drug stores, the hotels, and the news stands, all of which carried cigars and tobacco. The cigar store Indian stood for all that was antiquated in retail merchandising. The United Cigar Stores Co. was formed in 1900, and the principles which it adopted at that time are still in force. Reducing the location of his stores to a science, Mr. Whelan went a step further, and in the days when personnel administration was a name without meaning, he drilled his men with the principal idea of having them render service to customers. He standardized merchandise, standardized the appearance of his stores, standardized his methods of accounting, and, most important of all, succeeded in getting his clerks interested.

At the present moment, the United Cigar Stores Co. operates 1,500 stores and 700 agencies. It is the second-largest chain in the country, surpassed in size only by the Great Atlantic & Pacific Tea Co. The latest major development in its history was its acquirement by the United Retail Stores Corporation. Several small chains were absorbed during the process of development, but, on the whole, the progress has been systematic. Large cities were chosen first, in which the per capita consumption of tobacco was highest. Then smaller centers of population were covered. As fast as statistics show that a community is able to support a United Cigar Store, one is established there.

There is but one other important company in the tobacco retailing field, namely, the Schulte Retail Stores Corporation. In the past few years this company has expanded very rapidly. In 1918, with 113 stores, the company did a business of $4,000,000. From the same stores, in 1919, the company took in sales of $6,000,000, in addition to $2,000,000 from 51 stores opened during the year, or a total of $8,000,000, or twice the amount taken in during the previous year.

The General Cigar Co. has 77 stores, 25 of them in Chicago. In nearly all the large cities of the country there are local chains with branches running from 3 to 20. But the independent stores far outnumber the chain stores as yet.

In starting a tobacco chain, the location of the member stores is undoubtedly the most important consideration. Men will not go out of their way to buy standard brands which can be procured anywhere at a standard price. Hence the corner location policy of the United Cigar Stores Co.

The second requisite for success is an exceedingly rapid turn-over. Once in 30 days should serve as an average. This is necessary in retailing products on such a narrow margin of profit. The tobacco field has been particularly subject to cut-price wars in the past, but, as has been pointed out elsewhere, this policy rarely brings any actual advantage to the firms concerned.

Candy, Confectionery, Etc.—There are some fields which seem preëminently suited for manufacturers' chains, and the candy field is one of these. A Huyler store on one corner will not materially affect the sales of Huyler candy in an agency on the next corner. Thus the great problem of damaging agency sales does not cut a great figure. In the second place, a chain of candy stores offers a steady outlet for the company's products which, from their nature, must be disposed of within a comparatively short time.

As a matter of fact, candy is bought mostly by men and wherever they happen to be at the moment. Therefore, location plays an essential part in the success of the candy chain just as in the tobacco chain. The window display is very important. Windows have to be changed frequently because of the perishability of the product. Many candy chains arrange new displays daily except in the case of some special seasonal display, which may remain a week. The message which the candy stores are constantly trying to emphasize is the freshness and quality of their products. In the Loft stores, for example, candy is frequently displayed sliced through the middle to give a further effect of freshness.

It frequently happens that a number of chain candy stores are located close by each other and there is little to choose between the various locations. Assuming that the price appeal is approximately the same, recourse must be had to quality and service. Attractive window displays and local advertising will create an atmosphere of quality. Goodwill may be secured by good service. A candy store cannot sell too cheaply, or the quality will be suspected.

The principal chains in the candy field are as follows:

Huyler's	60
United Retail Candy Stores	25
Mirror	20
Loft, Inc	23
Schraft's	17
Page & Shaw	17 (10 additional stores in Canada and abroad)

In addition, there are a great many other chains, too numerous to mention, including Miller Brothers, the Goody Shops, Mary Elizabeth, Martha Washington, etc.

Several chains operate lunch counters or serve light lunches at tables in some of their stores. Schraft's and Huyler's are noteworthy examples. This service is only practicable in stores in or near shopping centers. Page & Shaw, in addition to manufacturing their own candy, also operate a chocolate factory and a box factory.

Tobacco and candy products are fairly limited in range compared with grocery and drug chains, but the Nedick's Orange Juice Co. is even more specialized. Through 55 stores in and around New York it sells orange drink and nothing else in the way of a beverage. Other things have been tried, but have not proved satisfactory. Although sales fall off in the winter, they do not care to put in hot drinks. As a sideline, candy and other miscellaneous edibles are sold.

The striking fact about the conduct of the stores is that the stores are open to the street. They are display and store in one. A uniform finish in white makes them easy to find. The fact that they are on the street, that there is no door to open, no steps to ascend or descend, has a strong selling appeal.

Bakeries.—The bakery chain is in many respects like the candy chain. That is, it is dependent on location for its business and, the product being perishable, the problem of left-over goods becomes extremely important. Owing to the necessity of supplying fresh products to the public, the bakery chain must do its own manufacturing, in many cases on the premises.

The Federal System of Bakeries of America, with approximately four hundred stores, is the largest chain in the bakery field. There are several small local chains of a few units each. The Federal Bakeries have picked out desirable city locations where there is a great deal of traffic, and have capitalized this situation with attractive window displays and· carefully conducted merchandising campaigns. By allowing the managers wide scope as to amount and size of bakings, choice of lines of goods to sell, and other local matters, the major difficulties have been overcome. Almost every store is a complete manufacturing unit. The home office at Davenport, Iowa, supplies material for window displays, merchandising ideas, formulæ, and necessary sales training for managers. The majority of the managers are trained at the company's own school.

The bakery field is a difficult one since the bakery has to contend constantly with the chain groceries, which also retail baked goods. The success of the Federal chain, however, shows that it is possible to surmount these difficulties by proper attention to chain store principles.

Restaurants.—As soon as we come to the restaurant field, the service problem is accentuated. The restaurant is the dividing line between the two types of chains. The restaurant field itself is sharply divided into the service and self-service type. At present, the bulk of the restaurant chains are of the latter type, approximately more nearly the original chain idea of a series of stores selling necessities to a large number of people, the sales being based on low price and convenient location.

In the service restaurants, Child's stands far in the lead. But it is a service chain conducted according to all the rules of chain store practice. It insists on suitable locations, serves standard low-priced food, stresses the display features, etc. This is directly contrary to the policy pursued by independent restaurants, where a reputation for fine cooking or excellent service will often draw customers out of their ways.

The self-service lunch rooms are always located on traffic. They will be found near railroad stations to catch early and late traffic, and in the business districts to catch business people at noon. The John R. Thompson Co. in Chicago and the Waldorf Lunch System, Inc., in Boston are the largest in the field. There are a great number of local and semi-local chains with from three to twenty branches.

The Waldorf System is typical of the self-service restaurant chain. It operates over one hundred restaurants in over thirty cities. The first Waldorf Lunch was founded as late as 1904, in Springfield, Mass., with an initial investment of only $1,800. The first Waldorf Lunch in Boston was started in 1906. The chain's great growth dates from 1919, when the Waldorf System, with 38 stores of its own, absorbed the Kinney & Woodward chain, having 14 stores, and the Baldwin chain, having seven stores, making a total of 59. In less than two years it added 30 more links, 20 of them from the absorption of the 11 stores of the Porter Capitol System, and nine from the Waldorf Co. of Providence, R. I.

The company has applied the policy of standardization to the retailing of food. The average amount of every portion is carefully calculated. For example, when a customer orders hash, he always gets the same amount. Each serving of hash has been carefully measured and done up in waxed paper before being sent to the member stores. All baking is done in the central commissary which operates twenty-four hours a day. The average meal during 1920 was thirty cents and the company made less than two cents profit on each meal. But during this period the company served 36,000,000 meals, and from this enormous turnover, it was possible to make substantial profits.

Hotels.—When we discuss the hotel chain we come to the largest enterprise which has yet been attempted along chain store principles. For example, the Hotel Pennsylvania, at New York, the largest hotel in the world, is a link in the Statler chain. The Bowman chain operates many hotels in the country. The United Hotels Co. of America operates 18 hotels in the United States and Canada. According to the Hotel Record, there are about one hundred so-called hotel chain systems in the United States, operating as many as three or four hotels under the same management.

Most of the hotel systems have a common accounting and purchasing system. The manager of each hotel, as is natural, exercises great authority in the hiring of help, ordering of supplies, adjustment of complaints, etc. But outside of material comfort, the hotel chain must furnish one indispensable element, which is service. We have already seen how important service is in the mere selling of commodities. But a great part of the hotel sales appeal is based on service, telephone, elevator, mail, waiter, almost everything the guest may desire. And the excellence of the service counts a great deal. Location, in other words, is not the entire story. A guest will have his favorite hotel of which he will be a steady patron as long as the service satisfies him. The management, therefore, tries to give uniform service in the entire chain, so that a guest going to another city will patronize the hotel owned by the same chain.

The Statler management will accept no excuse for failure to carry out policies as explained in the Statler Service Codes. Discourtesy is not allowed under any circumstances, even although the guest be unreasonable. For example, the following quotation is taken from the directions to front office clerks:

"Mail clerks and key clerks who recognize people and remember their names are more valuable to us than others who do not.

"You know that what the guest wants (and is entitled to) is a helpful and interested, as well as a courteous service. You are not through with any transaction until the guest is satisfied; or, if you cannot satisfy him, until you have called your superior and the matter is out of our hands."

The Hotels Statler have considered it worth the expense to advertise their policies nationally as a means of acquainting the public with them. It is another case of the chain organization's ability to pick out the fundamental basis of competition and use it as a sales appeal.

Miscellaneous.—The idea of a chain organization has spread also into widely divergent fields. But the principles of operation remain in all cases the same, although the stress may be laid on a different phase of the problem. There is the theatre chain, Keith and Shubert, and others. Here the success of the company depends upon the character of the amusements shown. Loew's, Inc. now operates 117 theatres. There are numerous moving picture chains.

There are two successful barber shop chains in New York where the chief problems are labor and location. There is a successful optical chain with 28 stores. There are chains of stores dealing in automobile accessories.

In starting a chain of enterprises of any sort the fundamental question is whether it is possible to apply the chain store principles as laid down in this volume. There is great opportunity existing, not only in old fields but in new and yet untouched fields. To capitalize these opportunities, it is necessary to heed carefully the methods and practices of others who have already been successful. It has been the purpose of this book to set forth, in so far as possible, the primary rules to be observed in conducting any chain enterprise as illustrated by the example of those who have been most successful.

BIBLIOGRAPHY

BOOK REFERENCES

Principles of Marketing, Paul W. Ivey, Ronald Press, 1921.

Marketing—Its Problems and Methods, C. S. Duncan, Appleton, 1921.

Market Analysis, Percival White, McGraw-Hill Book Co., 1921.

How to Run a Store, Harold Whitehead, T. Y. Crowell, 1921.

The Employment of Women in Five and Ten Cent Stores, Department of Labor, State of New York, Div. of Women in Industry, September, 1921.

Marketing Problems, Melvin T. Copeland, A. W. Shaw Co., New York, 1920.

Merchandising Advertised Products through Drug Stores, J. H. Cross Co., Philadelphia, 1920.

The Elements of Marketing, P. T. Cherington, The Macmillan Co., 1920.

Economics of Retailing, Paul H. Nystrom, Ronald Press Co., 1919.

Fortieth Anniversary Souvenir, The F. W. Woolworth Co., 1919.

Merchandising, John B. Swinney, one of Alexander Hamilton Institute business text books 1917.

Marketing Methods, Ralph S. Butler, one of the Alexander Hamilton Institute series of business text books, 1917.

Retail Buying, Clifton C. Field, Harper & Bros., 1917.

Retail Selling, James W. Fisk, Harper & Bros., 1916.

Psychology, a Study of Mental Life, R. S. Woodworth, Henry Holt, 1921.

Marketing Methods and Policies, Paul D. Converse, Prentice-Hall, Inc., 1921.

Personnel Administration, Tead and Metcalf, McGraw-Hill Book Co., 1920.

Succursales Multiples, Phillippe Moride,

ARTICLES ON CHAIN STORES

1922

Can Executives be Picked by Mental Tests? C. S. Yoakum, *Forbes Magazine*, Jan. 21, 1922.

The Chain Store Grocer, Alfred H. Beckmann, *American Grocer*, Jan. 4, 1922.

W. L. Douglas—A Shoemaker Who Stuck to His Last, *Printers' Ink Monthly*, January, 1922.

1921

A Success Built Upon Dealer Coöperation—The Walkover Shoe, *Printers' Ink Monthly*, December, 1921.

Selling Peanut Brittle, *Confectionery Merchandising*, December, 1921.

How He Turned Losses to Profits, O. D. Foster, *Forbes*, Dec. 10, 1921.

Possibilities and Obstacles in the Growth of Chain Stores, *Men's Wear*, Dec. 7, 1921.

How to Maintain Control of Chain Shops, Kagan & Podren, *The Haberdasher*, 1921.

How King Cash Builds Stores, *Business*, November, 1921.

In Retrospect and Prospect (S. S. Kresge Co.), *The Financial World*, Oct. 24, Oct. 31, Nov. 7, Nov. 14, 1921.

Growth of S. S. Kresge Co., *Boston Evening Transcript*, Nov. 8, 1921.

Analysis of Turnover, *Howell* H. Reeves, *Administration*, October, 1921.

Piggly-Wiggly, How it Has Grown, R. P. Crawford, *Forbes*, October, 1921.

Compiling the Selling Talks for Twenty-two Drug Stores, Felix J. Koch, *Drug Store Merchandising*, October, 1921.

Chain Stores to Invade the Sheet Music Field, *The Music Trade Review*, Oct. 8, 1921.

Chain Drug Stores in the United States, *The Druggists' Circular, Inc.*, September, 1921.

How One Drug Store Grew into a Chain, Louise M. *Holt*, *Drug Store Merchandising*, September, 1921.

How to Make Customers Want Candy, C. L. Ketcham, *Confectionery Merchandising*, September, 1921.

Chain Store Competition, Jay Burns, *Bakers' Review*, September, 1921.

Makes Men; Money Only By-product, *Forbes*, Aug. 20, 1921.

Use of *House* Organs in *Handling* Sales, Robert E. Ramsay, *Administration*, July, 1921.

The Chain and Its Weak Link, *Confectionery Merchandising*, July, 1921.

How Chain Stores Tell Which Locations Are Most Profitable, E. M. Wickes, *Printers' Ink Monthly*, July, 1921.

Chain Store Operation, Edward Wise, *Administration*, March, 1921.

When the Chain Store Gets on the Avenue, Edward T. Tandy, *Printers' Ink Monthly*, February, 1921.

Why a Buyer's Market *H*asn't Changed Our Plans, J. C. Penney, *System*, February, 1921.

Making Five Men's Wear Stores Pay in Iowa, *Chicago Apparel Gazette*, Feb. 9, 1921.

In Printers' Ink

Chain of Bakeries Makes Study of Contact with Consumer, Sept. 29, 1921, page 140.

Why So Many Retailers Swallow the Private Brand Argument, July 21, 1921, page 17.

Good, Old-fashioned Brand Name Advertising, the Specific for Substitution, June 30, 1921, page 3.

What the United Cigar Stores Company Has Accomplished in Twenty Years, May 19, 1921, page 17.

Advertising Is Determining What Products the Chains Shall Carry, April 28, 1921, page 136.

An Analysis of the Chain Store by Wholesale Grocers, April 28, 1921, page 177.

Starting a Chain of Retail Stores, Mar. 31, 1921, page 25.

How to Combat "Own Goods" Bonus in Chain Stores, Feb. 24, 1921, page 3.

Should Manufacturers Run Their Own Retail Stores? No. 1, Feb. 3, 1921, page 3.

Should Manufacturers Run Their Own Retail Stores? No. 2, Feb. 10, 1921, page 101.

1920

Piggly-Wiggly Stores: a Fast Growing Chain Stores System, W. J. Keary, *Financial World*, Nov. 29, 1920.

United Cigar Stores, *Boston News Bureau*, Nov. 5, 1920.

Great Atlantic & Pacific Tea Co., *Boston News Bureau*, July 29, 1920, Oct. 23, 1920.

Piggly Wiggly, *Dry Goods Economist*, Oct. 2, 1920.

Chain Drug Stores, *The Druggists' Circular*, May, 1920.

Lower Prices—Higher Profits, H. P. McBride, *System*, May, 1920.

J. C. Penney Co., *Boston News Bureau*, May 7, Oct. 25, 1920.

J. C. Penney Co., *Dry Goods Economist*, May 29, 1920.

Co-operative Merchandising for the Retail Clothier, M. D. Kobey, *Chicago, Apparel Gazette*, April 7, 1920.

An Insight to Chain Store Methods, J. B. Levey, *The Haberdasher*, 1920.

United Retail Stores Corporation, *Boston News Bureau*, Feb. 16, Feb. 27, 1920.

Meet Chain Stores Half Way, *The Haberdasher*, January, 1920.

The Chain Stores, John Morrow, *Magazine of Wall St.*, Jan. 24, 1920.

Schulte Cigar Stores, *Tobacco*, Jan. 8, 1920.

In Printers' Ink

Advertising's Business Partner, the Well-conducted Retail Store, Dec. 30, 1920, page 114.

Can Any One Plan of Marketing Monopolize Our Distributing System? Nov. 18, 1920, page 26.

Chain-store Methods to Revive Dead Country Stores, Sept. 16, 1920, page 133.

Visualizing the Magnitude of a Business with Chart Illustrations, Sept. 9, 1920, page 107.

Even Doughnut Holes, This Man Finds, Can Be Advertised, Aug. 19, 1920, page 53.

A Sidelight on Landing the Big Customer, June 10, 1920, page 93.

Drug Chain Concentrates Prescription Business in Centrally Located Stores, June 3, 1920, page 125.

Anti-chain Advertising Must Reach Fundamentals, May 13, 1920, page 145.

There's *H*appiness in Every Box, May 13, 1920, page 25.

The Chains and Local Advertising, April 15, 1920, page 231.

United Retail Stores Invade Many Fields of Merchandising, April 15, 1920, page 153.

National Campaign of Advertising for Kresge Stores, April 1, 1920, page 17.

The Winchester Plan—A New Step in Standardization, March 18, 1920, page 77.

A Chain Store Testifies for Advertising, March 4, 1920, page 178.

Creating Business for One's Competitors, Feb. 26, 1920, page 188.

Wanted—Two Men of Vision, Feb. 19, 1920, page 180.

S. S. Kresge Company Uses Paid Advertising, Feb. 19, 1920, page 49.

How to Keep Informed on Chain-store Developments, Feb. 19, 1920, page 44.

The Advertising End of the Chain-store Problem, Jan. 29, 1920, page 157.

Is Collective Buying the Answer to the Growing Chain-store Menace? Jan. 15, 1920, page 18.

New Rockefeller and Whelan Drug Chains Worry Manufacturers, Jan. 8, 1920, page 65.

1919

Is This to Be the Era of the Chain Hat Store? *The American Hatter*, November, 1919.

Fifty Dollars a Square Foot or Move, (Truly Warner), *The American Hatter*, November, 1919.

In Printers' Ink

Why I Make My Employees Partners, Oct. 16, 1919, page 3.

Chain Methods Make Overhead an Investment, May 29, 1919, page 109.

How F. W. Woolworth Built His Wonderful Distributing Machine, April 17, 1919, page 25.

The Small Chain a Growing Market for Manufacturers, April 10, 1919, page 101.

United Cigar Stores May Operate Exclusive Candy Stores, March 27, 1919, page 20.

Booklet to Celebrate Woolworth's 40th Anniversary, March 6, 1919, page 10.

A Chain Store Man's View of Service, Feb. 27, 1919, page 108.

The Five- and Ten-cent Store as a Means of Sampling, Jan. 30, 1919, page 37.

Shall Service be Scrapped or Capitalized? Jan. 23, 1919, page 6.

1918

Big Business of the Five and Ten Cent Stores, *American Industries*, ·Dec. 17, 1918.

The Day of the Chain Store, *Advertising and Selling*, May 1918.

Sebastian Spering Kresge, *Harry Davis, Magazine of Wall Street*, May 11, 1918.

Story of the Chain Stores, J. G. Donley, *Magazine of Wall Street*, April 13, 1918.

The Piggly Wiggly Stores and their Unique Advertising Copy, *Judicious Advertising*, April, 1918.

In Printers' Ink

Chain Stores or Exclusive Agents? Dec. 19, 1918, page 163.

Five- and Ten-Cent Stores are now Boldly "Trading Up," Dec. 19, 1918, page 129.

I'll Sell Anything, Drug Chain Owner Says, Sept. 5, 1918, page 17.

Fifth Avenue Trade as Diagnosed by the Woolworth Co., May 30, 1918, page 56.

Tremendous New Market Springs from Five- and Ten-cent Expansion, May 23, 1918, page 3.

How Liggett Built up the United Drug Co., Feb. 21, 1918, page 90.

1917

Man who at Twenty-eight Suddenly Had a Great Idea, (Woolworth) F. A. Patterson, *American Magazine*, October, 1917.

Systematizing Window Displays for Chain Drug Stores, F. A. Koijane, *American Druggist*, August, 1917.

Consumer and the Chain Grocery Store, C. F. Adams, *Outlook*, Jan. 24, 1917.

In Printers' Ink

In Piggly-Wiggly Stores the Product Has to Sell Itself, Dec. 20, 1917, page 17.

Philadelphia Jobbers and Retailers to Meet Chain-store Methods, Oct. 25, 1917, page 37.

Methods of the Man Who Founded Chain of 3,500 Stores, Sept. 13, 1917, page 83.

Chain Stores Advertise as Economy Measure, Aug. 9, 1917, page 119.

*H*igher Priced Goods in Variety Stores Mean Bigger Outlets for Manufacturers, May 31, 1917, page 3.

Chains Making Independents Better Merchants, April 5, 1917, page 101.

Increase of Selling through Irregular Channels, March 29, 1917, page 71.

Does the Consumer Really Want Service, After All? March 29, 1917, page 93.

Why Woolworth Is Starting a Store on Fifth Avenue, Feb. 15, 1917, page 65.

New Light on the Small Store versus the Big Store, Jan. 18, 1917, page 94.

1916

Big Dreams that Came True, H. Rood, *Everybody's*, November, 1916.

Five and Ten Cent Store Costs, *System*, June, 1916.

How I Watch the Sales of a Chain of 1,000 Stores, George A. Whelan, *System*, May, 1916.

In Printers' Ink

How Shall the Advertiser Regard the Newly Forming Chains? Dec. 28, 1916, page 88.

United Cigar's National Advertising Doubles Ricoro Sales, Dec. 14, 1916, page 3.

Chain-store Romance and Reality, Oct. 12, 1916, page 136.

Hosiery Store Shows which Way the Wind is Blowing, Oct. 5, 1916, page 8.

Jobber Advertises to Offset Chain-store Competition, Aug. 24, 1916, page 100.

A Mail-Order Business that Proved the Stepping-stone to a Women's Specialty Chain, Aug. 10, 1916, page 45.

How Penney Chains Find and Train Profit-Making Partners, May 4, 1916, page 41.

The New Regal Policy of Dealer Co-operation—April 20, 1916, page 41.

United Drug Company's New Premium Plan—February 24, 1916, page 131.

The Chain Store a Tonic with the Advertisers' *H*elp, Feb. 17, 1916, page 45.

How Jewel Tea Co. Built Resources of $16,000,000 in Sixteen Years, Feb. 3, 1916, page 17.

A Chain Store Man on the Chances of the Independent Retailer, Jan. 27, 1916, page 38.

1915

The Chain Stores, Barnard Powers, *Magazine of Wall Street*, November, 1915.

Whelan—Millionaire statistician, K. Banning, *System*, January, 1915.

In Printers' Ink

How a Woman Built a Million Dollar Chain of Stores, Dec. 16, 1915, page 11.

Building Big Mail-order Business on Retail Chain Foundation, Dec. 9, 1915, page 3.

Chain Stores Find the West a Difficult Field, Oct. 28, 1915, page 93.
Grocery Chain Store Practices, Oct. 14, 1915, page 58.
How the Site-buyer for United Cigar Stores Works, Sept. 2, 1915, page 68.
Campaign for a Five- and Ten-cent Store Chain, June 17, 1915, page 46.
Kresge Chain Reaching Out for Business by Mail, May 20, 1915, page 70.
The Five- and Ten-cent Store Outlet for Advertised Products, Jan. 14, 1915, page 3.

1914

Rapid Increase of Chain Stores, *Current Opinion*, December, 1914.
James C. Penney, F. C. Henderschott, *System*, June, 1914.
Money Sticking Out, Edward M. Woolley, *McClure's Magazine*, January, 1914.

In Printers' Ink

Manufacturers Forced to Start Chain Stores, Dec. 31, 1914, page 69.
Government Investigating the Chains, Dec. 10, 1914, page 84.
Chain-store Trading in England, Oct. 1, 1914, page 75.
Kellogg's Fight on Chain Stores, Sept. 17, 1914, page 23.
The Future of the Chains, Sept. 17, 1914, page 75.
Whelan Plans to Get Prosperity *H*ere Double Quick, Sept. 3, 1914, page 84.
What Do You Know about Chain Stores? July 23, 1914, page 140.
How Riker-*H*egeman is Generating Power for Rapid Expansion, July 9, 1914, page 3.
Copy that Boomed a Chain of Restaurants, June 11, 1914, page 82.
Inside Look into One Chain-store System, June 4, 1914, page 45.
Competitive Tactics of Chain Stores, April 9, 1914, page 82.
No Monopoly of Good Business Methods, Feb. 12, 1914, page 89.
Chain Store Series (Fourteen Articles), Sept. 10–Dec. 24, 1914.

1913

Retail Chain Store Evolution, *Printers' Ink*, Aug. 7, 1913.
Chain Stores, R. A. Bruce, *Printers' Ink*, July 10, 17, 31, Aug. 7, 1913.
F. W. Woolworth's Story, Leo L. Redding, *World's Word*, April, 1913.

1912

The Tower of Nickels and Dimes, *Hearst's Magazine*, October, 1912.
Chain Store Economies Practicable in Many Lines, John H. *H*anan, *Printers' Ink*, Mar. 21, 1912.

1911

Welding First Links in a chain store system, John P. Wilder, *Printers' Ink*, Dec. 7, 1911.
Gigantic Woolworth Chain, *Printers' Ink*, Nov. 16, 1911.

INDEX

CPSIA information can be obtained
at www.ICGtesting.com
Printed in the USA
LVOW12s2322290517
536237LV00012B/760/P